Reaching and Teaching Children Exposed to Trauma

Reaching and Teaching Children Exposed to Trauma

Barbara Sorrels, EdD

Gryphon House
www.gryphonhouse.com

Published by Gryphon House, Inc.
P. O. Box 10, Lewisville, NC 27023
800.638.0928; 877.638.7576 (fax)
Visit us on the web at www.gryphonhouse.com.

Reprinted May 2018

Library of Congress Cataloging-in-Publication Data
Sorrels, Barbara.
  Reaching and teaching children exposed to trauma / by Barbara Sorrels, EdD.
     pages cm
  Includes bibliographical references and index.
  ISBN 978-0-87659-350-9
1. Teacher participation in educational counseling. 2. Abused children--Education. 3. Mentally ill children--Education. 4. Psychic trauma in children. 5. Post-traumatic stress disorder in children. 6. Educational psychology. I. Title.
  LB1027.5.S558 2015
  371.94--dc23
                                        2015015093.

Bulk Purchase
Gryphon House books are available for special premiums and sales promotions as well as for fund-raising use. Special editions or book excerpts also can be created to specifications. For details, call 800-638-0928.

Table of Contents

Introduction

Four-year-old Katie* sat under the table barking like a dog. This was not a child enjoying dramatic play; this was one of the unpredictable and more bizarre behaviors that Katie displayed in child care. I invited her to join us in group time and offered to let her pass out the rhythm sticks. She responded with an exaggerated laugh that unnerved me and then crawled further under the table, out of my reach. I sat on the floor to make eye contact with her and presented some alternative choices of activities that she could do while the rest of the class had group time, but she shook her head and continued to laugh and bark like a dog. Not wanting to disrupt the routine of the other eleven children, I struggled to carry on with our normal routine. We made it through group time, and I breathed a sigh of relief as she came out from under the table when I announced it was time to go outside to play.

Two weeks later I noticed bruises on Katie's legs. Because she was a very active child, I first assumed they were the result of normal childhood activity. But when she came in with a bruise on her cheek, my emotional radar signaled alarm. I asked her how she got the bruise, and very matter-of-factly she replied, "My mommy hit me." What shocked me was that this was a highly educated, professional, churchgoing family that, from outward appearances, seemed to have it together. After numerous phone calls, meetings, and a visit from child protective services, I found out there were secrets behind those closed doors.

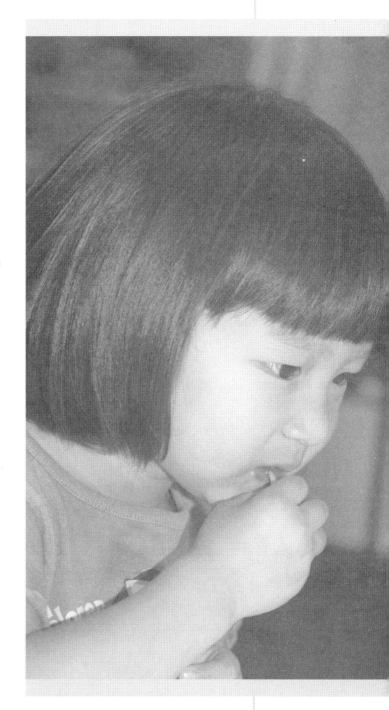

*Not her real name.

For many children, childhood is not the idyllic, carefree time that adults typically envision. There are many children like Katie in child care centers, Head Start programs, and public and private schools across America who have experienced various forms of maltreatment and trauma. Statistics from the U. S. Department of Health and Human Services indicate that in 2012, child protective services in the United States received 3.4 million reports of abuse or neglect involving 6.3 million children. Of those referrals, 62 percent were substantiated; 78 percent involved neglect, 18 percent involved abuse, and 9.3 percent involved sexual abuse. Infants suffered the highest rates of maltreatment with 26 percent of the reports involving children under three years of age; 20 percent of the victims were three to five years old.

According to Howard Bath, author of the 2008 article "The Three Pillars of Trauma-Informed Care," it is a fact that many, if not most, of the children who are in the child welfare system, the juvenile justice system, and mental health programs have been exposed to trauma in their early years. Many children exposed to trauma are identified as having special needs because most eventually receive the diagnosis of at least one of the following: attention-deficit disorder (ADD), attention-deficit/hyperactivity disorder (ADHD), oppositional defiant disorder, bipolar disorder, obsessive compulsive disorder, or depression. It is important to recognize that, in these cases, disorders are but a symptom of the underlying trauma. If we only address the symptoms and do not address the trauma that caused the neurochemical changes in the brain, we are only putting a bandage on the problem. The neurochemical changes resulting from the trauma of living in chronic fear and unmanageable stress cause profound changes in behavior. Early childhood professionals are typically the first people to see a child on a regular basis outside of the home and, therefore, play a key role in early identification of maltreatment and unhealthy patterns of development. That makes it crucial for the child care work force and those in early education to be trained and informed about the maltreatment of children.

It has been generally assumed that only those with advanced education and clinical skills can help traumatized children, but as Ricky Greenwald asserts in *Child Trauma Handbook*, a great deal of healing can take place in nonclinical settings with teachers, caregivers, coaches, and family members who are informed in trauma-based care. Bath also asserts that evidence indicates that trauma-informed environments in the home, child care center, and at school are a necessary ingredient in the healing process.

Dr. Bruce Perry is internationally recognized as one of the leading experts in child trauma. He and his team led the therapeutic recovery effort for children who escaped from the horrific fire in the Branch Davidian compound in Waco, Texas, in 1993. He comments in his book *The Boy Who Was Raised as a Dog* that

> Early childhood professionals are typically the first people to see a child on a regular basis outside of the home and, therefore, play a key role in early identification of maltreatment and unhealthy patterns of development. That makes it crucial for those in early education to be trained and informed about the maltreatment of children.

the most important thing he learned from that experience is that it doesn't take trained therapists to heal a child. It is the ongoing, daily interactions with loving, emotionally responsive and caring adults—be they a teacher, a caregiver, an aunt, or a grandfather—that bring about healing. Therapists and psychiatrists can certainly provide insight, determine the need for medication, and offer advice, but children find healing in the daily acts of love and nurture experienced in ordinary relationships. Because child care providers and teachers often spend more waking hours with a child than any other adult, they are key players in the path to healing. Therefore, it is imperative to train teachers and caregivers so they can effectively serve in our child care centers and schools.

Trauma-informed care and education means that caregivers and teachers understand how trauma changes the brain and affects relationships, self-regulation, sensory processing, learning, and behavior. Informed adults recognize the behavioral signs of trauma and know how to create environments that provide a sense of emotional safety and healing. They are able to look at children's behavioral challenges with compassion rather than anger and frustration. Trauma-informed caregivers know how to respond to maladaptive behavior in ways that maintain respect for children and help them learn new ways of being in the world.

Unfortunately, the burgeoning body of research regarding trauma-informed care and education is often unknown or ignored by professionals in the field. In fact, in the Child Trauma Academy 2013 winter webinar series, Dr. Perry described our educational culture as "child-illiterate." We currently have amassed more information and scientific research regarding the development of children than any other time in human history, but this body of information sleeps in university libraries. The current educational culture focuses on accountability and assessment, largely ignoring even basic principles of child development. Child care providers and teachers often feel that they are not qualified to address the social-emotional issues of maltreated children or that they will need to add one more thing to the complex demands currently placed upon them. One of the interesting findings, however, is that many aspects of developmentally appropriate practice (DAP) are parts of a supportive and healing environment to children who have been harmed. What early childhood educators have long known at an intuitive level has scientific evidence to explain and understand the benefits of DAP.

> It is the ongoing, daily interactions with loving, emotionally responsive and caring adults—be they a teacher, a caregiver, an aunt, or a grandfather—that bring about healing.

My own interest in trauma began in 1967 as a fourteen-year-old. On Sunday afternoons you would find me at DC General Hospital in Washington, DC, rocking babies on the abandoned-baby ward. The jail was across the street, and this was the ward where babies born to incarcerated moms were taken shortly after birth. Other infants were left on doorsteps, in city parks, or in trash cans. They remained in the hospital until they turned six months old and could be taken to the city orphanage.

These babies were not like those I saw in the church nursery, nor were they like my younger brother at home. They never cried, laughed, made eye contact, or tried to engage in play. I would sometimes spend hours just trying to get a baby to make eye contact. I wondered how and why this happened. A seed was planted in my soul to understand the behavior of children who were at risk. Throughout my high school and college years, I stayed involved in inner-city programs for children.

I began my teaching career caring for four-year-olds in the inner city in one of the most violent areas of DC. I cried on my way to work many mornings because I felt incompetent to meet the needs of the eighteen children in my care. Although I had some significant experience with children, I found this group to be exceptionally challenging. When they didn't want to clean up, they threw paint, blocks, or anything in front of them. They cursed, bit, hit, and seemed to bounce off the walls. In my heart, I knew these were not "bad" children: They were children who had seen more violence and trauma in their short lives than many others would see in a lifetime.

I moved on in my career and started two early childhood programs. Although I was no longer working in an inner city, I still encountered children across socioeconomic groups who struggled with behavioral challenges. In the 1980s, children started showing up at school with bottles of Ritalin and a label of ADD or ADHD. As I saw more and more children being diagnosed with this previously unheard-of condition, I began to notice a pattern. The vast majority of the children being medicated had experienced some sort of significant loss in their short lives—divorce, abandonment by a parent, violence in the home, or adoption. I had no idea how adoption could play into ADHD, but I just knew that I saw a pattern. It was also during this time that I encountered Katie and others who carried a diagnosis of reactive attachment disorder (RAD).

I read everything I could get my hands on to try to explain what I was seeing. The literature was scarce and bleak, mostly geared to mental-health professionals. It offered little hope other than medication for children with severe behavioral disorders. I had a hard time believing this could be true.

In the late 1990s, while working on my doctorate in early childhood education, I attended a conference where I heard Dr. Perry speak on brain development. I sat riveted as he confirmed what I somehow already knew: Trauma and loss profoundly change children. This discovery launched me into a passionate search to learn more. My motivation was both personal and professional: I had a drive to know, but I also had a desire to help the students I served as an early childhood education professor.

As students went out into the field, their number one struggle was classroom guidance and management. I began consulting with programs around the state, and I learned that the behavior of children is the biggest concern. Teachers and caregivers were increasingly seeing children with significant behavior challenges.

Recently, I "accidently" fell into the foster-care world in our state. A friend asked me to share what I knew about trauma with a group of foster parents. Their desperation and hunger to know how to help the children in their care were heartrending. Since that encounter, I have been immersed in the adoptive and foster-care world, training professionals, families, and clergy on the impact of trauma on healthy child development.

I am indebted to the work of Dr. Bruce Perry, Dr. Karyn Purvis and Dr. David Cross of Texas Christian University, Dr. Alicia Lieberman, Dr. Charles Zeanah, Dr. Vincent Fellitti, and the many others who are dedicated to helping children heal. Their wisdom and insight have informed my thinking, deepened my understanding, and changed my view of the world and of children. The extensive reading and education I have received through professional development have opened my eyes to the vast amount of knowledge that I have yet to learn. It continues to fuel my passion to understand more so I can help those on the front lines who live and work with children on a daily basis.

The purposes of this book are to help early childhood professionals understand how maltreatment and trauma impact healthy growth and development, to help caregivers know how to identify maltreated and traumatized children, and to teach practical strategies to create environments that bring about hope and healing for maltreated children.

Chapter 1

Defining Trauma

Betsy Groves, author of *Children Who See Too Much*, defines trauma as, "any event that undermines a child's sense of physical or emotional safety or poses a threat to the safety of the child's parents or caregivers." There are different levels of trauma, including acute and complex forms.

Floods, tornados, motor-vehicle accidents, or acts of terrorism such as the Boston Marathon bombing are examples of *acute trauma*, a single exposure to an overwhelming event. These events undermine a child's sense of physical and/or emotional safety and may cause nightmares and avoidance of anything that reminds the child of the trauma. A child who has had the experience of a tornado hitting his home can become panicked by merely hearing the local weather station mention a storm somewhere in the country. Certain triggers will evoke fear, but the child typically will not live life in a chronic state of being afraid.

Bessel van der Kolk, a psychiatrist who specializes in working with people who experience post-traumatic stress, defines *complex trauma* as, "the experiences of multiple, chronic and prolonged, developmentally adverse traumatic events, most often of an interpersonal nature . . . and early life exposure." In other words, complex trauma usually happens in the context of a relationship with a family member or caregiver who is in some way responsible for the

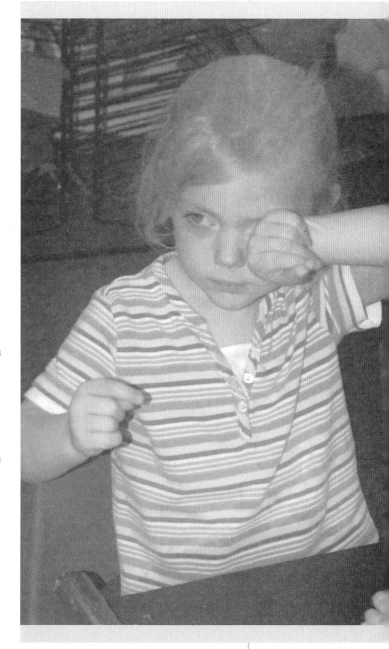

well-being of a child. It is the experience of being harmed or neglected at the hands of another person. It is chronic and ongoing, not a one-time event. This is the most toxic form of trauma and is the primary focus of this book.

Before looking at the impact of trauma, it helps to understand the ways relational trauma can manifest in the life of a child:

- **Physical Abuse:** The most obvious form of trauma is bodily harm from hitting, kicking, slapping, beating, burning, or punching. In 2009, the National Child Traumatic Stress Network Physical Abuse Collaborative Group published the *Child Physical Abuse Fact Sheet*. It states that approximately 149,000 cases of child physical abuse were reported in the United States, but the number is very likely much greater because not all abuse is reported. In many states, child protective service agencies are underfunded and overwhelmed with heavy caseloads, which means they can only respond to situations that are imminently life threatening. Many children fall through the cracks and never come to the attention of the authorities, or the circumstances of their lives are regarded as non–life threatening and remain unaddressed.

  Abuse at the hands of a family member or caregiver is psychological poison. As Alicia Lieberman and Patricia Van Horn assert in their book *Psychotherapy with Infants and Young Children*, when the person who is supposed to protect the child is the one who willfully and intentionally harms the child, the child is put into an impossible psychological dilemma. The natural instinct of a child is to run to a parent for protection, yet at the same time, the stress response of the brain tells the child to run from the source of threat. The child has nowhere to turn, and the psychological impact is long lasting and severe. Children who experience abuse in the early years of life are often diagnosed with ADD/ADHD because they live in a chronic state of alarm, hypervigilant to any possibility of threat. They have difficulty forming lasting relationships because they are unable to trust others and typically resort to aggression to solve conflict. Later substance abuse is a common issue as it is a way of assuaging their emotional pain. They often carry within themselves a deep sense of worthlessness and the false belief that they somehow deserve the abuse, which often leads to risky behaviors. Some develop manipulative strategies to deal with their abuser, and manipulation becomes a way of handling all relationships.

  Research has found that invasive medical procedures in the first three years of life are often processed in a child's psyche as abuse. An infant does not have the capacity to understand that the tubes, needles, and pain he endures are necessary to save his life. He only knows that the people around him cause pain. Early medical trauma can cause a pervasive sense of anxiety across the lifespan because the development of the regulatory system may be affected, which can interfere with the attachment process.

- **Neglect:** The definition of neglect, or deprivation, is inadequate responsiveness to the needs of a child. Neglect can happen in both subtle and profound ways. Gross neglect of the basic survival needs of food, water, sleep, medical attention, or shelter can literally threaten a child's life. Poverty of experience, having a chronically depressed parent or caregiver, and lack of sensory stimulation also are forms of neglect and can have serious emotional and cognitive repercussions. Though more subtle, these forms are, nevertheless, profoundly harmful. Decades of research have l ed experts to agree that the effects of neglect are far more destructive and profound than outright abuse. Significant language delay, learning deficits, a pervasive sense of anxiety, mental health issues, an inability to form lasting relationships, and an inability to cope with stress are some of the common outcomes.

- **Sexual Abuse:** Sexual abuse involves a wide range of behaviors, from the obvious forms of bodily contact, such as fondling, kissing, and intercourse to others that don't involve contact. Sexual exploitation for pornographic purposes, witnessing sexual activity between adults, and exposure to pornography and flashing are also destructive forms of sexual abuse. Children exposed to sexual abuse often have no personal boundaries and initiate and accept inappropriate forms of physical contact. They often act in a provocative manner later in life, making them a prime target for sexual predators and abusive partners. Some, but not all, grow up to be perpetrators of sexual abuse because this is their "normal." Many will struggle with intimacy and have difficulty sustaining lasting relationships.

- **Emotional Abuse:** This form of trauma often flies under the radar and can remain undetected for years—even throughout childhood. Emotional abuse occurs when an adult intentionally subjects the child to terrifying events, taunts, humiliation, or chronic shame. Examples include parents telling children they are stupid, they will never amount to anything, or they can't do anything right, or stepchildren rejected by a stepparent and treated like outsiders. Emotional abuse instills within the child a deep sense of shame and humiliation that paralyzes and prevents her from living up to her potential. The child may go through life viewing herself as somehow defective, unworthy of love and affection. The child may live in the shadows and try to go through life unnoticed and invisible.

- **Domestic Violence:** Domestic violence includes actual or threatened physical and/or emotional abuse between family members or intimate partners. A 2009 survey by the National Child Trauma and Stress Network indicates that between fifteen million and seventeen million children in the United States—30 percent—live in homes where they are exposed to intimate-partner violence. A review of court records reveals that children younger than six are disproportionately represented in this population.

  Living in the context of domestic violence gives a child a distorted sense of love and relationships. Abuse at the hands of a spouse or partner is their "normal," and they often repeat the cycle and end up marrying or living with an abusive partner or becoming an abuser themselves. Because of the ego-centric nature of children, they often believe they are somehow the cause of the violence at home. They may grow up to view themselves as ineffective and helpless as they are powerless to stop the violence. To them, conflict is handled by aggression rather than words and negotiation.

- **Abandonment:** Being abandoned by a primary caretaker is a traumatic event. Even children who are given up for adoption at birth and placed into loving and nurturing families can experience a traumatic stress response. Abandonment may happen through death, divorce, or incarceration. Divorce is so commonplace in our culture that it goes unrecognized as a source of trauma. But the breakup of a family typically results in a rupture of an attachment relationship to one degree or another, and this is painful to a child of any age. They often grow into adulthood cynical about marriage or live in fear that any relationship they have will inevitably come to an end. Trust issues are very common.

In 1998, I attended the annual conference of the National Association for the Education of Young Children (NAEYC) in Toronto, Canada. There I heard Dr. Bruce Perry speak on the most recent findings about the brain. Research allows us to understand how a child's brain develops and gives us insight into the needs and conditions that support healthy growth and development.

Basic Principles of Healthy Brain Development

The brain begins to develop just days after conception with the first cells rapidly dividing and prolifically producing millions and millions of neurons. Many different types of neurons are produced in the brain, each designed with specific capabilities. In the next step of brain development, the cells migrate to specific locations where they will do their work. Once in their assigned locations, they begin to connect with other neurons to fulfill their functions. The brain is at its most vulnerable during this period of cell division, migration, and differentiation. It is highly susceptible to the destructive effects of substance abuse, smoking, and toxic stress. When mothers live in the context of domestic violence during pregnancy or experience some sort of significant loss or threat, the resulting stress crosses the placenta and affects brain development. (We will take a deeper look at how trauma affects the developing brain in Chapter 3.)

The development of a baby is an interactive project and not the result of a simple unfolding of nature. It is a dynamic process that involves both nature and the environment. Genes provide the basic blueprint for development, but experience fine-tunes or customizes the brain to function and adapt to a particular environment. Small differences in the beginning have a disproportionate effect on the trajectory of a child's life and leave their mark in significant ways.

The architecture of the brain is developed through two kinds of experiences: *experience expectant* and *experience dependent*. When a child is born, there are certain kinds of experiences that are expected to be common to all members of our species. As Charles Nelson, Nathan Fox, and

Charles Zeanah point out in their book *Romania's Abandoned Children: Deprivation, Brain Development, and the Struggle for Recovery*, it is assumed that all children will have opportunities to see patterned light, listen to language, and gaze at faces because these are some of the most basic life experiences common to all mankind. Experience-dependent development, on the other hand, is unique to the individual. For example, not all children have the opportunity to learn to play a musical instrument or learn gymnastics, which establish certain patterns of connection in the brain. The resulting brain development that occurs from these experiences will only happen for those exposed to these opportunities. The brain develops as a result of the quantity and quality of life experiences. The number of connections and the complexity of the connections in the brain are determined by the richness of life experiences.

There is nothing easy about caring for a group of infants when it is done well.

The brain stem is the only part of the brain that is fully developed at birth, and its primary purpose is to ensure survival. The limbic or emotional brain functions only partially at birth, and the cortex, or the thinking part of the brain, is relatively undeveloped. In other words, the brain develops from the bottom up: It moves from more primitive, reflexive types of functioning to complex thinking.

The brain stem controls most of our vital life functions, such as breathing, heart rate, and blood pressure. It organizes in utero around the consistent, predictable rhythm of the mother's heartbeat, and, because it develops prenatally, it is the hardest part of the brain to change. All sensory input—whether received through the eyes, ears, skin, nose, or mouth—enters through the brain stem and is sorted, processed, and disseminated to other parts of the brain to be acted upon. The effects of early trauma are primarily rooted in the brain stem.

The first three years of life lay the foundation for future mental health. Our most emotionally stable and competent child care providers need to be caring for our youngest children. There exists the mistaken notion that infant child care is just about rocking babies. I've heard people comment that they just want to rock babies and not work with older children in child care because the older ones are too hard to handle. There is nothing easy about caring for a group of infants when it is done well. Infant care providers need a great deal of knowledge and understanding to facilitate the growth of a stable foundation for mental health.

Exposure to relational trauma transcends socioeconomic class, race, and ethnicity. Neglect and abuse happen behind the closed doors of the rich and educated as well as the poor and unschooled. They are often more difficult to detect among the affluent because outward appearances are carefully guarded.

The true rates at which young children are subject to trauma is difficult to assess because the private nature of many forms of trauma can fly under the radar and not come to the attention of the community. It is suspected that the true rates of abuse and neglect are far greater than those reported.

Children who experience trauma are often unable to communicate their distress through words. Some fear retribution from their abusers, and some develop defense mechanisms against even remembering the experience. But as van der Kolk asserts, the body is an historical organ, and it keeps score. Even though the child may not consciously be able to recall the event, the trauma is literally encoded in the psyche and in the cells of the body, and its effects are felt throughout the biological system.

Traumatized children often communicate their distress through behaviors that frustrate caregivers and teachers who do not understand the negative effects of maltreatment on children's growth and development. These hurting children are often reprimanded, punished, sent to time out, and have privileges taken away by well-meaning but misinformed adults who aren't able to "hear" the messages being communicated. Labels such as "challenging," "defiant," "uncooperative," and even "bad" are attached to these children, and the labels often follow them throughout their school careers. This underscores the importance of caregivers and teachers recognizing the signs of trauma.

Characteristics of Traumatized Children

Young children communicate more through their behavior than they do through words. Different children will display different characteristics depending on the timing, intensity, and nature of the abuse or neglect. Some children will exhibit many—if not all—of the characteristics described below, and some will intensely demonstrate just a few.

Infants

- **Difficult to soothe:** Infants who were exposed to substances or toxic stress in utero may be chronically fussy and hard to comfort.

- **Resistant to touch:** Babies who suffered prenatal insult, early medical trauma, prematurity, early neglect, or abuse may resist being held. They may arch their backs and refuse to mold to the caregiver's body. Some will forcefully throw themselves backward to the point that they are upside down. They will often try to wiggle out of the arms of the adult and may loudly protest.

- **Sleep dysregulation:** Some infants will have difficulty falling asleep, while others will violently startle, scream, or cry out. Some will appear awake, with eyes wide open, but seem unaware of what is going on.

- **Feeding issues:** The brain and the "gut" are intertwined, and stress has a profound impact on digestive issues. Infants may chronically spit up or have gas or constipation issues.

- **Dull, listless appearance:** Babies who have suffered neglect often have expressionless faces. They will lay listless in their cribs and stare into space. They rarely respond to initiations from the caregiver to interact or play.

- **Lack of eye contact:** Infants will avert their eyes or look past the caregiver, seemingly staring at something behind them. Others may look at their caregiver as if they are looking through them and not at them.

- **Rocking:** Infants may incessantly rock back and forth in their cribs or while sitting on the floor. All babies may occasionally rock, but when the behavior is persistent and intense, it is cause for concern.

- **Head banging:** Children may hit themselves on the head with their hands or bang their heads on the wall or floor.

- **Sudden lack of motor control:** When infants experience a lack of safety, they may suddenly be unable to perform motor activities that they have previously demonstrated a capacity to do. For example, a baby may suddenly lose the ability to crawl. The child may collapse in spread-eagle fashion and just lie on the floor. Or, if you are holding a baby and he becomes overwhelmed, he may start yawning and lurch forward, losing postural control.

- **Temper tantrums:** All babies have meltdowns now and then, but traumatized infants have them on a regular basis. They have very little frustration tolerance.
- **Lack of play:** Around four months of age, babies typically become very playful and begin to issue invitations for interactions with caregivers. Traumatized and neglected infants show little interest and ability to engage in playful interactions.

Toddlers

In addition to the characteristics mentioned above, toddlers may also display the following:

- **Language delay:** One of the hallmarks of trauma and neglect is a significant delay in language development. Children from hard places lack rich verbal interactions with caring and sensitive adults. Babies learn to communicate out of an innate drive to connect with those who love and care for them. They imitate the sounds and nonverbal expressions of communication of those around them. Maltreated infants and toddlers typically have little experience with reading, singing, nursery rhymes, chants, and games.
- **Alternately fearful and aggressive:** Their actions can be highly contradictory and extreme. Temper tantrums are frequent. They hit and bite other children even without provocation.
- **Excessively negative and oppositional:** Though it is the nature of children between eighteen and thirty-six months to demonstrate some level of opposition and defiance, traumatized children may demonstrate this to an extreme. They will have temper tantrums throughout the day, particularly during times of transition.
- **Withdrawal:** While some children demonstrate their dysregulation through aggression, others withdraw and become pulled into self. They rarely interact with others or respond to initiations to interact and play. They may sit quietly and stare into space. There are children who are simply slow to warm up by nature, but after an initial reticence, they wholeheartedly engage in play. Maltreated children never warm up and consistently remain withdrawn or actively resist interaction.
- **Random and erratic play:** Though toddlers are known for their perpetual motion and relatively short attention spans, children who experience trauma may demonstrate a frenetic level of activity. They randomly roam around the room, picking up toys, only to throw them down after a few seconds. Their behavior almost seems like a wind-up toy, with little purposeful engagement of any sort.
- **Difficulty with separation:** Entry into child care and leaving a family member or guardian is difficult and triggers meltdowns. Because people

have inconsistently come and gone in these children's lives, they struggle with separation. They are very fearful of letting someone go because, in their world, that person is likely to not come back.

■ **Refuse to be comforted when hurt:** Maltreated children will often resist efforts by adults to comfort them when they fall and often turn to things rather than people for solace.

Three- to Five-Year-Olds

In addition to the behaviors described above, the following may also appear:

■ **Precocious self-care:** Children from hard places have often had to shoulder responsibility for their own daily survival needs and demonstrate the capacity to do things that typically developing children don't do yet. At the same time, they are unable to do things that are typical for their age. For example, a four-year-old may be able to prepare a bottle for her baby sister yet not be able to use scissors.

■ **Indiscriminate attachment:** Some children are not able to distinguish the differences among an attachment figure, an acquaintance, and a stranger. Sometimes people mistake their behavior as just being very outgoing and friendly. They will initiate not only conversation but physical contact with a total stranger. If a visitor comes into the room, they may run over and hug the person and strike up a very animated conversation.

■ **Inability to play:** For several different reasons, maltreated children often do not know how to play. Mom is typically a child's first play partner, but when she is abusive or neglectful, playful interactions are few and far between. In other instances, young children are forced to deal with inappropriate psychological stress or responsibilities that rob them of the time and energy to play. Some children are so overwhelmed that all of their inner resources are spent merely trying to cope and survive.

Maltreated children find it very difficult to engage in any kind of play that involves the use of symbols. Dramatic play, blocks, and play that depends on language are very difficult for them for reasons that will be discussed in a later chapter.

■ **Unusually controlling:** Chaos typically characterizes the lives of children who have experienced abuse and neglect. To compensate, they spend an enormous amount of energy trying to manipulate and control everything and everyone in the child care or school environment. Sometimes their efforts seem helpful and appropriate, but there is an intensity and pervasiveness that is extraordinary. For example, I had a severely maltreated and neglected five-year-old who assumed the role of caretaker. She noticed every detail regarding the needs and activity of all the children in the group. If someone needed glue, she jumped to get it for him. If someone needed a cotton ball for an art project, she frantically scrambled to find one. She relayed messages to adults in the room regarding the needs of other children. She made individualized lists reminding others of what they were supposed to be doing. At first glance, her behavior might be construed as helpful, but in reality, this child had a high need to control her environment to feel safe. A child with a high need to control finds it very difficult to relax and just be a child.

- **Seemingly random acts of aggression:** For maltreated children, feeling vulnerable is extremely unnerving and causes a great deal of anxiety. Emotional closeness and intimacy can be very threatening and feel unsafe; feelings of vulnerability can be more frightening and uncomfortable than feelings of aggression. Moments of emotional closeness may trigger a sudden and unprovoked act of aggression. For example, reading a book or telling a story with a group of children is often a special and intimate time. It is a common occurrence in an early childhood setting for the "holy hush" to settle over a group of children who are fully engaged in a story. That magical moment may be disrupted by a sudden outburst from a child with a trauma history. She may suddenly reach over and pinch another child, hit him with a stuffed animal, or sling a blanket at him. This aggressive behavior catches adults off guard because it seems so unprovoked and random.

- **Visceral reactions to frustration:** Children who experience trauma often struggle with strong emotion. Because they frequently lack the ability to use words to identify what they feel, they express emotion through their bodies. They have very little tolerance for frustration, and their reactions to anger and frustration often look like those of a toddler.

- **Gorges or hoards food:** Starvation in utero or in the first years of life touches the psyche of children at the most primitive level. Substance abuse and malnutrition in a pregnant mom can rob the developing baby of necessary nutrients and can result in prenatal starvation. According to Dr. Karyn Purvis, a child who experienced starvation in utero will act like a child who was starved after birth (Purvis, e-mail correspondence, 2010). Children may gorge to the point of throwing up. Some take food out of other children's lunches or backpacks. This is often perceived as "stealing," but it should be recognized as a survival mechanism. This behavior will be addressed in later chapters.

- **Difficulty with transitions:** Maltreated children tend to be rigid and inflexible in their behavior, and transitions often trigger defiance, aggression, and anxiety.

- **Memory problems:** Living in a state of chronic fear damages the physical architecture of the brain and can impair a child's short-term memory. Maltreated children may not remember what they are supposed to do next, and their behavior is often mistaken as noncompliance.

- **Hypervigilant:** Maltreated children are hypersensitive to any indication of a threat to their physical or emotional well-being. They notice every sound, movement, or change in the environment, making it very difficult for them to settle down and focus. It isn't that they aren't paying attention at all; on the contrary, they are paying attention to everything and cannot screen out what isn't important.

- **Misinterpret facial expressions and body language:** Traumatized children stay highly attuned to facial expressions and body language; however, they are prone to misinterpreting nonverbal cues. Their profound sense of shame and worthlessness causes them to filter everything through the lens of "She doesn't like me," or "There's something wrong with me." The frown on your face may be because of a headache, but the child with a trauma history will believe it is directed at him.

- **Developmental delay:** Children with a trauma history often seem significantly younger than their age. (Though a developmental delay may be apparent at younger ages, it usually becomes obvious to caregivers by age three.) Their behavior and responses to everyday events may appear more like a young toddler than a three-year-old. Generally speaking, according to *Understanding the Effects of Maltreatment on Brain Development* by the U. S. Department of Health and Human Services, children exposed to chronic violence, abuse, neglect, and trauma are developmentally about half of their chronological age.

I'm sure by now that you recognize these characteristics in some of the children you work with. The burning question is, "What do I do to help them?" We will address these behaviors and offer practical strategies in later chapters of the book, but first, you need to understand the why before knowing what to do. When teachers and caregivers understand the science or the rationale behind a particular teaching strategy, they are more likely to do it.

Chapter 2

The Stress Response and Fear-Based Behavior

Many adults in our culture have bought into the myth of the resilient child, believing children are inherently so at birth, that resilience is hard-wired into all children and not a function of life experience. I believe we have bought into this myth because our culture needs resilient children. We need very young children who can tolerate being away from home and from family for long periods of the day. We need children who can navigate smoothly between two homes because of a divorce in the family. We need children who can manage a fast-paced life with packed schedules and little down time for play. We need children who can sit still for long periods of time and bubble in answers on standardized tests. Even a cursory glance, however, at the world around us is enough to debunk the myth of the inherent resilience of children.

A record number of children are being medicated on a daily basis to allow them to function in school. Increasing numbers of children are being diagnosed with autism, sensory processing disorder, ADD, and ADHD. Rates of abuse and neglect are escalating, and schools in at-risk neighborhoods are failing. If we look at the facts, we find that children aren't quite as resilient as we would like to believe, but Research has given us some valuable insight into how children become resilient.

All children are inherently malleable; only some children become resilient. Resilience is developed through a dynamic interaction between biology and experience. Some children have a biological tendency toward resilience, but even the most genetically inclined child can be derailed if he lives in a particularly stressful environment. Warm, responsive relationships with at least one caring adult can tip the scales in favor of resilience.

The behavior of children from hard places can be challenging and overwhelming, leaving caregivers and teachers feeling incompetent and frustrated. The defiant and oppositional behavior of children can be taken personally and interpreted as saying, "I don't like you." When a child consistently pushes the adult away and challenges every request, it can wear down even the most committed professional and lead her to believe she is ineffective. Working with children then loses its joy, and the daily task of caring for children becomes drudgery. Some caregivers burn out and leave the field altogether: In a presentation at the annual Head Start Association conference in 2013, early childhood researcher Michael Wells reported that the behavior of children is one of the top reasons why Head Start teachers leave their jobs.

> The challenging behaviors of traumatized children are driven by fear—not rebellion and defiance. Scared children do scary things because they are afraid and not because they are trying to get on the last nerve of the people who care for and teach them.

All behavior carries meaning; children do what they do for a reason. However, the reasons are not always readily discerned. An in-depth understanding of child development and trauma will enable adults to more accurately "hear" and understand the messages children communicate through their actions. Decades of research indicate that the challenging behaviors of traumatized children are driven by fear—not rebellion and defiance. Scared children do scary things because they are afraid and not because they are trying to get on the last nerve of the people who care for and teach them. When children live in dysfunctional environments characterized by violence, abuse, and neglect, they develop strategies to survive. I used to refer to the behavior of maltreated children as "maladaptive." I no longer look at it that way. Their behaviors are adaptive strategies to a dysfunctional environment. For example, when food is chronically withheld from a young child, survival instinct will drive the child to take food from whatever source he can find. At home, he may get up in the night and sneak food to hide under the bed. When he accompanies someone to a convenience store, he may stuff food in his pockets and later be beaten for stealing. So when this child comes to child care, he may gorge himself on snacks or may take food out of other children's cubbies because he wants to get all he can when he can. In the child care setting where food is plentiful, his behavior seems maladaptive because it doesn't fit the context.

To recognize and accurately interpret the messages communicated by the adaptive behavior of young children, we must understand how trauma impacts brain development and healthy growth.

The Neurochemistry of Fear and The Hope Connection

We are indebted to Dr. Karyn Purvis and Dr. David Cross, developmental psychologists at Texas Christian University, and their work on the neurochemistry of fear. In 1998 they were approached by adoptive parents for help with their behaviorally challenged children, most adopted from orphanages in Eastern Europe. These dedicated parents were at the end of their rope in trying to help their children. Purvis and Cross launched a research study that eventually became known as The Hope Connection. It started as a three-week day camp targeting children with behavioral challenges stemming from early neglect and/or abuse. As the study unfolded, they witnessed significant behavioral changes in struggling children. As they sought to understand why their intervention had positive effects on children's behavior and attachment, they began to look at the neurochemical profiles of these children before, during, and after camp. What they found astounded them.

Prior to entering camp, most of the children had a neurochemical profile that looked like that of an adult diagnosed with post-traumatic stress disorder (PTSD). PTSD develops after a person experiences a terrifying ordeal that involves some sort of severe threat or injury. The experience is so profound that it results in chemical changes in the brain. Purvis and Cross refer to PTSD in children as, "the neurochemistry of fear."

What was so amazing about The Hope Connection was the remarkable change in the brain chemistry and behavior of the children. As they were immersed in an emotionally safe, sensory-rich, attachment-rich environment, significant changes in behavior were observed. There was a correlation between the change in brain chemistry and the observed behavior of the children. By the end of camp, their brain chemistry began to approach normal levels with corresponding behavioral changes. It was one of the first studies to show that the brain could change as a result of changes in the environment. To understand how this can happen, it is necessary to understand the stress response and the effects of trauma on the brain.

Understanding the Stress Response

Our brains are exquisitely designed for self-preservation and programmed to respond with lightning speed to anything that threatens our emotional or physical well-being. The brain constantly receives and processes data from the senses to determine what is safe and what is not safe. Every sight, sound, or sensation is processed through the brain stem, and messages are sent throughout the brain to initiate an appropriate response.

When something is deemed unsafe, a well-orchestrated symphony of electrical impulses and neurochemical cocktails instructs the entire body to instantaneously mobilize to address the threat. All systems of the body divert energy and resources to defend against the perceived danger. Changes in heart rate, blood pressure, respiration, glucose levels, and muscle tone occur in preparation to fight, flee, or freeze. As soon as the danger is either eliminated or goes away, the body returns to a state of calm and all systems return to normal functioning.

However, when children live with chronic neglect, abuse, or violence, the stress response system remains stuck in the "on" position, and the brain and body are never able to return to a state of equilibrium or calm. The implications are profound and lifelong. Living in a chronically fearful state is like trying to drive a car with one foot on the brake and the other on the gas. This situation is exceedingly toxic in the first five years of life when the developing brain is establishing connections and determining "set points" of self-regulation. There is evidence that chronic stress actually damages certain parts of the brain, impairing healthy functioning across the life span.

What is the difference between toxic stress and manageable stress? A number of factors determine whether the stress will have long-lasting effects and a negative impact on a child: timing, intensity, chronicity, degree of control, predictability, and social support.

- **Timing:** The timing of trauma is a critical factor in terms of the negative impact and lasting effects. As a general rule, the younger the child is at the time of trauma, the greater the likelihood of severe emotional, physical, and mental impact. The brain is most vulnerable in utero and during the first year of life when the basic architecture is being established. With each passing year, the brain becomes a little more stable and a little less vulnerable to stress.

- **Intensity:** Events that are highly intense and severe are more toxic than those that are milder in nature. For example, suppose a child is abruptly kidnapped by an abusive, noncustodial parent who then leads police on a dangerous chase with the child in the car. He wrecks the car but manages to flee into the woods carrying the child on his back. There is a three-day manhunt to find them, and the child is finally rescued as the police hold the parent at gunpoint. This scenario is far more intense and traumatic than a child who goes for a visit with a very loving noncustodial relative who fails to return the child to the custodial parent in a timely manner. Even though the relative is in contempt of court, the child is well cared for until he is found by police and returned to the custodial parent without incident. Being separated from the primary caregiver would certainly be traumatic, but the experience would not be as intense as that of the first child. The experience of being violently abducted by an abusive individual is likely to overwhelm the child's capacity to cope.

- **Chronicity:** A child who lives with chronic neglect or abuse is more likely to suffer toxic effects than a child who experiences a single abusive event at the hands of a momentarily overwhelmed parent. Chronic trauma keeps the stress response stuck in the "on" position, and the brain and central nervous system never have a chance to recover.

- **Degree of control:** If a child feels that he has some control over the circumstances of the abuse or neglect, it can buffer the level of psychological impact. For example, the oldest child in a group of siblings hears their drunken father come home and warns his brothers and sisters to pretend they are asleep. He slips out of bed to confront his father and provoke him into a rage instead of waiting for him to stagger into their room and begin his tirade. After slinging curse words and slapping the child around, the father staggers off to bed, leaving the rest of the children untouched. The oldest child goes back to bed knowing that his father typically stays in a drunken stupor until long after they get up and leave for school.

- **Predictability:** Anticipated or familiar events or circumstances are more manageable than unpredictable or novel ones. Predictability and familiarity allow the child to access his coping skills and prepare for the stress. If a child knows that his dad usually flies into a rage when his mom returns from grocery shopping because he believes she spends too much money, the child can prepare for the tirade by hiding in the closet, going out to the backyard, or psychologically preparing himself in other ways. On the other hand, if abuse and neglect are unpredictable, the child remains in a hypervigilant state and unable to turn off his stress response, which is a toxic state for the brain.

- **Social Support:** The key difference that tips the scale from toxic stress to manageable stress is the presence of another person who can offer

When the individuals
were asked what
helped them to
overcome their
adversity, the majority
identified a relationship
with a supportive adult
as a decisive factor.
In most cases, they
named a teacher.

support, empathy, encouragement, or some kind of assistance. Warm, responsive relationships in the life of a child can buffer toxic stress. A little bit of kindness can go a long way. A landmark study known as the Kauai Longitudinal Study tracked 698 children born in 1955 on the island of Kauai. Of the 210 children who were born into poverty and suffered many adverse childhood circumstances, one-third grew up to be competent, caring adults. When the individuals were asked what helped them to overcome their adversity, the majority identified a relationship with a supportive adult as a decisive factor. In most cases, they named a teacher.

The Impact of Cortisol

Cortisol is often referred to as the "stress hormone." It is actually both a hormone and a neurotransmitter that is involved in our daily functioning. The slow rise in cortisol gives us our morning boost of energy to get out of bed. It begins while we are sleeping, reaches its high point at midmorning, and slowly tapers off throughout the day, reaching its low point at bedtime. This typical ebb-and-flow pattern is established in children by age four. However, it is very different for maltreated children.

When the threat of danger is detected, there is an instantaneous surge of cortisol throughout the brain and body that triggers the fight, flight, or freeze response. Elevated levels of cortisol remain until the threat is over or has been eliminated. Once the danger has passed, the production of cortisol subsides. But when children live with constant threat, the flow of cortisol never turns off.

During the first year of life, babies are developing cortisol receptors in their brains. These receptors sweep up excess cortisol once the brain has signaled the faucet to turn off. Research indicates that children who live with chronic stress develop fewer cortisol receptors than well-nurtured children who live in relative safety, so their brains are not able to remove excess cortisol as efficiently. These children recover more slowly from stressful events.

Chronically elevated levels of cortisol cause damage to the *hippocampus*, a part of the brain involved in memory and information processing. Too much cortisol in infants also affects parts of the cortex, impairing their ability to read social cues. Maltreated children, therefore, have difficulty processing and retrieving information, which affects their ability to think and manage their behavior.

Babies are subject to the effects of cortisol even in utero. The placenta is designed to protect the developing baby. However, extreme adversity experienced by the mother, such as poor nutrition, worry over financial concerns, domestic violence, and substance abuse, compromise the protective function of the placenta. Excessive amounts of cortisol and other stress hormones cross the barrier and pose a threat to the baby. It isn't the cortisol itself that is lethal to cells but the presence of high levels of cortisol makes the developing baby more susceptible to the destructive effects of too little oxygen, nutrients, and other critical elements.

In his book *Life in the Womb: The Origin of Health and Disease*, physician Peter Nathanielsz asserts that when the compromised placenta fails to protect from elevated stress hormones and becomes inefficient at transporting oxygen and other vital nutrients, the baby responds by secreting his own cortisol. The baby is then exposed to elevated levels of cortisol from three sources—the blood stream of the mother, that which crosses the placenta, and that which is produced by his own body. The brain is most vulnerable to these adverse effects in utero and can cause significant impairment to healthy brain function.

Cortisol is not the only neurochemical involved in the stress response of the brain. Here are some others to be aware of:

- **Epinephrine and norepinephrine:** elevate in response to threat and contribute to the fight, flight, or freeze reaction; affect children's ability to maintain focused attention
- **Dopamine:** a neurotransmitter that facilitates communication within the brain. At optimum levels, it helps the brain control fluidity of movement, clear thinking, information processing, memory, joy, and pleasure. Abuse, neglect, and chronic stress alter the production of dopamine causing changes in demeanor and functioning. Imbalanced levels of dopamine are associated with such conditions as schizophrenia, autistic-like behaviors, compulsion disorders, lack of joy, aggression, poor memory, and shyness.
- **Serotonin:** most well-known for its influence on depression (people who are depressed typically have low levels of serotonin). It also affects mood, appetite, memory, sleep, temperature regulation, compulsive thinking, behaviors, and feelings.
- **Phenylethylamine (PEA):** amplifies the effects of other neurotransmitters and controls energy and mood. It is also associated with creative thinking and clear cognitive functioning. When PEA levels are not in balance, it is associated with mood disorders, ADD/ADHD, depression, autism, lethargy, and racing thoughts.

When you are dealing with a child who has experienced recurring maltreatment and trauma, you are dealing with a child who has a different brain than that of a child who has not lived with unmanageable stress. Not only is the child neurochemically different, the connectivity of the brain is different as well. Chronic stress inhibits the brain from connecting in complex and stable ways.

The disorganized behavior of the child reflects the disorganization in the brain. When you try to change behavior, you are also trying to change the brain.

States of Arousal

My first encounter with Sammy was memorable. I was at the door of my classroom, welcoming my new group of four-year-olds, but when I greeted Sammy, I didn't get the response I expected. He looked at me and said, "You are nothing but a G– d– f'n SOB." I knew immediately it was going to be an interesting year.

I quickly learned that Sammy was "king" of the classroom and was known for his vicious biting. This group of children had been together for two years and had learned to acquiesce to his every demand for fear of being bitten. He would bite at the slightest provocation, often drawing blood. It was obvious that the children tried to keep their distance from him, moving to the opposite end of the playground or to another part of the classroom when he came near. Although I didn't have the benefit of all the knowledge that we now have regarding the brain, Sammy clearly lived in a hyperaroused state and had a very quick trigger. His chaotic behavior reflected the chaotic state of his brain, which, in turn, reflected the chaotic circumstances in which he lived. Sammy grew up in a home and community surrounded by domestic violence and drugs. Unfortunately, this was before we fully understood the impact of these conditions on children's growth and development, and these kinds of situations were common in the community in which I worked. Only when life-threatening violence was evident did these children come on the radar of the authorities.

Children like Sammy can turn on a dime. In a matter of seconds, they can move from a state of calm into a total behavioral collapse. They may be enjoying the water table one minute and writhing on the floor in a violent tantrum the next. For some, this is a way of life: Daily living is punctuated by meltdowns in which property is destroyed and people can be harmed. If you are dealing with a child who struggles with violent tantrums, it is critical that you seek the advice and help of a therapist who can guide you in the best way to deal with the behavior. Never, ever attempt to restrain a child without training in how to properly perform a therapeutic hold. Children have been harmed and even killed by people who did not know how to safely contain a child. It should only be done by a trained individual and under the supervision and direction of a therapist.

In dealing with children like Sammy, it is helpful to understand arousal states because adults can unwittingly set children off. Perry believes that one of the biggest mistakes caregivers make with a traumatized child is misunderstanding his internal state and unintentionally doing or saying things that cause the child to instantaneously melt down. For example, I was in a classroom of five-year-olds. Johnny was lying on the floor playing with a train set when the teacher announced it was time to go to the large-motor room. Most of the children ran to line up at the door, but Johnny sat up and merely stared at them. The teacher told him to get in line, and he shouted, "No!" The teacher tried to lift him off the floor, pulling him up under his arms, and he began to scream and thrash. He lifted his feet off the floor and let his body go limp. Within seconds, this seemingly contented child was in full meltdown mode as a result of a simple request.

Perry has identified five arousal states that can give us insight into the stress response of children and their behavior: calm, alert, alarm, fear, and terror. These state systems have enormous implications both for children and for the adults who care for and teach them.

The State of Calm

Children who enjoy the benefit of predictable, consistent, and nurturing experiences with sensitive and attuned caregivers are able to spend a significant amount of time living in a state of calm. They feel physically and emotionally safe most of the time and have supportive adults nearby to help them when they encounter things that are frightening or overwhelming. Living in a state of calm allows the child to have access to the creative and reflective parts of the brain. The child is able to develop internal capacities of self-awareness and empathy and can think about the future and approach life with an appropriate degree of flexibility. He handles transitions well, can purposely engage and complete a task, and can respond to instruction and correction without shame.

Never, ever attempt to restrain a child without training in how to properly perform a therapeutic hold.

When it is time to stop painting and go outside, he is able to comply even if he really doesn't want to go outside. He adjusts to new situations well because he has both the emotional support and sense of personal competence to deal with appropriate levels of change.

The State of Alert

When a child encounters something new or novel, his state of arousal moves up the continuum to a state of alertness or attentiveness as his brain makes sense of and processes new information. As long as the newness is in appropriate amounts, the child can manage and can flow back and forth between the calm and alert states of being. The child continues to have a high degree of access to higher-level thinking and can thoughtfully respond. This is why it is so important that teaching and learning be developmentally appropriate and individually matched to the child's particular level of ability.

When expectations are not age appropriate and are not matched to the child's particular level of interest and ability, the child will likely move from a state of alertness into a more hyperaroused state of alarm. For example, a very well-nurtured and regulated three-year-old placed in a child care or school environment where he is expected to identify letters, sounds, and rhyming words and quietly sit at a table to do worksheets is not likely to remain in a state of calm. If these inappropriate expectations are a significant part of his day, he is likely to move up the continuum into more dysregulated states of arousal. It would not be unusual to see increased levels of stress and behavior issues as the day progresses. On the other hand, the same three-year-old placed in an environment with appropriate expectations and activities will flow in and out of states of calm and alertness throughout the day. He comes to group time where they read a story about the habitats of different kind of bears. The conversation is lively, engaging, and of an appropriate length to match the attention span of a three-year-old. The day has an appropriate balance of teacher-directed and child-directed activity whereby children are able to choose activities and rest and relax as needed. This child's arousal state allows his brain to process information and learn new things. The pace, content, and method of teaching is very important to maintaining optimum arousal states for behavior and learning to be at its best.

A child in a calm or alert state may move up the arousal continuum and into a more dysregulated state if the teacher or caregiver shouts, issues too many directives, or displays her own distress or anxiety. For example, Tiffany is sitting in the manipulative center putting together a puzzle. She accidently drops the puzzle, scattering pieces all over the floor. This can cause even the calmest child a degree of stress and can move the child up the continuum. If the teacher is reassuring and says something such as, "Oops. That's okay. We all make mistakes sometimes. Let me help you pick up the pieces," the child will be able to return to a state of calm rather quickly and will return to the enjoyment of the puzzle. But if the teacher is irritated with the situation, grits her teeth, and tersely says, "Pick it up," the child will remain in a state of alertness and may even move up the continuum to higher levels of arousal. Even after the pieces are gathered, the child may not be able to enjoy putting the puzzle together because she remains in a more dysregulated state.

The State of Alarm

A child living in a state of alarm becomes less able to use his cortex and executive functioning. He is living out of the emotional or limbic brain and is less able to engage in complex thought or empathize with other people. He will often appear to be anxious and preoccupied, making it hard for him to concentrate and learn. When this child comes to group time, he is not thinking about the story being read; he is watching the facial expressions of the teacher and is focused on the fact that the child next to him is too close. This child will react emotionally to anything novel and unexpected or anything perceived as threatening. His reaction to things may seem irrational to adults who don't understand the dynamic.

These children are easily escalated into higher levels of arousal when adults raise their voices, lob words at them across the room, shake a finger at them and scold, or use harsh and threatening tones of voice. A child in a state of alarm will need a great deal of support and understanding from adults to regulate and not move into a higher state of arousal.

Most children who have suffered maltreatment will remain in a state of alarm, even at their best. Their stress system remains in a constant state of hyperarousal, and they are easily triggered into more reactive states. This is why they are perceived to fly off the handle so quickly. Caregivers and teachers need to be very intentional and mindful of their own emotional states when dealing with a child who operates out of a state of alarm. When adults become anxious or overwhelmed by the child's behavior and respond with coercive dictates, yelling, and ultimatums, the child is guaranteed to escalate, and the situation become emotionally charged.

This is the challenge of caring for and teaching maltreated children. Their dysregulated and confusing behavior causes teachers and caregivers to become stressed and frustrated, which causes the adults to respond in an emotional and less-thoughtful manner, which in turn escalates the child into more challenging behaviors. As the child becomes more out of control, the adults become more stressed, and they are caught in a vicious cycle. Children in a state of alarm are deescalated by slow, sure, deliberate movement; gentle but invited touch; quiet "motherese" or "parentese" talking; soft music; and singing.

State of Fear

Children who operate out of a state of fear have little to no access to their cortex or executive functioning. They act primarily out of the limbic brain and the brain stem. They will be very reactive to people and their environment and unpredictable in their reactions. It is often difficult to determine what sends a child into a state of fear. A smell, a sound, or a look triggers the memory of past abuse and maltreatment, and he is suddenly in the throes of a fight, flight, or freeze response. Often, these memories of trauma are unconscious, and the child doesn't even know why he is afraid. The only thing he knows is that he no longer feels safe. Adults often describe these children as "turning on a dime." Relatively calm one moment, they suddenly become irrational the next, yelling, screaming, making irrational statements, or throwing a temper tantrum.

If adults act out of frustration or fear and begin to yell, make abrupt movements, lunge toward the child, or shout ultimatums and directives, the child likely will move to the highest level of arousal and become violent. It is important to remember that children in this state of arousal have very limited access to language, and you are not going to be able to talk them down or rationalize with them. It becomes mostly about who you are, rather than what you do. It is critical to maintain a calm demeanor and not become reactive.

I recently met a three-year-old who was placed into a loving foster home at three months of age. When she was eighteen months old, her biological father was given custody, and she returned to his home. Within three weeks, the child was covered in welts and bruises from beatings, and she was returned to her foster home. After this experience, she began having seemingly random temper tantrums and meltdowns at home, at childcare, and in public. Her family finally realized that the sight of a man wearing a ball cap triggered her violent behavior, as her biological father was always seen wearing a ball cap. This is the challenge of working with maltreated children; the reasons for their behavior are not always readily apparent. Adults need to trust the reality of the child and think like a detective.

State of Terror

When a child moves into a state of terror, he acts exclusively out of the brain stem, and his behavior is purely reflexive. The child feels as if his very life is at stake. Language shuts down. Thinking shuts down. The child goes into survival mode and may become highly aggressive and violent. He may hit, scratch, bite, kick, scream, slap, punch, and pinch. Never attempt to physically restrain a child unless you have been properly trained and are certified to use a therapeutic hold. It is possible to suffocate a child by improperly restraining him. When children reach this point of dysregulation, the support of a child therapist or mental health expert is critical.

A plan must be in place for dealing with a child in an emotional and behavioral collapse, because it will inevitably happen if you work with maltreated children on a consistent basis. If a child reaches this point of dysregulation, it is best to remove the other children from the scene to a safe place rather than try to remove the out-of-control child.

Remain in proximity to the tantruming child without putting yourself into harm's way. Never leave a child who is in a state of total collapse alone. Provide an identified safe place for the child to rage. There are commercially made safe places designed for this purpose—typically a soft, padded, open circle with a padded floor where the child can safely rage. Put soft pillows, stuffed animals, soft blankets, or any other item that is calming to the child inside the ring. Sit close by where the child can see and hear you calmly speaking to him. Sometimes offering the child something to eat or drink can de-escalate him. Say something like, "I'm going to put a granola bar and some water beside you in case you need it, and I'm going to sit right here in case you need me. I'm here to help you when you are ready."

In a trauma-informed classroom, tantrums are expected and plans are in place should a child have a meltdown. During large group, small group, and on an individual basis—before a tantrum occurs—talk about the purpose of the safe place and the reasons why children go there. Talk about how it feels to be so angry and upset that you have a hard time controlling your arms and legs. Point out that the safe place can help children feel safe when they feel out of control. Read scripted stories about common stressors in the classroom that may cause children to go into a rage, and identify the safe place as a good place to be.

You can't force a child in meltdown mode to go to a safe place, but you can notice the signals of a meltdown before it becomes a full-blown tantrum and can ask the child if he needs to go to the safe place. You can offer to help him go to the safe place. If the child is small enough, you can offer to carry him to the safe place. If the child refuses, simply sit down next to the child. You can put your hand on the child's back if he is facedown or on the child's shin if he is belly up to see if he is receptive to touch. If he is, gently rub his back or lower leg (never above the knee). If the child starts to de-escalate, offer to help him to the safe place. If he still refuses, simply continue to sit next to him and periodically let him know that you are there to help him if he is ready.

Your movements should be slow and deliberate. Any fast movement toward the child may be interpreted as an aggressive act and may further send him into terror. As soon as the child begins to de-escalate, calmly let him know you are there. Offer to rub his back, rock him, or wrap him in a quilt, or offer some water and a granola bar. Do whatever you know helps the child calm down.

Possible Triggers that May Escalate Arousal States

- A new child or adult
- A stranger entering the space
- Noise level
- A smell
- An unexpected noise
- Change in lighting
- Change in schedule
- Too many transitions
- Harsh words or tone of voice
- Angry or fearful facial expressions

- Quick movements
- Unexpected touch
- Harsh touch
- Another child crying
- Someone taking something away
- New room arrangement
- New piece of equipment
- Nap time
- Someone approaching the child too quickly
- An adult towering over a child

- Disorganized materials
- Unpredictable schedule
- The absence of a caregiver
- A particular texture
- Taking the child's shoes off while lying down
- Someone approaching while the child is lying on a cot
- Tickling a child

Fight, Flight, or Freeze Response

> Understanding that aggression is the language of fear profoundly changes how adults view and respond to children's maladaptive behavior. An aggressive child is a scared child.

When the brain determines that danger is present, the brain and body will deal with it in one of three ways: fight, flee, or freeze.

The child who operates in **fight** mode becomes verbally and/or physically aggressive. She may swear or call people names. At the extreme, the child may become physically violent and pinch, hit, kick, spit, and flail about. In the child's mind, she is literally fighting for her life.

Understanding that aggression is the language of fear profoundly changes how adults view and respond to children's maladaptive behavior. An aggressive child is a scared child. Understanding this basic principle helps adults to look at children with compassion rather than anger.

Common Behaviors of Children in Fight Mode

- Child yells or screams
- Child is argumentative
- Child curses
- Child throws self on floor
- Child kicks, hits, spits, bites, or head-butts other children and adults
- Child destroys property
- Child makes violent threats
- Child uses objects to jab or hit other objects or people in the room

Other children will **flee** or seek to get away from the perceived threat at hand. When an adult raises his voice or reprimands a child, she may hide under the table or pull a jacket over her head and refuse to look at or talk to the caregiver or teacher. If a child perceives the teacher is annoyed with her on the playground, she may run in the opposite direction when called or may hide behind a bush. In extreme cases, she may literally leave the property and run away.

Common Behaviors of Children in Flight Mode

- Child covers face with hands, buries face in arms, pulls jacket over head, pulls hat down over face, wears sunglasses
- Child hides someplace in the room out of sight of caregiver or teacher
- Child literally runs out of the building or room
- Child hides under a blanket
- Child sits in the corner of the room and just watches
- Child sits under a table
- Child appears to be daydreaming
- Child falls asleep when things are chaotic, noisy, or overstimulating
- Child becomes absorbed with things and seems oblivious to people

The initial reaction to a traumatic event is always **freeze**, even if for a split second, as the brain assesses the situation. However, some individuals will remain in freeze mode if the threat is particularly overwhelming or if the individual is a very young child. The freeze state is called *dissociation* and is the brain's way of preparing the body to get hurt. Blood flow and heart rate decrease to limit the loss of blood from potential injury. The body produces a surge of natural painkillers and opioids to blunt the perception of pain and produce a calm state that allows the individual to put psychological distance between herself and the trauma at hand. Conscious memory shuts down but "body memories" of the trauma are stored.

Dissociation is more prevalent in female children and is the primary defense mechanism for infants and toddlers. In response to the initial alarm state, a baby will attempt to signal the caregiver for help through movement, facial expressions, and crying. If no one is around or if her cries are ignored, the baby will use the only coping mechanism she has available—dissociation. A baby does not have the physical capacity to become aggressive and fight back, nor does she have the ability to run. Her only option is to psychologically distance herself from the experience. It is the mind and body's way of protecting itself.

The degree of dissociation lies on a continuum from mild to severe. In the mildest forms a baby may seem to be in an in-between state of wakefulness and sleep or may appear listless and "checked out." Some infants will actually go to sleep as a way of escaping the trauma. As children get older, you will see some of the same behaviors such as appearing to be "checked out" or daydreaming. In extreme cases the child may seem to be in a trance-like state and unable to hear or see you.

At the most extreme end of the dissociative spectrum, both children and adults may have an out-of-body experience that is often described as being a bystander to the events that happen to them. As van der Kolk describes in *The Body Keeps the Score*, it is as if the person is standing on the sidelines watching what is happening and has no perception of actually feeling the pain or being a part of the event. When maltreatment is so severe and chronic that it triggers an out-of-body experience on a regular basis, the likelihood of the child developing a serious mental illness increases.

Although the freeze or dissociative response is often seen in infants, it is not uncommon for older children to display this primitive defense mechanism as well. In addition to the symptoms listed above, toddlers in a state of dissociation may wander around the room as if in a daze and not pause to focus on any one thing or activity. They may stare into space and seem to be daydreaming. Some will regress, and more infantile behaviors will reappear or persist. Others may whimper and tremble for no apparent reason or may respond to unfamiliar noises, people, or sights by "checking out." Some may display repetitive motions such as rocking or swaying and may fail to gain weight and grow.

The child who becomes uncooperative, shuts down, tunes people out, and seems unable to hear or understand anything may actually be in a mild dissociative state. In their books, Bruce Perry and Maia Szalavitz assert that children who are diagnosed as "oppositional defiant" are actually children who live in freeze mode. They are so overwhelmed by fear that memory shuts down, and they are unable to process and respond to instruction. Their lack of compliance is misinterpreted as rebellion.

According to Perry in the *Textbook of Child and Adolescent Forensic Psychiatry*, some children who are able to describe the experience speak of "going to a different place," taking on the identity of an animal or superhero, or leaving their body and watching the event unfold much like watching a movie. This dynamic creates a profound sense of learned helplessness in children.

Common Behaviors of Children in Freeze Mode
- Babies will appear lethargic and spaced out
- Child is unresponsive to name being called
- Child is unresponsive to commands, requests, or questions
- Child appears to daydream a lot

The Role of Memory

Memory plays an important role in how we perceive and respond to the world and affects the way we deal with and process a traumatic event. The brain is an historical organ and acts as a virtual filing cabinet for our memories. To reach and teach children exposed to trauma, it is important to understand some basic facts about the development of memory.

During the first two years of life, all children experience what Daniel Siegel and Mary Hartzell, authors of *Parenting from the Inside Out*, term *childhood amnesia*. Most people are unable to intentionally recall specific events or experiences from these early years. However, during this time, there is a preverbal form of memory operating called implicit memory. *Implicit memory* plays a role in the formation of the earliest connections in our brains. Additionally, one of its most important roles is the creation of mental models. Our brains are not big enough to store every specific detail about every specific experience in life; instead, they make associations and create generalizations about our experiences. For example, if a child grows up in the context of domestic violence in the first years of his life, he will not remember specific incidents of violence, but his brain will make generalizations about relationships, creating an internal working model that tells him relationships are not safe. Later in life, he may have no conscious memory of the violence, but the implicit memory of these early experiences will be the filter through which he processes life. He likely will have difficulty with trust and intimacy, though he will not be aware of the cause. Mental models created in the first years of life influence how we think about ourselves, our families, and the world around us. I often hear potential adoptive parents comment that they want to adopt a baby because he or she won't remember the abuse, creating less likelihood of serious developmental concerns. This couldn't be further from the truth. Early experiences are encoded in the brain through implicit memory. Implicit memory is operating at birth, and there is evidence that it may even be operating in utero. Every experience that a person of any age has results in a particular firing of neuronal connections in the brain. The brain "remembers" these patterns of connecting—even in babies—through the nonverbal implicit memory system. As Siegel and Hartzell assert, the implicit memory system encodes emotional responses, behavioral responses, perception, and bodily sensations.

For example, a toddler is subject to sexual abuse until the age of two, when her mom leaves the abusive father and later marries a very loving man who is a good father to the child. At ten years of age, the child goes to a slumber party. All the little girls are in their sleeping bags, and the father of the house climbs the stairs to tell the children that it is time to turn out the lights and go to bed. The sound of his heavy footsteps triggers an implicit memory in the little girl with a history of abuse. She suddenly feels terrified, starts to cry, and begs to go home. She has no idea why she suddenly feels scared; she just knows that she wants to get out of there. Such implicit memories can be triggered by smells, sounds, faces, textures, tastes, or any other bodily sensation associated with a traumatic event.

Daniel Siegel, in *The Developing Mind*, writes that sometime after age two, the hippocampus in the brain develops, allowing *explicit memory* to develop. This means that events can be consciously recalled and processed. Explicit memory actually makes processing a traumatic event somewhat easier because the memory can be brought to mind and shared with another person through language.

Often when we are dealing with behavioral issues with a traumatized child, we are bumping up against her history and stored memory. For example, Susie is a three-year-old adopted child who was in and out of foster care during the first two years of life. When she was about eighteen months old, her biological mother kidnapped her and her three-year-old sister after a supervised visit. As the caseworker walked with the children to the car, the biological mother was waiting in the bushes and snatched Susie out of the arms of the caseworker. The mother had arranged to have another woman grab the three-year-old. The children were gone for three days before being found by the police. The event happened in December when there was snow on the ground and Christmas decorations everywhere. Police found the children unkempt and hungry in a disheveled, filthy home with a group of drug addicts.

Shortly afterward, the children were adopted into a loving home and enrolled in child care. Susie liked to climb and would climb on anything and everything in sight. However, when an adult grabbed her from behind to pull her off a piece of equipment, she would become hysterical. She would thrash and scream violently and try to get away. In December, when snow began to fall and Christmas decorations began to appear, she became very aggressive toward others. She was asked to leave the center because of her "oppositional behavior." Sadly, this same story played out four more times in four more centers.

Children from hard places may carry many explicit memories of trauma that repeatedly play across their minds. They may be so preoccupied with these memories that it is difficult for them to focus on anything else, and this is one of the reasons why they sometimes struggle to learn. Sometimes they re-enact the event over and over again in the dramatic play center, draw pictures of it, or compulsively talk about it. Often the memories of a traumatic event don't play out in a cohesive narrative fashion but appear in the child's mind as a series of disconnected images. These memories are multilayered and complex, making it challenging to help children process their experiences. The brain is driven to make sense of the world and the experiences of life, but sometimes a child's life experiences are so far out of the range of "normal" that the brain struggles to gain mastery over them. Perry asserts in his booklet *Effects of Traumatic Events on Children* that different parts of our brain are designed to store different types of memories.

State Memory

The brain stem encodes *state memory*, the anxiety or arousal state associated with a particular traumatic event. Even if the event happened during the period of childhood amnesia, a state memory can be triggered and the child may react in unpredictable ways.

Motor Memory

Motor memories are stored in the midbrain and cerebellum and are the body memories that lie within our muscles, joints, and tendons. Whenever there is a traumatic event, the midbrain encodes information about the position or movements of the body. For example, I encountered a situation where a childcare center reported behavioral difficulties with a four-year-old girl. She would become hysterical when they pulled her shoes off at nap time, which the center staff viewed as noncompliance. Her foster parents disclosed that she had been sexually abused during the first two years of life—the period of childhood amnesia. Though she likely has no conscious memory of the abuse, having her shoes removed while lying down triggered a motor memory of her trauma. Her therapist suggested letting her sleep with her shoes on or allowing her to sit in a chair to have her shoes removed.

Emotional Memory

The limbic brain is responsible for storing the *emotional memories* of an experience. For example, we have all probably had the experience of hearing a favorite song from our teen years that triggers the memory of a particular event or person. Immediately the emotions of the past wash over us. We may once again experience the thrill of driving down the road in our first car or the pain of breaking up with our first boyfriend or girlfriend. So it is with children. Hearing another child cry can trigger the memory of younger brothers and sisters cowering in the corner as mom and dad slugged it out and the accompanying feeling of helplessness. If a child falls down on the playground, the sight of blood can trigger the memory of seeing someone get shot and the terror of the moment. If a childcare provider innocently grabs a child's arm to keep him from tripping over a toy, this can trigger the memory of the child's alcoholic dad coming home at night and pulling him out of bed for a beating. The child may become violent as the fear washes over him.

Cognitive Memory

The cortex is responsible for encoding *cognitive memories*. These are easily recalled and include specific facts about an incident, such as who, what, when, and where it happened. A family member may arrive to pick up his child wearing a ball cap turned backward. Another child looks up and sees him and begins to cry and scream because his abusive father always wore a backward ball cap. A police car drives by the playground with the siren on. A child begins to cry because she remembers the night the police responded to the domestic violence in her home and she was taken to a shelter in the back of a police car.

Traumatic memories can take years to process. It is important for teachers and caregivers to document triggers that they notice in children and to pass this information along to therapists, family members, and any professionals working with the child. The more information that is available, the better the team will be able to help the child.

Not only are these memories activated in children, but they can be activated in the adults who care for and teach children. We all have certain circumstances that evoke strong emotions in us. It may be a particular child or it may be a particular circumstance, but we suddenly find ourselves experiencing emotions with an intensity that can be frightening. For example, suppose there is a caregiver who suffered sexual abuse as a child, but she has kept these awful secrets for twenty years, telling no one. She is changing the diaper of a baby who has experienced sexual abuse, and every time the baby gets a diaper change, the baby thrashes about on the changing table, screaming. Though abuse is suspected, the authorities are still in the process of trying to prove the case; hence, the baby remains in the home. The behavior of the baby triggers the repressed memory stored in the caregiver's brain, and suddenly the adult's heart is racing, her breathing becomes shallow, and an overwhelming sense of anxiety and fear wash over her. The adult may not even be aware of where the feelings are coming from, or she may begin to have images flash before her eyes like snapshots. It is possible that the adult may even become aggressive toward the baby or remain so wrapped up in the clutches of fear and anxiety she is not able to comfort the baby. Our own trauma memories can prevent us from caring for the children entrusted to our care in a warm and responsive manner.

> It was once believed that traumatic memories in the early days of life had no impact on the life of an individual. We now know this is not true.

It is important to note in this discussion that scientists now believe that memories are even stored during the prenatal period. In *Neurofeedback in the Treatment of Developmental Trauma*, Sebern Fisher states that the amygdala comes online between the fifth and sixth month of pregnancy, at which time the developing baby begins to feel fear. The fetus feels and hears the mother's pounding heart and hears the angry voices outside the womb. Children who are exposed to alcohol, drugs, smoking, or toxic levels of stress hormones marinate in a state of stress and fear during a significant part their prenatal experience. Because they are robbed of essential nutrients and oxygen, these babies grow and develop in a chronic state of alarm that alters the stress response of their brain stems and stores templates of fear in their state memory. As Nathanielsz reports in his book *Life in the Womb: The Origin of Health and Disease*, it is well known that prenatal trauma and stress critically alter the development of the stress-response system of the brain and are linked to high blood pressure, heart disease, stroke, and mood disorders.

Chapter 3

The Effect of Trauma on Relationships

The behavior of maltreated children is often difficult to understand and can be very disruptive to the flow of the classroom. Most caregivers and teachers usually just want to know how to "fix" the behavior. Anyone who works with children needs to recognize that there is a vast difference between simply managing behavior and truly healing a child. Managing behavior is basically about getting through the day with the least amount of stress and pushback. It largely involves power and control, reward and punishment, or bribery. Adults may tiptoe around, hoping that nothing is said or done that will set the child off.

Creating a trauma-informed environment designed to facilitate emotional healing and effect lasting change means focusing on relationships instead of solely on behavior. In their book *Hold on to Your Kids*, authors Gordon Neufeld and Gabor Maté assert that the ability to influence the behavior of a child is directly proportional to the strength of the attachment relationship that a caregiver has with that child. Children who have been harmed in the context of a relationship can only be healed in a relationship. It's about changing a child's heart, not just the behavior, and this will never happen without a relationship of trust and unconditional acceptance.

> Children who have been harmed in the context of a relationship can only be healed in a relationship. You will never truly change a child's heart without first establishing a relationship of trust and unconditional acceptance.

Uri Bronfenbrenner, the renowned developmental psychologist, once said that every child needs to know that there is someone who is absolutely crazy about him, that he is the apple of someone's eye. He needs to have a relationship with at least one adult who takes great delight in meeting his needs. Children who are afforded such a relationship come to believe that they are lovable and worthy of care. However, this fundamental birthright has been stolen from those who have suffered maltreatment. When children are abused, neglected, shamed, or humiliated, they don't think, "What's wrong with these adults?" Instead, they think, "What is wrong with me?"

The Internal Working Model

During the first year of life, children are developing an internal working model of the social world, a filter or a set of beliefs that will shape a child's thinking about himself and his interactions with other people. It may be positive or negative, depending upon the availability and responsiveness of a child's caregivers. Infants whose needs are met with warmth, sensitivity, and acceptance develop a positive view of self and the world. Infants whose needs are ignored or met with harshness and abuse develop a negative view of self and others. For better or for worse, an individual's internal working model serves as a template for how the social world works, and it follows the child into adulthood. The outcome of a positive internal working model is a healthy sense of self-esteem, self-confidence, and trust.

Self-esteem relates to the child's feelings toward himself. Children with a positive internal working model view themselves as loveable and worthy of care. They come to child care expecting their needs to be met in a timely and affectionate manner. Because they view themselves as loveable, they can accept the love and care extended to them by the adults in their world. Maltreated children, however, often believe that they deserve the poor treatment they receive. They typically carry a great deal of shame at their core, which differs from guilt. Guilt is feeling bad about what one has done; shame is feeling bad about who one is. A person can change behavior but not who he or she is. Shame is toxic to healthy growth and development.

Children with a base of shame or negative internal working model show up in child care not expecting to be treated well or that their needs will be met with warmth and affection; therefore, when they encounter adults who offer unconditional acceptance and meet their needs in timely and affectionate ways, it elicits enormous feelings of vulnerability and fear. When their experience contradicts their internal working model, maltreated children often find it difficult to accept the love and care extended to them. Their challenging behaviors are often an effort to "prove" that they are unlovable and to push people away to escape their feelings of vulnerability.

The internal working model also affects self-confidence, a child's understanding of his ability to accomplish things and make an impact on his work. Everyone has an innate drive within to master our world. Children whose needs are met in timely and affectionate ways come to view themselves as capable and effective at eliciting the care they need from others. They are able to venture out into the world with confidence and curiosity. Children who suffer maltreatment, on the other hand, interpret abuse or neglect as a confirmation of their own ineffectiveness. They see themselves as so incompetent and flawed that they can't even get their basic needs met by others. They are afraid to try new things and approach even the simplest task with an "I can't do it" lens.

Finally, a negative internal working model undermines the child's capacity to trust in the goodness and availability of others and to believe that the world is a safe place. The capacity to trust is the foundation of mental health and allows the child to live with a sense of hope and optimism and invest his energies in exploration and mastery of his environment. However, when neglect, abuse, and trauma erode the capacity to trust, the child lives in a constant state of aloneness and isolation. She arrives in child care unable to accept affection and care. Relationships are viewed with suspicion and fear, and attempts to reach out to her may elicit seemingly irrational responses, such as averting her eyes or literally pulling away from an embrace. She may run, act silly, or become aggressive toward the person trying to connect. Fear drives the behavior, not rudeness or defiance. Maltreated children have a tendency to switch off all feelings of vulnerability as a way of self-protection. Emotions become blunted, and there is a dullness of soul often reflected in the eyes. Trust can only develop in the absence of fear; the two are incompatible.

There is nothing simple or easy about caring for a wounded child. One of the most important things to remember is to not take it personally. You are bumping up against the child's history, which can cause you to bump up against your own feelings of inadequacy and lack of confidence. We can never lose sight of the fact that humans are wired for relationships. The brain requires it, and healthy growth and development depend upon it. In the heart of even the most defiant and angry child is, at the very least, a thread of a desire to connect with others. This becomes the primary task of a healing environment—to develop a secure attachment relationship with every child.

Before we look at strategies to deal with these behaviors, we must first address three questions you need to ask when things are not going well in a classroom:

- Is there anything that I, as the adult, am doing to contribute to the problem?
- What is the environment doing to contribute to the problem?
- What is going on within the child?

Am I Contributing to the Problem?

- **Are my expectations appropriate for the age and developmental level of the child?** Because of the culture in which we live, we expect children to master academic skills at younger and younger ages. Understanding ages and stages and developmentally appropriate practice is critical.

- **Have I established a relationship with the child?** My ability to influence a child's behavior is directly proportional to the strength of my attachment with that child. I will never be able to change a child's behavior without a relationship.

- **Do I look at the child with compassion and respect instead of irritation and anger?** The behavior of harmed children is sometimes exasperating, but without a fundamental attitude of compassion and respect, we will never be able to connect. Adults often think they can hide their feelings from children, but we all leak. Our demeanor and feelings about a particular child will spill all over him if we aren't mindful and self-aware.

What Is the Environment Doing to Contribute to the Behavior?

The environment is the second teacher and has a direct effect on a child's behavior and learning. Trauma-informed teachers check carefully to avoid environmental features that trigger challenging behaviors. For example, in my first year of teaching in the inner city, we had a sand lot for a playground. There was no equipment whatsoever, not even a ball. So, the children threw sand and fought with each other. The environment set them up for inappropriate behavior. Not enough materials, a disorganized and cluttered classroom, too many children, too many transitions throughout the day—any and all of these can trigger behavioral challenges.

What Is Going on with the Child to Cause This Behavior?

Understanding the child's history is critical. The more you know about the child's past, the better you will be able to meet his needs. Family members and caregivers are not always forthcoming with information, but as you establish relationships and a bond of trust with them, they often share important details that help you better serve the children. For example, knowing about complications during pregnancy, premature birth, family trauma, divorce, incarceration of parents or family members, or catastrophic illness and injury in the family can contribute another piece to the puzzle of understanding the reasons for a child's behavior and can help you know how to help him.

The Power of Being Wanted

In his book *Anatomy of the Soul*, psychiatrist Curt Thompson says, "A baby is born looking for someone looking for him." Emotionally healthy moms begin to "look for" their baby when they first feel the baby move. Movement typically confirms the reality of the baby, and moms actively begin to prepare psychologically and in practical ways for the child's arrival. Parents and family members begin to hold an image in their minds of what they imagine a child will look like and what life will be like with her. A joyfully anticipated baby will instinctively know she is celebrated and wanted. Others will become keenly aware that no one is looking for them.

There are many reasons why the birth of a baby is not celebrated. Mom may be addicted to substances or in the depths of depression. The baby may be just one more mouth to feed or the result of rape, prostitution, incest, or a one-night stand. Anecdotal evidence cited by Purvis and Thompson suggests that babies have an instinctive awareness of their aloneness or sense of being unwanted. I recently had a woman who was adopted at birth approach me after a conference. In her teenage years she often left home for days on end, sleeping in parks or going home with virtual strangers. She said she finally realized why she did it: "Something happened to me before I was born. I think I wasn't wanted. I ran away because I needed to know someone was looking for me." She went on to explain that when she ran, she would always leave clues for her adoptive parents to find. She wanted to be found and needed to know that they cared enough to look.

Consider the first weeks and months of life from the perspectives of two different children:

A baby is born to a mom living in the chaos of domestic violence. Throughout the pregnancy, the unborn baby is subject to the effects of toxic stress suffered by the mom and the chaotic sounds and sensations of the violent world outside the womb. Because of the conditions in utero, the baby's stress response is altered, and the child cries with a sharp, piercing sound for hours on end. His exhausted mother is overwhelmed by her circumstances. She does her best to try to soothe the baby, but she is so preoccupied with her own fear that she is unable to attune to him and read his cues. During a feeding he turns his head away from her and the bottle, but she doesn't realize that he is trying to tell her that he has had enough. She grows anxious because she thinks if she can just get him to eat more maybe he won't cry as much. She continues to prod and try to poke the bottle into his mouth, but he brings his little fists up to his face and continues to look away. Her anxiety increases, and her body becomes tense. The baby senses her anxiety and begins to cry. Dad walks in the door and begins to scream at the mom, "Can't you keep that baby quiet? What kind of a mother are you?" At the sound of the father's angry shouting, the baby begins his piercing wail. The mother plops the baby in his crib and throws a blanket over him in an attempt to protect him, then she runs out of the room, slamming the door to confront her husband and hopefully keep him from harming the baby. As the child lays in the darkness alone, he hears chaotic voices and the sound of furniture falling. There is no one to attune to him or meet his needs.

But let's imagine a different scenario for this same baby. The mom shows up to the hospital to have her baby, and the nurses notice her black eye and the large knot on her head. They alert the hospital social workers, and after the baby is born, the mom tells them the whole story. Together, they make arrangements to move her into a home for battered women and children, where she can get the rest and care she needs and the resources to create a new life for herself and her baby.

After six weeks, the infant is enrolled in a high-quality child care center so that his mom can attend classes to get her GED. Because of the prenatal stress the baby endured, he cries a lot and can be rather irritable. The child care provider is aware of the baby's history and understands that this little guy needs some extra tender loving care. When he cries, she carefully reads his cues. She determines that he most likely just needs some comfort and attention. She picks him up, and immediately he quiets and snuggles against her body. She rocks him for a bit and quietly sings and looks into his eyes. He feels the calm and steady rhythm of her heart and the warmth of her body and breath. As the relationship between this baby and his caregiver continues over time, she will become increasingly adept at reading the baby's cues and understanding his needs.

This process of reading and responding to a baby's cues is a dance that we call *attunement*. It is a fundamental ingredient in all satisfying relationships throughout the human lifespan. One of the most powerful needs we all have is to be understood, to know that someone truly "gets" us. For example, a baby hears a loud noise and begins to cry loudly in his crib. As the caregiver picks him up, her face mirrors the expression on the child's face. She frowns and sympathetically asks, "Aw, did that scare you?" She holds him close and gently rocks him until he is calm. In this simple interaction, her touch, her facial expression, and her voice communicate, "I get you. I understand your distress. I know you are afraid." Over time, as this type of interaction occurs day in and day out, the child begins to believe that the world is a safe place where people can be counted on to meet his needs. Trust is born in his heart.

Attunement is instinctive to most adults, but many things can undermine this essential dynamic both at home and in child care settings. A mother who is the victim of domestic violence is going to find it difficult to attune to her children, as will family members who are addicted to substances and those who are clinically depressed.

Attuned caregivers are important for all children but for those with a history of trauma, attuned care is a critical ingredient for mental health and healing. Attuned caregivers have the potential to buffer the effects of overwhelmed caregivers at home. Many things can disrupt attunement in a child care or preschool setting:

- High ratios of children to staff
- A high percentage of children with special needs and not enough help
- High staff turnover

- Preoccupation with personal issues
- Conflict between adults in the classroom
- Fatigue
- Unpredictable work environment
- Lack of support from administrators
- Lack of training, which leads to feelings of incompetence

Attachment versus Bonding

We are genetically wired to live in relationships with other people. At the moment of birth there is biological bond between a mother and a child. Nature jumpstarts the relationship through hormonal changes that give moms a biological drive to nurture and protect their children. Moms have an innate desire to initiate bonding behaviors such as holding, cuddling, smelling, rocking, and gazing at their newborns. The infants typically respond by snuggling, cooing, clinging, and gazing, back. Infants can recognize mothers by their voices and by their smell, which also facilitates the bonding process.

Unfortunately, many things can override the bonding process and the biological drive of a new mom to nurture and care for her child, such as drugs, alcohol, clinical depression, and domestic violence. A mind altered by drugs can cause a parent to respond to the cries of the baby with harshness and violence rather than love and affection. The shroud of untreated post-partum depression can be so debilitating that a mom does not have the emotional capacity to respond to her baby. Victims of domestic violence may throw a blanket over the crib when violence breaks out in the hope that it will muffle the sounds and somehow protect the baby.

Also, a baby who is difficult to soothe, the presence of a birth defect, or a premature birth can undermine the bond that is typically present. The child may remind the parent of an abusive partner and be unconsciously rejected.

In healthy development, bonding behaviors continue through the first weeks and months of life, producing a secure *attachment*—the strong emotional bond that is present between people and endures over time. It is the human drive to maintain physical, emotional and psychological closeness to family members and caregivers and to those with whom we have a biological, emotional, and social connection. Unfortunately, maltreatment, neglect, and trauma can thwart and undermine this instinctual drive.

Types of Attachment Patterns

An *attachment pattern* is a template or habitual way of perceiving and responding to relationships with other people. Research has identified four basic ones:

- Secure
- Insecure avoidant
- Insecure ambivalent
- Disorganized

Secure attachment is the healthiest and most desirable pattern because it predicts the best outcomes for mental and emotional health. There are two forms of organized but insecure attachment patterns, which means the child has a plan for responding and interacting with others, but it is not the optimum way of relating and presents some challenges to both the child and the caregiver. It doesn't mean that the child had abusive or "bad" parents, just that the child did not receive optimal levels of nurturing care. Last is the disorganized attachment pattern, which indicates maltreatment or neglect of some sort. Researchers including Marinus van Ijzendoorn, Carlo Schuengel, and Marian Bakermans-Kranenburg have found that, of maltreated children, 80 percent will display disorganized attachment. Understanding the different attachment patterns and how they form can help teachers and caregivers better understand the emotional needs of children and the behaviors that they often display.

Secure Attachment

Children with secure attachment are often described as well-adjusted and pleasant to be around. They get along with other children, respond well to appropriate adult authority and requests, and accept comfort from others when hurt or upset. They know that others are there for them (a "secure base") and are able to approach the world with an overall sense of hope and curiosity. Securely attached children have confidence in their own abilities to cope with challenges. This is not to say that securely attached children don't have their moments—they do—but they respond well to instruction and correction. These children feel free to express negative emotions and do so without feeling shame and rejection. They have a flexibility that allows them to adapt to the daily ups and downs of life without undue stress.

Research has given us insight into the biological reasons why securely attached children are better able to handle stressful life events than insecurely attached children. According to researchers such as Megan Gunnar, Charles Nelson, and Melissa Nachmias, securely attached children do not release high levels of cortisol as insecurely attached children do. And, as Sue Gerhardt points out in her book *Why Love Matters: How Affection Shapes a Baby's Brain*, there is evidence to suggest that securely attached babies develop more cortisol receptors in the first year of life.

Securely attached children typically have nurturing families who have a reasonable degree of emotional strength and maturity. They respond quickly and warmly to the child's distress and basic needs with an appropriate degree of nurturing. Even though parenting an infant is a demanding task, these families find great pleasure and joy in meeting the needs of their child. Playful interactions are a normal and regular part of the relationship, and mutual delight between parent and child is obvious.

In the classroom or child care setting, securely attached children demonstrate a high degree of competence. They aren't overly demanding of adult attention but aren't afraid to ask for help when they need it. They are usually listed among the most well-liked children in any group and are often looked up to by others. Secure attachment gives children a base that is critical to successful learning and functioning in school. Robert Karen states in his book *Becoming Attached* that studies have found securely attached children are more responsive to instruction and demonstrate a higher degree of persistence when they encounter challenging tasks. They can engage in more creative play and have the capacity to create imaginary worlds, unlike children who lack securely attached relationships.

Insecure Avoidant Attachment

Children with insecure avoidant attachment do not find relationships to be particularly satisfying. They have a level of self-sufficiency and fearlessness that makes them seem mature beyond their years. Intimacy and closeness are uncomfortable for them, and often they take more enjoyment in things rather than people. It is not unusual for them to avoid eye contact and "suck it up" when they get hurt or are distressed, rebuffing adult attempts to console or comfort them. If they fall off the climbing equipment, they will act like it doesn't hurt and walk away.

Three different types of avoidant attachment have been identified by Sroufe. There is the shy, very withdrawn child who may seem emotionally flat but who, from time to time, may have a surprising, out-of-character emotional meltdown that seems to come out of nowhere. There is the obviously disturbed child who may have unusual twitches or "quirks" and may seem to live in his own world most of the time. And then there is the aggressive bully who is persistently angry, blames others for everything that goes wrong, and may lie to avoid being found out. These children are loners, and alienation, isolation, and self-protection often characterize their journeys through life.

An avoidant attachment pattern is fostered in both obvious and subtle ways, but the overall dynamic can be described as "dismissive." Even though physically present, the parent or caregiver is emotionally unresponsive or even rejecting of the child's display of feeling. Some homes are overtly and harshly dismissive of emotion, and others are more nuanced. For some families, the neediness of their children overwhelms them, and they lash out in anger and frustration. In *Anatomy of the Soul*, Thompson says the child internalizes the message that emotions are not okay and not important and that the world is an emotionally barren place where feelings don't matter. Many issues—mental illness, domestic violence, addiction, clinical depression, catastrophic illness or injury, poverty, or other trauma—may sap the emotional resources of a parent and leave him or her with nothing to give the children. For example, a single mom is struggling to survive emotionally and financially or a father is trying to deal with two small children and a mentally ill wife. These are not bad people. They love their children and want the best for them but are overwhelmed and lack an adequate support system to help them with life's challenges.

In other families, the dismissive nature of the parent is subtler. These task-oriented parents effectively meet the outward needs of food, clothing, shelter, and education, but they ignore the needs of the heart. The neediness of their children is an inconvenience and source of irritation that results in a socially acceptable form of emotional neglect. The children are expected to function according to schedules and expectations that may not be developmentally appropriate. Perfection is the goal, and competence in everything they do is expected. Outwardly, these children may appear to have everything they need—designer clothes, every toy and gadget on the market, lessons in everything from tennis to voice to piano to martial arts, and enrollment at the best schools—but they lack genuine warmth and connection with their parents.

Researchers such as Karen have observed teacher interactions with avoidantly attached children and have found that these children are least likely to evoke a warm response from their caregivers and the most likely to provoke their teachers to anger. The avoidant child's aloof, sullen, or oppositional demeanor and seemingly arrogant self-sufficiency alienate the adults who care for him. This dynamic further reinforces the child's belief that people are not available and that he is not worthy of love and affection. Because interaction with things seems safer than interaction with people, these children often are more concerned about their "stuff"

than they are about relationships. They gravitate toward electronic games and technology, because interacting with machines is a way of avoiding interactions with people. According to Karen, relationships are a constant struggle.

Avoidant children may seek the attention of adults through negative behaviors, such as demanding to sit on their laps or wanting to sit next to them at every group time. They may push their way to the front of the line to hold the teacher's hand while jeering at the other children. If they are sent back to their place, they often pout and scowl. Teachers generally don't even expect compliance from an avoidant child. Attachment researcher and expert Allan Sroufe, as quoted by Robert Karen in *Becoming Attached*, once said, "Whenever I see a teacher who looks as if she wants to pick a child up by the shoulders and stuff him in the trash barrel, I know that kid has an avoidant attachment history."

Insecure Ambivalent Attachment

Children with insecure ambivalent attachment demonstrate emotional extremes. They can be demanding, clingy, and difficult to satisfy—nothing is ever quite right—and they have low tolerance for frustration. Their behavior can be unpredictable and disruptive as they often resort to temper tantrums or crying as a manipulative tool to get their way. The child may be fidgety and compulsive with poor concentration skills, easily upset and tense. Or, the child may be the fearful and clingy type who lacks initiative and gives up easily when he encounters a challenge. Ambivalent children are difficult to soothe: Ambivalently attached babies cry more at one year of age than children with other forms of attachment. According to researchers including Thompson, Karen, and Purvis, they live with a pervasive sense of anxiety and insecurity. As they get older, they are more likely to be the victims of bullies and more likely to succumb to substance abuse.

Sometimes whiny and demanding children are viewed as "spoiled" or indulged. In *The Boy Who Was Raised as a Dog*, Bruce Perry and Maia Szalavitz point out that people assume such children become that way because they have been given too much or feel too good about themselves. An adult's inclination is to punish them and hopefully coerce them to change, such as sending them to time out until they straighten up. Love, for them, is usually conditional; they are loved and accepted only when they have their act together. What many people don't realize is that whiny and demanding children typically have unmet emotional needs and unexplored potential. Their behavior is not the result of too many good things—it is the result of too few, and we take away the very thing they need: unconditional love and acceptance.

Karen reports in *Becoming Attached* that Sroufe and his students have looked at the interaction patterns of teachers with ambivalently attached children in the classroom and have found that teachers are usually more indulgent toward them than they are with other children. He asserts that teachers view these children as emotionally immature and incapable of following rules, so teachers cut them more slack and hold them to a lower standard.

According to Thompson, the child with ambivalent attachment is typically cared for by people who are consumed by their own anxiety. Their preoccupation with their own worries and concerns makes it difficult for them to attune to their child's needs. They are very unpredictable in their ability to read their child's cues and respond inconsistently, being very attentive at times but ignoring them at other times. There is yet another dynamic that creates an ambivalent attachment pattern and that is the intrusive parent. In this type of relationship, the parent is constantly imposing his own agenda on the child. For example, the child may be playing with his Legos, when his dad sits down next to him and insists on reading a story.

Once again, it is important to understand that these adults are not bad people—they are typically overwhelmed by life and simply don't have the resources to cope or the emotional resources to provide consistent nurturing and care. They may be burdened by financial or health issues, marital problems, or addictive behaviors. They have the best of intentions but are unable to provide the consistency of care required by babies and young children.

Disorganized Attachment

When researchers first began recognizing children's attachment patterns, they encountered a few who did not fall neatly into a single category and who displayed characteristics of both avoidant and ambivalent attachment. Their behavior was very chaotic and unpredictable. Therefore, a fourth category, disorganized attachment, was identified. It indicates that the child has either been the victim of or witness to chronic violence. In a study of maltreated infants, Vicki Carlson, Dante Cicchetti, Douglas Barnett, and Karen Braunwalk found that 82 percent of them had disorganized attachment at one year of age. Without appropriate intervention, the disorganized orientation of these children will remain unchanged. As they grow, they can be very challenging in the child care or classroom setting. The disorganized child typically lives in a chronic state of alarm that easily escalates into fear or terror. They are prone to acts of aggression or violent meltdowns. At other times they may be withdrawn to the point that they seem almost nonresponsive. They are highly attuned to nonverbal cues or nuances that people don't like them but often misinterpret tone of voice, body language, and facial expressions of their caregivers and react

Many children spend most of their waking hours outside the home; therefore, the relationships that form with young children in centers and schools have the power to set the trajectory of a child's life.

in ways that may seem bizarre or strange. They can be highly reactive to sensory cues in the environment, interpreting sights, sounds, and other sensations as threatening.

Children with disorganized attachment live in homes where parents or caregivers are scared or scary. Mom may live in a state of fear because of an abusive and violent husband or boyfriend, making it impossible to respond to the needs of her child. Or, the mom or dad may be the perpetrator of the abuse. The natural human tendency of a child is to turn to a parent for comfort when he is afraid. But when the person who is supposed to be the source of comfort is the source of the abuse, as researchers Lieberman and Van Horn point out, the child is put into an impossible psychological dilemma. Abuse by a parent is psychological poison. Unfortunately, the challenging and chaotic behavior that disorganized children exhibit often elicits anger, frustration, and shame from caregivers and teachers who don't understand that the behavior is a function of the trauma.

In his 2014 webinar on the neurosequential model of therapeutics, Perry stated that approximately 40 percent of children in the United States have a secure attachment relationship with at least one parent; however, the rate is on a downward spiral. For many children in child care, the attachment relationship they have with caregivers is stronger than the relationship they have with parents or guardians. Many children spend most of their waking hours outside the home; therefore, the relationships that form with young children in centers and schools have the power to set the trajectory of a child's life.

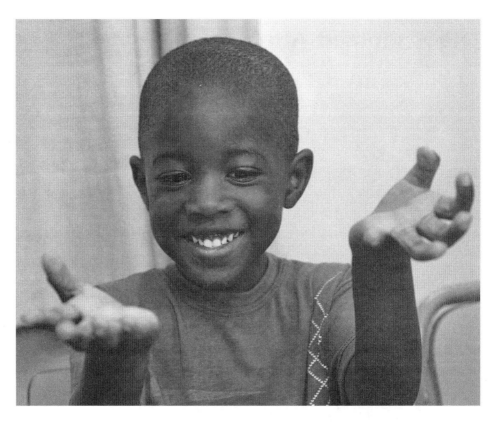

Types of Attachment

Attachment Type	Characteristics	Home Dynamic
Secure	<ul><li>Well-adjusted</li><li>Pleasant</li><li>Responds well to appropriate authority</li><li>Responds well to appropriate requests</li><li>Accepts comfort when hurt or upset</li><li>Confident</li><li>Curious</li><li>Has a drive to master her world</li><li>Takes appropriate risks and tries new things</li><li>Persistent, able to cope with challenges</li></ul>	<ul><li>Parents are nurturing</li><li>Parents have emotional strength and maturity</li><li>Parents respond quickly and warmly to the child's distress and basic needs</li><li>Parents find joy in meeting the needs of their child</li><li>Parents play with and interact with their child</li></ul>
Insecure avoidant	<ul><li>Self-sufficiency beyond the child's years</li><li>Uncomfortable with intimacy</li><li>Seemingly fearless</li><li>Difficulty accepting help or comfort when upset or hurt</li><li>May seem withdrawn and emotionally flat, with unexpected meltdowns</li><li>May seem persistently angry and blame others for anything that goes wrong</li><li>May be sullen and oppositional</li><li>May lack empathy</li><li>May be aloof, a loner</li></ul>	<ul><li>Parents may be dismissive of child's needs and emotions</li><li>Parents may be overwhelmed by child's needs</li><li>Parents may lash out in frustration at child</li><li>Parents often overwhelmed by responsibilities or circumstances, such as mental or physical illness, domestic violence, addiction, poverty, or single parenthood</li><li>Parents often lack a support system</li><li>Parents may provide for child's physical needs but ignore child's need for emotional connection</li></ul>
Insecure ambivalent	<ul><li>Demanding and clingy</li><li>Difficult to satisfy</li><li>Low tolerance for frustration</li><li>Uses temper tantrums or crying to manipulate</li><li>Fidgety</li><li>Compulsive</li><li>Poor concentration skills</li></ul>	<ul><li>Parents respond inconsistently to child's needs—sometimes in a loving, nurturing way, sometimes in frustration and anger</li><li>Parents often overwhelmed by responsibilities or circumstances, such as mental or physical illness, domestic violence, addiction, poverty, or single parenthood</li><li>Parents often lack a support system</li><li>Parents are intrusive</li><li>Parents are not adept at perceiving and reading the child's cues</li></ul>
Disorganized	<ul><li>Lives in constant state of alarm</li><li>Hypervigilant</li><li>Misinterprets social cues</li><li>Highly reactive to sensory cues in the environment</li><li>Displays behavior that seems bizarre or strange</li><li>Prone to meltdowns</li><li>May vacillate between a hyperaroused state and a withdrawn state</li><li>Unpredictable behavior</li></ul>	<ul><li>One or both parents are abusive</li><li>Chronic domestic violence</li><li>Parents are profoundly neglectful</li><li>Very little interaction or human contact</li><li>Parents may be mentally ill and/or addicted to substances</li><li>Family may be constantly moving to avoid authorities</li></ul>

Connecting with Children

A child who has been harmed in the context of a relationship can only be healed through a warm responsive relationship with an invested adult. That is the fundamental principle of healing environments. Our culture has bought into the myth that all children are inherently resilient. Children are malleable. Some become resilient. Research indicates that those that do become resilient to one degree or another do so because of a relationship with a loving adult. This is the challenge and responsibility of early childhood educators. Most teachers and caregivers go into the field because they love children, but they often find that establishing a warm, loving, and responsive relationship with a maltreated child is not as simple as it might seem. This becomes a critical factor—caregivers and teachers who find caring for a maltreated child overwhelming will never be able to create a healing environment.

Nature has endowed babies with certain characteristics that endear them to adults. It is often their cuteness and helplessness that draws us in and makes us want to connect. But it can be a very different story trying to establish a relationship with a maltreated and neglected four-year-old who meets your efforts to connect with aggression or withdrawal. The blank stare, the frozen smile, and the sullen face often repel instead of invite you to come close. The child may withdraw from your touch and resist your initiations by scowling and walking away. She pushes back when you seek to comfort her and laughs when others are hurt. It can be difficult for even the most trauma-informed adult to look past the behavior to see the hurt in the child's soul and continue to reach out in the face of repeated rejection. It is easy to take it personally and conclude the child doesn't like you. Never forget that challenging behavior is a cry for help and not a desire to get on our last nerve. Aggression is the language of fear: The more intense it is, the deeper the wounds and the more sensitive the heart.

In the best-case scenario, maltreatment of children comes to the attention of teachers, caregivers, and others in the community. These community helpers can take steps to assist the family in learning new ways of parenting or make sure the child is removed from the abusive setting and placed in a loving foster or adoptive home. Sadly, in many cases, abuse and neglect fly under the radar, and it can be a long process before the child gets help and protection. Sometimes the public entities that are supposed to protect the child are slow to respond. This makes establishing attachment relationships with all children critical. Fortunately, early childhood professionals can do much to facilitate attachment relationships.

> Never forget that challenging behavior is a cry for help and not a desire to get on our last nerve. Aggression is the language of fear: The more intense it is, the deeper the wounds and the more sensitive the heart.

To establish a secure attachment relationship, a child must believe and know that the adult is safe. How does one convey this message? Primarily through nonverbal means—touch, tone of voice, facial expressions, and body language. The first language that a baby understands is that of touch. Touch is critical to human life; without adequate amounts of it in the early days of life, babies will literally die. The manner in which you hold and touch an infant communicates volumes in terms of how you feel toward that child. Babies who are lovingly caressed and gently held in the earliest weeks and months of life come to know and understand that they are deeply wanted, loved, and worthy of tender care. Those who are harshly handled, rarely stroked, or left to languish for long periods of time in a crib come to believe that they are unwanted, unloved, and undeserving of care. Receiving adequate, nurturing touch throughout the day is an important element in a trauma-informed environment.

This sounds easy enough but is more difficult than it might seem because some maltreated babies are touch avoidant. Their experience has taught them that touch is not satisfying and may even be painful. This can be learned through abuse, neglect, or early medical trauma. Premature babies are typically prodded and poked to ensure their survival; however, this life-sustaining touch loads in the biological system in much the same way as abuse. The touch-avoidant child may arch her back, stiffen, cry, or throw her head back when picked up and held. Caregivers can misinterpret the child's behavior to indicate that the baby doesn't like them and wants to be put down. Unfortunately, I encounter situations where after a day or two of this behavior, the baby is left to "cry it out" in a crib. I have heard people say, "Oh, she doesn't like to be held, so we just let her be." Over time she usually does stop crying, but this does not mean that she is okay. It may mean she has learned that no one will respond so there is no point in crying. With the touch-avoidant baby, caregivers must start with small doses of nurturing touch throughout the day. They have to carefully read the signals and cues from the infant to determine when enough is enough and to avoid overwhelming her.

Make the most of daily routines to provide small moments of nurturing touch. Never prop a bottle in the crib to feed an infant; holding a baby during a feeding is important. Some maltreated babies will avert their eyes as if they are looking at something behind the caregiver or may turn their heads and overtly avoid eye contact. Occasionally, gently stroke your finger along the baby's cheek that is closest to you. Usually this gentle touch causes a baby to at least glance at the caregiver. Calmly sing and talk to the baby.

During diaper changes, handle the baby with gentleness and respect. Playfully interact and count her fingers and toes. Take time to rub warm lotion on her or gently massage her legs and feet. As the baby becomes more accepting of touch, slowly increase the length of interactive touch. Caregivers have reported significant changes when they have persistently worked with the baby over a period of weeks. Some babies are difficult to soothe, and listening to a baby cry for long periods of time despite your best efforts can unravel even the most dedicated and invested caregiver. Sometimes the continual crying distresses the other babies in care, and you soon have a chorus of crying babies. This is one of the challenges of caring for infants in group settings and is why ratios are very important. Babies require an intense investment of time, energy, and attention. National standards recommend a one-to-three ratio in infant rooms. When ratios are higher, it is extremely challenging to adequately meet the needs of not only maltreated infants but also typically developing children.

A common fear often expressed by both parents and caregivers is the belief that babies will be "spoiled" if they are held too much and will come to expect it all the time. Experts agree that *there is no such thing as holding a baby too much*. In fact, some maltreated infants will have a strong need for lots of touch. Purvis points out that the path to healing must recreate and recapture the path of typical development. A harmed baby may crave loving touch as he attempts to recover what he lost in the course of his developmental trajectory.

Here are some tools for your toolbox.
- Some touch-avoidant babies respond to swaddling long past the age that others begin to protest. Try swaddling the baby and rock, walk, sway, or gently bounce her. Be highly attuned to the baby's cues of resistance to being swaddled and do not swaddle a baby against her will. Some babies may accept swaddling when they are upset because the tightness helps them feel safe, but pay attention to their cues for when they have had enough. They will begin to wiggle and squirm as if trying to get loose. Follow the lead of the baby. With older babies and toddlers, simply putting a blanket around them and rocking may help them calm.
- Several times a day, gently apply infant massage. *It is important to receive training in massage techniques by a trained professional.* Massage is very beneficial for all babies—not just those who have experienced maltreatment—because it stimulates the central nervous system, promoting the production of growth hormones and activating the parasympathetic nervous system. According to Tiffany Field in her article "Infant Massage" in *The Journal of Perinatal Education*, premature babies who receive infant massage will gain 47 percent more weight than those who do not and will be released from the neonatal intensive care unit (NICU) six days earlier on average. To offer the most benefit, it is advisable to become certified in infant massage. However, even without formal training, a caregiver can certainly be attuned to how a baby prefers to be held and what kind of stroke a baby prefers. Some like to be held with their head on the caregiver's shoulder; some

prefer to be cradled in her arms. Some like to be patted; some like to be stroked; and others prefer to be rubbed. Pay close attention to figure out if an infant prefers a firmer or a softer, lighter touch.

- Develop a signature touch with each child. This means that every time you touch a child, you initiate contact by touching him in the same place and in the same way. With consistency, the signature touch will activate the parasympathetic nervous system and activate a calming response.
- Rub the baby with warm lotion. Put the lotion bottle in warm water before applying to make sure it is an appropriate temperature. Cold lotion is not very comforting.
- Carry the baby in a baby carrier or sling. Maltreated babies often want to be held frequently because the rhythm of your breathing and the sound of your heartbeat help them to feel safe.
- Rock the baby often.
- Play soothing music or white noise, or sing to the child.
- Play games throughout the day that involve touch, such as patty-cake and This Little Piggy.
- Avoid approaching babies and picking them up from behind. Approach them within their range of vision, and tell the baby what you are doing. For example, "I'm going to pick you up so we can change your diaper."
- During the first weeks and months of life, we don't put babies on eating and sleeping schedules. We feed them when they are hungry and let them sleep when they are tired. Within a few months, typical children will slowly establish a fairly predictable pattern of eating, sleeping, and eliminating. However, it is common for maltreated children to have difficulty settling into a predictable routine. The chaos they experience in their homes disrupts the biological rhythms of their bodies, and the dysregulation carries over into the child care setting. Their eating and sleeping patterns may be erratic for a long period of time, especially if the domestic violence or chaos in the home is ongoing. However, when the child care environment is predictable, consistent and responsive, the infants will usually settle in over time. Their patterns of eating, sleeping, and eliminating will gradually become more predictable, but they may require a great deal of time and patience to soothe, feed, and meet their needs.

Strategies for Connecting with Preschoolers

As children get older, trying to establish an emotional connection often becomes more challenging as patterns of behavior become more ingrained and the heart of the child becomes walled off. However, consistently offering small acts of kindness can scale the walls of even the most wounded children.

Communicating Acceptance

- Communicate a sense of "you matter to me." Greet children by name at the door each morning and welcome them to child care. Let them know that you are "looking" for them.
- Have a place to store personal belongings. Label each space with a child's name and picture.
- Display photographs of children on the walls and on furniture.
- Display framed pictures of each child's family.
- Display children's work on the walls.
- Celebrate birthdays.
- Send cards to or call children who are absent.
- Incorporate children's interests into the curriculum.

The Importance of Touch

Touch is important throughout childhood and remains one of the primary ways we connect with children. Nurturing touch communicates a sense of safety and is an important component of a healing relationship. Hugs, high fives, pats on the back, and a hand on the shoulder are intentional forms of touch that send messages of affirmation and acceptance so desperately needed by children who have been harmed. In the early stages of a relationship, always ask a child if he would like a hug. If he resists, then ask if he would like a high five, handshake, or fist bump. If the child still refuses, simply say, "That's okay. Maybe tomorrow."

Some maltreated children have no idea what affectionate touch is. Their hugs often feel more like an attack rather than a sign of affection, such as surprising you when you lean over and jumping on your back while wrapping their arms around your neck. It is important to help these children establish appropriate boundaries. Just as you are always going to ask for permission to hug them, insist that they also ask for permission to hug you. If they jump on your back, tell them that is not okay. Say something like, "It's not okay to jump on me because it could hurt me. If you want a hug, you need to ask me and I will always say yes. But you must ask with respect." Walk the child through the situation, and practice asking for hugs.

The policies and practices deemed appropriate by some school districts across the Unites States alarm me. Increasingly, I hear reports that schools and child care centers forbid any kind of nurturing touch: Adults are not allowed to hug, rock, or have a child other than an infant sitting on their laps. Although I understand that the intent of such policies is to protect children, depriving them of nurturing touch will only increase the likelihood of the child seeking and accepting inappropriate touch. Touch is such a fundamental human need, and the drive to be touched is so strong that children will seek to meet this need one way or another. If they have no idea what appropriate touch looks like or feels like, they will accept whatever form of touch is given.

With children who are avoidant of touch, adults must help the children become comfortable with skin-to-skin contact. Because the brains of maltreated children remain in a constant state of hypervigilance, they often misinterpret the accidental bumps and jostling that happen in the context of play and ordinary routines as aggressive acts, and they are quick to retaliate. "He pushed me!" is a common complaint heard many times a day. It is not unusual for harmed children to respond with aggression. They perceive the accidental human contact as a threat, and they are primed for a fight.

We can help children who are touch avoidant by creating an environment with lots of touch offered in fun and playful ways. Musical games and activities are great ways to provide playful touch. Games such as "London Bridge Is Falling Down" or "Ring Around the Rosie" provide a context in which children hold hands and playfully bump up against each other.

> Touch is such a fundamental human need, and the drive to be touched is so strong that children will seek to meet this need one way or another. If they have no idea what appropriate touch looks like or feels like, they will accept whatever form of touch is given.

Some children, boys in particular, enjoy rough-and-tumble play; however, this is often forbidden in childcare and school settings. Research indicates that rough-and-tumble play can make important contributions to children's development. In addition to the playful touch it affords, it requires children to become proficient at reading nonverbal cues. They must be attuned to the body language and facial expressions that signal when it is someone else's turn or when another child has had enough. Adult supervision is always a must and, like most things, children from hard places may need additional coaching to successfully navigate this form of play. According to Frances Carlson in her article "Rough and Tumble Play 101," adults may need to point out when traumatized children become too rough or when they aren't picking up on the nonverbal cues that another child doesn't want to play.

When children have playful touch on a consistent and daily basis, they become desensitized and will slowly begin to feel more comfortable with hugs, handshakes, and other appropriate forms of body contact. Over time, they will typically begin to accept intentional touch without it triggering a stress reaction. Here are some more tools for your toolbox.

- **Parachute Games:** Parachute play is an activity enjoyed by most young children. While working together to raise and lower the chute, children accidently bump into one another with their arms, elbows, torsos, and legs in a nonthreatening context.

- **Duck, Duck Goose:** Ordinary childhood games such as Duck, Duck Goose can be adapted to include more nurturing touch. Instead of chasing one another around the circle, the goose and the duck can run in opposite directions, meeting halfway around the circle. When they meet, the goose can choose to greet the duck with a hug, a high five, or a handshake.

- **Musical Hoops:** Instead of walking around a line of chairs, as the music is playing, have the children walk around several large plastic hoops lined up on the floor. When the music stops, the teacher calls out a body part, and everyone has to put that body part in a hoop. After each round, a hoop is removed until only one or two hoops are left, and everyone clusters to put their indicated body parts in the hoop.

- **Hand-Clapping Games:** Games such as Miss Mary Mack incorporate touch in a nonthreatening, fun manner.

- **Checking the Weather:** Have children sit in a circle with their hands on the shoulders of the person in front of them. Tell them that they are going to "check the weather." Begin by having them lightly tap their fingers on their partner's back as the raindrops begin to fall. Add other movements to represent the wind, lightning, thunder, and pounding raindrops. Gradually have the rainstorm subside and return to a sunny day. Note: Some children may get carried away with the pounding of the thunder, so demonstrate what appropriate "thunder" looks like. Remind the children that it is your job to keep everyone safe and you won't let anyone be hurtful. If necessary, have an adult partner with a child who struggles with being too rough.

- **Nail polish and face paint:** Use washable, water-soluble nail polish and face paint to do children's nails and create fun pictures on their hands or faces.
- **Playdough jewelry:** Let the children make playdough rings, bracelets, crowns, and other items to put on one another.
- **Bandages and slings:** Enhance dramatic play by putting adhesive bandages and slings in the dramatic-play center for a hospital theme.

Creating Healthy Boundaries

Some children are indiscriminately attached. This means that they have no primary attachment figure, and they approach any new person as if that person were their best friend. The indiscriminate child will hug anyone and everyone in sight. They may run to an adult and throw their arms around the person's legs and cling for dear life. The adult may have to literally peel the child off her body. Indiscriminately attached children have often spent some portion of their earliest years in an orphanage or experienced multiple placements in foster homes, learning how to quickly endear themselves to the adults around them as a survival mechanism. An indiscriminately attached child is often very charming because this is how he has learned to get his needs met. However, there is often a falseness about the friendliness that can seem unnerving.

Explain to the child that we meet all kinds of people. Some are strangers, some are acquaintances, some are friends, and others are family. Help the child understand appropriate ways of greeting the different categories of people encountered during the day. We might smile or say hello to a stranger in our school, but we should never hug a stranger. We might shake hands with an acquaintance or give the person a high five, but hugs are reserved for family and friends. Help children know the appropriate way to greet parents or guests who enter the classroom.

As with reluctant children, always ask permission to hug an indiscriminately attached child, and require that the child ask permission to hug you. Reassure the child that you will always say yes, but permission is required. Keep these boundaries in place until you are confident that the child knows the difference among strangers, acquaintances, friends, and relatives and understands how to appropriately greet them. Once the child has well-defined boundaries, you can resume more spontaneous interactions.

Similar principles apply to sexually abused children. Victims of sexual abuse often have no physical boundaries because theirs have been violated, and unwelcome touch is their "normal." They may touch other children or adults in inappropriate places and inappropriate ways. These children are not "perverts"; they are children whose innocence and childhood have been stolen. If you have a child in your care with a history of sexual abuse (assuming it is on the radar of proper authorities), it is important to be intentional in helping the child establish a new standard for appropriate boundaries.

One way to do this is using large plastic hoops. Explain to children that we all have an invisible bubble around us that is our personal space. When people get too close to us or touch us without permission, it can make us feel uncomfortable. Give the children hoops to put around their waists, and talk about how the area inside the hoop is their private space. Others should not get inside their space without their permission. With another adult or child, demonstrate what it would look like to greet someone while inappropriately invading space. For example, rush forward in such a way that the hoops overlap. Pretend to roughly pat or hug the person and say, "What's up?" Point out that when we respect another person's space, our hoops don't touch. Have the children practice greeting their partners with their hoops overlapping. Teach them words to say when someone invades their space in a way that makes them feel uncomfortable, such as, "Please stop!" or "Please step back!" Have them practice greeting each other appropriately without overlapping the hoops. Practice this until you see improvement in behavior.

If you observe a child touching others in inappropriate places, have a one-on-one conversation discussing the fact that there are private places on our bodies that no one should touch without our permission. Using dolls, point out that the "bathing suit" areas on a boy and a girl are no-touching zones. If the behavior persists, it is important to get mental health consultation or get a therapist involved.

Avoid tickling children you know have been sexually abused. It can evoke memories of inappropriate sexual touch and provoke aggressive or extremely withdrawn behavior.

As with the indiscriminately attached child, insist that children who struggle with boundary issues always ask permission to hug you or their classmates. Help them understand that it is okay for people to say no. Honor the children's requests for a hug. Likewise, always ask permission to hug them. Keep these boundaries in place for at least four to six weeks, at which time you should see some positive changes in behavior.

Tone of Voice and Body Language

For many maltreated children, their survival has depended upon being able to pick up on subtle nuances indicating that they are about to be harmed or that domestic violence is about to break out. This same orientation to their environment plays out in child care as their brains pay more attention to the unspoken messages we communicate than the spoken words. These children vigilantly monitor our nonverbal communication, looking for any nuance that we don't like them or are about to harm them. Unfortunately, their emotional radar often misinterprets the unspoken messages through the lens of their history, and they assume the worst. The frown on your face may be from a headache, but the maltreated child interprets it as anger. It is therefore critical to be very mindful of our body language, facial expressions, nonverbal communication, and tone of voice.

If I could change one thing about our culture, it would be how we talk to children. When I visit child care centers and schools, I pay attention to the sounds coming from classrooms. People say things to children in ways they never would to adult. Patterns of communication can become so ingrained that we don't even notice our tone. I am convinced that the only way it will ever change is to develop trusting relationships with our colleagues to the point that we can hold one another accountable for the way we speak: "That sounded a little harsh. Maybe you need to go back and say it again." "Did you notice how Johnny recoiled from your touch, and you ignored his body language? Did you see how afraid he was?" These kinds of interactions make us better caregivers and teachers, but it takes an enormous amount of vulnerability and trust among colleagues.

The human brain is wired for *motherese* or *parentese*—that high-pitched, singsong, lilting voice we use with infants that communicates a sense of safety. In the first weeks and months of a child's life, we do not talk to a baby in the same tone of voice we use in ordinary conversation. Unfortunately, babies and children who are harmed or who live with domestic violence hear threatening words spoken in angry tones accompanied by violent acts. They become attuned to any inflection or change of tone that may remotely indicate threat. This makes it imperative that caregivers and teachers be keenly aware of their tone of voice. This does not mean that we don't speak in a firm tone of voice when the situation warrants, but it is never okay to be harsh.

In ordinary conversation and in teaching moments, talk to children in a friendly, playful tone of voice. A playful tone of voice helps the child to feel safe. Save the "I mean business" tone for those moments when firmness and limit setting are necessary.

Eye Contact

The way that we look at someone can communicate volumes. For example, a glare communicates anger and can cause a child to recoil and pull away, and soft eyes communicate safety and can beckon a child to come close. The best way to understand soft eyes is to watch someone interacting with a baby in a playful and nurturing way. Usually an interaction with an infant elicits soft eyes in an adult. This sounds easy to emulate but can be difficult in everyday life when the stress of dealing with a traumatized child in a group setting can challenge even the most experienced and knowledgeable teacher. In a fleeting moment, the look of softness can turn into a look of frustration, anger, or exasperation. As you turn away from a frustrating encounter with a child, he likely will detect even a slight rolling of the eyes. Knowledge of your own state of mind and body and honest feedback from trusted coworkers can help you become increasingly aware of the messages you communicate.

Look children in the eye when you talk to them, and give them your total attention. Being fully present communicates a sense of value and worth to a child who feels unworthy. The early childhood environment is an extremely busy place, and adults easily can be preoccupied with the logistics of getting through the day. Maltreated children *need* to have moments where they are the center of your attention with eye-to-eye contact. Play games that involve a back-and-forth volley of some sort. For example, when I throw a beach ball or a Frisbee back and forth with a child, he has to look at me, at least briefly, to aim. These kinds of games acclimate children to making eye contact.

If you have a child who consistently averts his gaze or seems to look past you, gently stroke your finger under the child's chin. Typically, a child will make eye contact for at least a split second. Say something like, "Thanks for letting me see those beautiful eyes." In every interaction, try to get the child to make even brief eye contact just once, but never force it. For example, as I'm talking to a child, I might lightly stroke my finger under his chin as he looks at the floor. If he pulls away or seems distressed, I do not push the issue further; however, if he continues to look down but doesn't seem upset, I might say something silly such as, "I didn't know you have purple eyes!" (Humor is often the key to scaling the walls of fear.) If the child looks at you, continue with something like, "Oh, no! What am I thinking? You have blue eyes, not purple!" If the child ignores your comment, though, don't keep trying to get him to make eye contact.

When a child who has historically avoided eye contact starts to connect, he will often only be able to tolerate small doses of face-to-face interaction. Be very aware of the child's body language and cues that he is uncomfortable and avert your gaze when necessary.

Playful Engagement

At the heart of a secure attachment relationship is a sense of mutual joy and delight. The adult communicates that she genuinely enjoys being with a child, and the child truly enjoys being with the adult. This is easy to say but difficult in reality. The ongoing behavioral struggles of children from hard places can wear down even the most loving adult. Play is often the context in which we can create and experience short moments of authentic joy in being with a particular child and is often the first thread of connection with a maltreated child. Small moments of meaningful interaction throughout the day can multiply over time to have a significant impact on the child.

Observe children at play to discover what a child truly enjoys, and join him. If the child ignores you or turns his back to you, subtly mimic him. For example, if a child is playing cars in the block center and pushing a car along the floor saying, "Vroooom," do the same thing. If the child is sitting cross-legged, sit cross-legged. But be sensitive to the child's reaction: Your imitation must not be so obvious or exaggerated that you appear to be mocking the child or being a copycat. Look for ways throughout the day to share a playful moment. As you laugh and play together, children will begin to feel safer about entering a trusting relationship with you.

Playful engagement is important to babies and toddlers as well. It is easy in child care settings to focus only on the physical needs of the baby—diapering, feeding, and sleeping—and neglect to simply play, but it is not enough to simply provide custodial care. Around four months of age, a baby actively begins to initiate playful interactions, and these invitations need to be accepted and reciprocated.

Peekaboo and chase are games that infants and toddlers initiate and enjoy. These games are ways to experience mutual delight with infants and toddlers and to communicate that someone is—to use Thompson's phrase—looking for them. Pay close attention to other games that infants and toddlers initiate, and join in.

Find Ways to Say Yes

When adults respond to a baby's cry in a timely manner with warmth and sensitivity or playfully reciprocate a toddler's invitation to engage in a game of chase, they fill a child's psychological "bucket" with yeses. This legitimizes the child's needs and affirms his existence. When children experience abuse and neglect as a way of life, their psychological buckets are filled with nos. When a baby cries and no one responds, the legitimacy of his needs is negated and the essence of who he is denied.

Helping wounded children heal means we have to find ways to fill their buckets with yeses. We can do this in many ways.

- When we honor a child's preference for scented playdough instead of plain, we say yes to his legitimate desire.
- When we notice a child's fascination with butterflies and bring in books about the insects and plant a butterfly garden, we say yes to her interests.
- When we notice a child's struggle to keep his hands quiet while listening to a story and give him a fidget to hold, we say yes to his needs.

We also fill a child's bucket with yeses through affirmation. I like to make "I notice you" statements. For example, "I noticed that you worked long and hard at building that bridge. Even when it fell down, you didn't give up. You kept trying until you got it," or "I noticed that when it was your turn to paint at the easel, you let your friend Casey have a turn." "I notice you" statements simply describe the behavior that you see and let children know the specific behaviors that you are affirming. This is how children develop a conscience and internalize a value system.

Look for ways to say yes to children throughout the day. Little yeses along the way are like tiny drops that accumulate to water the souls of wounded children.

Invite Dependence

In my work with parents, I challenge them to thoughtfully ponder the question, "What do you want your children to know and be able to do when you launch them into the world at the age of eighteen?" The most common answer is, "I want my child to be independent." Our culture places a high premium on independence. We want children to grow up fast, usually for our own convenience. However, Neufeld and Maté warn that when we push children and ignore their dependency needs, we push them into the arms of their peers. To become independent, a child must first be allowed to be dependent.

Most maltreated children have had no one to depend on to meet their needs. Many appear to be very self-reliant, often with a pseudomaturity that belies their age, and find it very difficult to ask for help. They are more comfortable turning to a peer for help than they are to an adult.

Humans require a long period of dependence before they can truly be independent. Part of the healing process is allowing children to recover what they lost, which means we need to allow children from hard places to be dependent past the age at which independence typically is achieved. For example, a five-year-old who has been in the foster system for three years continually asks to be pushed on the swing. While most five-year-olds are quite proud of the fact that they have learned to pump and can swing independently, this is a small way that the harmed child can experience dependency on an adult.

It is not unusual for harmed children to demonstrate behaviors much younger than their chronological ages and to be dependent in ways that are not typical for their age. As Perry asserted in his 2013 webinar, maltreated children are typically half of their chronological age. Adults sometimes deny their dependency needs by saying such things as, "Big boys don't do that," or, "Only babies do that. Don't act like a baby." Recognizing a child's need to be dependent can help adults be more understanding and patient.

Be aware of how you respond to children when they ask for help. It is not uncommon for adults to chastise children for not paying attention. Trauma-informed teachers recognize that children from hard places sometimes don't process information as quickly as other children and may have some impairment of short-term memory. Celebrate the fact that the child had the courage to verbalize his needs. Give him the minimal amount of help needed to successfully accomplish the task.

Another way of inviting dependence is to be aware of what Neufeld and Maté term *orientation voids*. When a child enters an unfamiliar environment, he is unsure of what to do, what to say, and how to act. There is a certain sense of "lostness" as the child adapts to a new environment. An attachment relationship works much like a compass, orienting the child to his world. Through observation and interaction with an attachment figure, children learn what is important, what is valued and what is not, what is expected, and what is frowned upon. This void is an opportunity to invite dependency: Take the child under your wing, so to speak, and show him around the classroom. Introduce him to the other children. Show him how things work. "Here, let me show you how the wagon attaches to the bike." "Here, let me show you how we do things around here at snack time." "Here, let me show you how to put the paint smock on." The first interactions a child has in a child care or school setting are critical because the first person with whom a child interacts is often his "go to" person or "compass." It is crucial that these first interactions are positive.

> To become independent, a child must first be allowed to be dependent. Most maltreated children have had no one to depend on to meet their needs.

Sameness

Children want to be like those they respect and admire. Look for similarities between you and a child. It might be hair color, freckles, the same interests, or the same family car. I was once in an early childhood setting to observe an adopted child who had experienced trauma. The time I had with her was short, so I was hoping to connect quickly. I walked over to the table where she was sitting, and she pulled some lip balm out of her pocket and put it on her lips. I pointed to my lips and exclaimed, "Pink lips!" and then pointed to hers, "Pink lips!" Her face broke into a smile, and she shouted, "We're the same!" Sameness can break down the barriers of resistance.

Grouping

The actual grouping of children can help facilitate attachment relationships for all children and especially for maltreated children. Many schools and child care centers have implemented a process called *looping*, where teachers move up with the children for a number of years. A teacher may start out teaching a group of three-year-olds and move up with them as four-year-olds to be their teacher for another year. Typically, teachers loop for two years, but it can be carried out over several years.

Another approach is *multiage groupings*. This is carried out more often in child care centers than schools but could be effective in both settings. Infants and toddlers may be grouped together, as are three-, four-, and five-year-olds. Based on the work of Lev Vygotsky and his research on the *zone of proximal development*, it is recommended that children be grouped with other children no more than two years older.

A third method is through *nurture groups*. If two or more adults are in the room, the children are divided into the same number of groups as there are adults. The assigned teacher carries out all of the routine interactions with the child throughout the day, including welcoming the child in the morning, diapering, toileting, feeding, settling in for a nap, and separating at the end of the day. This arrangement provides those anchors of consistency and familiarity that help the child feel safe and secure. The teacher can get to know the individual children and their needs on a deeper level. Teachers interact and play with all children throughout the day, but the assigned teacher assumes primary responsibility for those transitional and more intimate moments of the day.

Chapter 4

The Effect of Maltreatment on Sensory Processing

When Jimmy arrives at child care in the morning, his teacher can recognize his heavy footsteps coming down the hall. He often wants to keep his jacket on and tightly clutches it around his body. The collars of his shirts are frayed, as he chews on them constantly. When he comes to group time, he has a tendency to sit on other children, which causes a great deal of jostling and pushing. Rarely a day goes by that Jimmy doesn't spill his drink at lunch or snack time. He loves rough-and-tumble play but often doesn't know when to stop. Other children tend to shy away from him because he is so physically aggressive.

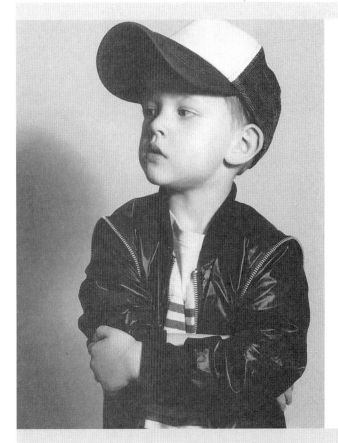

Sarah, on the other hand, insists on wearing flip-flops in the dead of winter. Her mother reports that Sarah cuts the tags out of all her clothes and will only wear certain fabrics. She frequently complains that the sheet on her cot is scratchy, and she refuses to put her hands in the fingerpaint or sensory table. Meal time can be challenging as she avoids eating any kind of finger food.

Cody appears to be a clumsy child, bumping into other children frequently during interest centers. His clumsiness angers others, who often exclude him from play. His favorite spot in the room is the rocking chair, and he also loves to sit on the floor and spin around on his bottom. Out on the playground, he prefers equipment that spins and is often seen turning cartwheels or spinning around like a top.

Is Jimmy just a careless child who doesn't pay attention to what he is doing? Is Sarah just a willful child who insists on doing things her way? Is Cody an overactive child who just needs to learn to sit still? Are all of these children behavior challenges? The answer to each of these questions is no! These are children with sensory processing disorder.

Defining Sensory Processing Disorder

Sensory processing disorder has been described as a traffic jam in the brain. It is a malfunction of the sensory processing system. To understand the disorder, we must first know some basic things about the system.

Our brain constantly takes in information about the world around us through our senses. It is estimated that a billion bits of information bombard the brain at any given second. If the brain tried to process and pay attention to all of this information, it would be quickly overwhelmed. Therefore, filters in the brain sift through the mass of information to identify what is important and what can be ignored. In her article, "What You Should Know about Your Brain," Judy Willis estimates that approximately 2,000 bits of information per second are actually allowed to enter the sensory processing center of the brain. This system must analyze and organize the information so that the brain can appropriately respond.

The reticular activating system (RAS) is known as the gatekeeper of the brain and is the point at which information is filtered. Once the RAS allows information to enter, it goes to one of two locations: the *prefrontal cortex*, which is the thinking part of the brain where the information is thoughtfully processed and reflected upon, or the more reactive *limbic brain*, where the amygdala and hippocampus evaluate the information and decide if danger is present. If so, the fight, flight, or freeze response is activated.

Effective filtering and processing of sensory input allows us to function in daily life with a feeling of safety and security. We can direct and sustain focused attention, move freely without fear, and efficiently carry out a myriad of both fine and gross motor tasks without giving these activities much conscious thought or effort.

But, when these bits of information are not efficiently filtered and processed, there is a virtual traffic jam in the brain as it tries to figure out what is important and what is not: Does that smell mean that something is amiss in my environment? Does that loud noise mean there is an eminent threat, or is it just the lid blowing off the trashcan? Does that person's tone of voice indicate she is angry with me, or does she have a headache?

If the information coming into the brain is not organized, the individual likely will respond in ways that may seem inappropriate or even bizarre. The feel of cotton rubbing against the skin may cause a child to cry out in pain. Another child may become hysterical and cower in the corner at every loud noise. A slight brush on the arm may cause a child to clutch her arm in pain and accuse the child behind her of hurting her. Sensory processing disorder can cause children to experience a pervasive sense of anxiety and can compromise feelings of safety and security, leaving children feeling overwhelmed and distracted.

> Sensory processing disorder can cause children to experience a pervasive sense of anxiety and can compromise feelings of safety and security, leaving children feeling overwhelmed and distracted.

Maltreated Children and Sensory Processing Issues

According to Purvis, in the general population approximately one out of twenty children will be diagnosed with sensory processing disorder (SPD). However, eighteen out of twenty maltreated children will be diagnosed with SPD. The brain stem plays a central role in the sensory processing system. Because the brain stem is largely developed in the prenatal environment, it is most susceptible to the ill effects of drugs, alcohol, and toxic stress. A disorganized or underdeveloped brain stem will not be able to efficiently analyze, organize, and respond appropriately to incoming stimuli.

In the earliest weeks and months after birth, the brain is extremely vulnerable to the effects of the environment. The sensory systems of maltreated children are often assaulted by a myriad of sensations that overwhelm them emotionally, physically, and psychologically. They can be exposed to screaming voices; the sounds of objects crashing to the floor; intense visual images of adults assaulting one another; the sensation of being hit, kicked, or otherwise abused; the smell of blood, gunpowder, drugs, or alcohol; and the frenetic movement of people fighting, arguing, or trying to protect themselves. Lieberman and Van Horn assert that the disjointed and vivid images, sounds, smells, and sensations are difficult for young children to process in any coherent kind of way. The chaotic input overwhelms the developing brain, resulting in disorganization of the sensory processing system.

Our Eight Senses

Sensory processing disorder can affect all eight of our senses. Yes, you read that right—we have eight senses, not just five. Most people are familiar with sight, sound, hearing, taste, and touch. We also have three others that are less well-known—vestibular, proprioceptive, and interoceptive.

Children with sensory processing disorder will typically fall into one of three categories: sensory seeking, sensory avoidant, or a combination of the two. The child who is *sensory seeking* will crave certain kinds of sensory input. The child who is *sensory avoidant* will recoil from certain kinds of sensory stimuli and may even become aggressive or belligerent. It is possible for a child to be sensory seeking in one domain and sensory avoidant in another. Before we take a look at the three sensory systems that are unfamiliar to many, we will briefly address the tactile system, as disorganization in this sensory system can also be a manifestation of trauma.

Tactile System

The skin is our largest organ and has millions of receptors that help us to know the boundaries of our bodies, discern a light touch from a heavy touch, and discriminate different sensations. Our sense of touch has both protective and discriminatory functions. When a fire ant crawls across our foot, we are alerted through our tactile system, and we slap it off. When we touch a hot stove, the tactile system causes us to jerk our hand away. The discriminatory portion of the system allows us to know when we are touching or being touched; to determine what part of the body is being touched; to identify the pressure of the touch; and to perceive the nature of an object as it relates to texture, size, shape, material, and temperature.

Well-nurtured children are cuddled, stroked, and held in many different ways throughout the day. Caregivers count their toes, rub their feet, pat their tummies, and caress their cheeks. This tactile input helps stimulate and strengthen the connectivity of the tactile system. Because maltreated children lack the sensory stimuli and nurturing touch that typical children receive in the context of the attachment system, it is not uncommon for them to be either *hyposensitive* (low sensitivity) or *hypersensitive* (high sensitivity) to touch.

A child who seeks tactile stimulation will often appear to not notice being touched if it is done with too little pressure. Another child may brush up against her while waiting to go down the slide, and she will not even notice. Some will have difficulty perceiving when something is too hot or too prickly. Many such children put their hands on everything in sight, obsessively rub unusual fabrics, and constantly have something in their hands to fiddle with. Some will refuse to eat with utensils and will use their fingers past the typical age that children become proficient with using utensils. They may have a drive to touch every bite of food before it goes into their mouth. The child who seeks touch and is constantly touching and hanging on other children can be annoying to others and can find it difficult to make friends. Some adults may think the child is intentionally trying to provoke when she is simply trying to get tactile stimulation.

Avoidance of tactile stimulation is sometimes called *tactile defensiveness*. These children find touch disturbing and unpleasant. In an early childhood setting where hands-on learning is a critical component, hypersensitivity to touch can undermine learning and overall function. Language is affected because the ability to identify attributes and use descriptive words often requires touching the object first. These children can miss out on the pleasure of affectionate touch as the gestures are perceived as "hurting" or "scratchy." They might avoid messy activities such as fingerpainting or gluing; they may become extremely upset when they get paint or glitter glue on their hands. Some refuse to eat any kind of finger food, and others will walk around the room keeping their hands in their pockets and will avoid using any kind of tools at all. As a result, their life experiences are significantly narrowed, and they don't learn basic skills such as using scissors, paintbrushes, or eating utensils.

Dressing the hypersensitive child has challenges. They can be very picky about the textures of their clothing and may refuse to wear certain kinds of fabric. Often, the tags are cut out of all their clothes, and if one is inadvertently left inside, the child can become unglued, claiming that the tag is scratchy. They may refuse to wear socks and prefer wearing sandals, even in the middle of winter. The smallest degree of dampness around their shirtsleeves can send them shrieking.

Like the vestibular and proprioceptive behaviors, tactile defensiveness can be misinterpreted as challenging behavior. When children balk at participating in highly tactile activities, their resistance is often misconstrued as being uncooperative. Their messy eating habits can evoke negative messages from both children and teachers. Through careful observation, teachers and caregivers can identify patterns in behavior to discern sensory issues in maltreated children.

Vestibular System

Our brain has a powerful drive to know where our head is in relationship to the earth at all times. This is the primary job of the vestibular system. A canal of fluid between our ears, called the *vestibular canal*, acts much like a carpenter's level: As the head moves, the hairlike cilia within the canal detect movement and send messages to the brain regarding the position of the head and the movement of the body. The vestibular system allows us to keep our balance when walking on an uneven surface or on a balance beam. We can close our eyes while riding in a car and still know that we are moving.

The vestibular system is a powerful organizing factor for all other senses. When the vestibular sense fails, effective functioning of all senses is often compromised. People who have vertigo (essentially a malfunctioning vestibular system) report being nauseated, dizzy, and unable to balance or function normally. Some remain curled up in bed in a fetal position until the condition is corrected.

The vestibular sense comes online during the second trimester of pregnancy, and it is the mechanism by which the baby knows to enter the birth canal head down. The sense is fully developed by four months of age and requires ongoing stimulation to continue to function at maximum capacity. According to Purvis, there is a correlation between attachment disorders and vestibular issues.

Children who suffer maltreatment and neglect do not get what is called *competent holdings*. Well-nurtured babies are picked up and put down multiple times a day. They may be rocked, cradled, and carried in slings or backpacks. They may ride in baby carriages, swing in infant swings, and jump in a baby jumper or ExerSaucer. All this movement gives them lots of vestibular stimulation. The neglected baby, on the other hand, is often left to languish for long periods of time in a crib or infant seat. She is rarely rocked and often has little to no experience with sensations associated with different kinds of movement or positioning of her body. I have encountered foster babies who cannot lift their heads, roll over, or sit up because of a profound lack of opportunity to move.

As Carol Kranowitz points out in her book *The Out-of-Sync Child*, a child with vestibular issues will experience difficulties with everyday skills and activities related to the following:

- **Gravitational security:** Gravitational security is confidence that we are firmly attached to the earth. It allows us to walk and move around without the fear of falling. Most children enjoy turning somersaults, jumping out of a swing, or doing a cartwheel. But for the child with gravitational insecurity, any activity where her feet leave the ground evokes a great deal of fear and anxiety.

- **Movement and balance:** Children with vestibular issues will move at extremes—they will either move a lot or move very little. They may appear clumsy and have difficulty with balance. Walking on an uneven surface is terrifying, and the fear of falling so pervasive that they become very controlling and rigid in their everyday interactions. They may refuse to play group games or participate in music and movement activities. Their rigidity may be misinterpreted as defiance.

- **Muscle tone:** Babies with low muscle tone will appear to be "floppy" and may be late meeting typical developmental milestones for sitting, crawling, walking, or running. As they grow older, sitting upright at a table is very tiring. They may prop their heads up on their arms, lay their heads on the table, or drape themselves over a chair. For children whose vestibular sense has not been adequately stimulated, there is nothing wrong with the muscles; the messages from the brain are scrambled and the body doesn't know what it is supposed to do.

- **Bilateral coordination:** This is the ability to get both sides of the body to function cooperatively as a team. When children first begin to go up and down stairs, they do so using *parallel steppage*: the child raises a foot to the next step and places the other one on the same step beside the first foot. As coordination improves, they begin to use bilateral coordination, and they move up a flight of stairs smoothly with each foot touching every other step.

  Around the age of three or four, typical children can coordinate both sides of their body to *cross the midline*. Draw an imaginary line down the center of your body. When you cross your right foot over your left, you are crossing the midline of your body. When you scratch your shoulder with your opposite hand, you are crossing the midline. The capacity to cross the midline is a critical skill required for reading a line of print. The eyes have to sweep across the midline to read all of the words. Children with a dysfunctional vestibular system may have difficulty with everyday experiences that involve bilateral movement and crossing the midline. They may use parallel steppage long after it is age appropriate, have difficulty putting on their own socks, or struggle to cut a piece of paper with scissors.

- **Auditory language processing:** Interestingly, the auditory and vestibular systems are intertwined because the cilia also detect the vibration of sound being processed in the inner ear. Children with a dysfunctional vestibular system many have difficulty processing language. Some will have difficulty discriminating sounds, which means they will struggle with recognizing rhyming words and the sounds of letters. Others will find it very difficult to listen to someone speaking when there are other sounds in the environment. A child care center is a busy and noisy place, which means some children will struggle with being able to concentrate on what adults are saying and may not appear to be listening or following directions. These children may not talk much in the classroom, as they find it difficult to organize their thoughts; however, a burst of language may suddenly bubble up when they are swinging or jumping. Some will spontaneously start to move around the classroom as they speak due to an unconscious drive to stimulate the vestibular system. When asked to respond to a question in group time, they may rock back and forth or stand up and move about.

- **Visual-spatial processing:** This involves the ability to organize visual information into meaningful patterns and understand how objects or shapes might change as they move through space. Children who struggle with spatial issues will have difficulty with paper-and-pencil tasks because of a lack of eye-hand coordination. Discriminating the forms of basic shapes, letters, numbers, colors, and words will be a challenge. Children with spatial issues will often bump into other children because they have difficulty judging distances between objects and people.

Teachers can recognize children with vestibular problems by carefully watching their movements. Remember, children will always tell us what they need through their behavior if we have the capacity to be astute observers. The child who is *sensory seeking* with regard to the vestibular system will seek out lots of vigorous, big-body movement and will crave certain kinds of play. They love to resist gravity by hanging upside down on the monkey bars and may even hang upside down off the edge of their chair to look at a book. They are passionate climbers and love to jump off high ledges or platforms. They love to swing and don't get dizzy when they play on a merry-go-round or a Sit'N Spin. They enjoy rocking chairs and rocking boats and often dart from one physical activity to another. They may seem reckless as they move without hesitation despite their tendency to be a "bumper and a crasher."

The child who is *sensory avoidant* with regard to the vestibular system will clearly resist certain kinds of movements and activities. She may resist swinging in a swing, spinning on a Sit'N Spin, or playing games that require walking in a circle. Linear movement is not always a pleasant sensation, and some will become dysregulated riding in a car or a wagon or on a bike. If she is sitting in group time and an adult comes up from behind to move her over to make room for another child, she may become very agitated and loudly protest. If you are doing the Hokey Pokey, the sensory-avoidant child may fall down when you get to the part where you "turn yourself around" or may even become angry and swat at the person next to her. The sensation of turning around undermines her sense of security and disorients her to the point of not being able to function.
The behavior of children with a dysfunctional vestibular sense can be misinterpreted as defiant or challenging. When they bump into other children,

they are scolded for not paying attention. When they balk at playing group games that involve turning around, they are deemed uncooperative. Teachers need to carefully watch children to identify patterns that may indicate sensory issues. All of these things put together can cause a child—especially a maltreated child—to feel very unsure and insecure in her everyday experiences. The emotional environment is already threatening, and when you layer the burden of sensory issues on top of that, it can create enormous challenges for everyday life in a group setting.

Proprioceptive Sense

The word *proprioceptive* comes from the Latin word meaning "one's own" and refers to the sensations and messages communicated to the brain through the joints, ligaments, muscles, and tendons. Proprioception is largely about motor planning and motor control. As Linda Gilkerson and Rebecca Klein assert in the book *Early Development and the Brain*, these messages inform the brain about the position of the body. When you sit at the dinner table, the proprioceptive sense allows you to know where your feet are without actually looking at them. This system allows us to know where our body is in space and to adjust the force exerted by our muscles to do everyday tasks such as picking up a glass, writing with a pencil, turning a doorknob, or taking the lid off of a container.

While the vestibular and tactile senses can work independently of proprioception, the proprioceptive system works in sync with the vestibular and tactile systems to carry out tasks. Proprioceptive issues are common among maltreated children. Those who display clinical signs of a proprioceptive problem will have difficulty with the following:

- **Motor planning:** With regard to proprioception, children with motor-planning issues will struggle to figure out what their body needs to do to complete a task. The simple act of getting on a tricycle requires trial and error and an enormous amount of concentration.
- **Modulation of movement:** Children will struggle to know how much strength or pressure is needed to complete a task. They often reach for a cup of water with too much intensity and knock it over or grasp it too tightly and spill the contents. They throw balls too hard at other children and press down with such force on a crayon or pencil that they tear the paper or break the points. Sometimes they grasp writing utensils so lightly their writing is hardly visible.

Caregivers and adults can recognize children with proprioceptive issues through careful observation. The sensory-seeking child may walk with a heavy, stomping footstep because she wants feedback to know where she is in space. She chews on her hair, clothes, pencils, and toys. She often doesn't want to take her jacket

The behavior of children with a dysfunctional vestibular sense can be misinterpreted as defiant or challenging. Teachers need to carefully watch children to identify patterns that may indicate sensory issues.

off and may prefer to wear clothing that would normally be considered too tight or may cocoon herself in a sheet during rest time and want more blankets piled on. Being a crasher and bumper, she craves rough-and-tumble play.

The sensory-avoidant child is the one who seems to flounder in space. Her body is uncoordinated, and she often bumps into things and into people.

The behaviors of the sensory-seeking or -avoidant child can be mistaken for challenging behaviors. The child who sits on other children during group time may not be doing so to irritate another or to stake claim to a particular location in the group. She may literally not know where her body is in relation to other children. Only when she bumps up against another body does her brain get adequate stimulation to know where she is in relationship to other people or objects in the room. The child who constantly bumps into others either by accident or on purpose may not be doing so out of disrespect but because she does not have the coordination to control her movements, or she may be bumping into children to know where her body is. This is one reason transitions are often difficult for children from hard places. Lining up to go outside is challenging for someone who struggles to know where her body is in space. Providing visual cues on the floor for lining up can help the child know where to place her body in relationship to other children. For example, little feet can be placed on the floor by the door to indicate where children are to stand when going outside or to another part of the building.

Interoceptive Sense

The interoceptive system sends information gathered from the internal organs to the brain. It helps children know when they need to use the restroom, when they are hungry or full, or when they feel ill. It allows them to recognize when they are tired or too hot or too cold.

It is not uncommon for children from hard places to struggle with potty training and eating issues. Although emotional factors may play into these behaviors, the interoceptive system may also play a part. I met a four-year-old who had no perception of when he needed to use the restroom—he had no awareness of even being wet when he soiled his clothing. Some children struggle with constipation because they are unaware of the sensation of needing to use the restroom. This may cause them to soil their pants because they don't realize they have to go until it is too late, and they can't make it to the toilet.

Food issues can present in many different ways. Some children gorge on food to the point of making themselves sick because they can't sense when they are full. Others will become dehydrated because they don't realize they are thirsty. Recognizing thirst is especially important for children who have had prenatal fetal alcohol exposure. Purvis and Cross warn that they dehydrate faster than typical children because of their different neurochemical makeup. I know of a foster child who had a mild heat stroke in child care because the adults in the child care center told him to stop drinking so much water.

Some children will play until they literally drop because they are unable to detect when their bodies are tired. For some, the transition from activity to sleep is almost instantaneous. One moment, they are actively playing, and the next moment, they are curled up in the corner sleeping. Helping children recognize signs of fatigue is important.

Characteristics of Children with Sensory Processing Issues

Understanding sensory processing gives teachers and caregivers a different lens through which to interpret perplexing behaviors. However, it is important to realize that many children have quirky responses to sensory input at one time or another. It is only recognized as a disorder when it interferes with a child's ability to feel safe and to function in the world. A disorder disrupts a child's capacity to learn, play, and enjoy relationships with others.

Sensory processing issues can also present in ways similar to trauma behavior. For example, an infant may resist being held or cuddled for tactile reasons and/ or emotional reasons that indicate an attachment issue. A child may become upset during diaper changes, which can indicate a sensory-processing issue and/ or abuse. When puzzling behaviors are a persistent concern, an evaluation by an occupational therapist is in order.

Characteristics of Sensory Processing Disorder with Infants and Toddlers

- Have an extreme startle reaction to noise, which results in crying or screaming
- Cry or arch their backs when held
- Are distressed by diaper changes
- Become upset when face or hands are wiped with a wet cloth
- Have erratic sleep cycles
- Cry excessively throughout the day
- Seem uncomfortable most of the time
- Are distressed by certain motions such as rocking, bouncing, swinging, and so on
- Have difficulty sucking, chewing, or swallowing
- Don't recognize when diaper is wet or soiled
- Prefer to be naked
- Are distressed by bright lights
- Become inconsolable when other babies cry
- Don't enjoy interactive games such as peekaboo or This Little Piggy
- Can't switch toys from hand to hand; use one hand to explore
- Are unable to bang toys or clap hands together in front of body
- Are distressed by food or dirt on face or hands
- Have difficulty accepting solid foods
- Avoid foods of a certain texture or consistency
- Avoid equipment that involves movement: rocking horses, swings, bouncers, and strollers
- When not teething, constantly chew on clothing, toys, or fingers
- Avoid toys and materials of a certain texture
- Prefer toys and materials of a certain texture
- Refuse to be put in certain positions; will only lie in a certain position
- Have difficulty staying asleep more than thirty minutes
- Are unable to self-soothe
- Require a particular sound to go to sleep: fan, white noise, vacuum, or music
- Ask for heavy blankets put on them to go to sleep
- Show excessive use of a pacifier
- When they begin to walk, only walk on tiptoes
- Crave movement
- Approach toys and people with intense and uncontrolled touch; seem to not understand the concept of *gentle*

Characteristics of Preschoolers with Tactile Defensiveness

- Resist being touched or hugged
- Resist wearing socks and/or shoes; prefer sandals
- Avoid messy activities
- May crave messy activities—can't keep hands out of the paint cups, playdough, and so on
- Have the tags cut out of their clothes
- Become upset or even aggressive when other children bump into them
- Avoid games and activities that involve touch
- Will only wear clothing made of certain fabrics; complain that their clothing hurts them
- Will only accept a sheet or blanket made of a certain fabric
- Constantly rub toys or materials made of a certain fabric
- Resist having hair brushed or hands or face washed
- Are distressed when the wind blows on their faces
- Avoid clothing with belts around waist, avoid turtlenecks
- Avoid walking barefoot on grass
- Are picky eaters

Characteristics of Preschoolers Who Are Tactile Sensory Seeking

- Crave touch; touch everything in sight; can't keep hands to themselves
- Don't seem to be aware of someone touching them
- Don't seem to feel pain
- Bite and hit themselves; bang their heads
- Seek out materials of distinct textures
- Crave messy play
- Crave vibrating toys
- Crave spicy, sour, or salty foods

Characteristics of Preschoolers Who Are Sensory Avoidant of Vestibular Input

- Avoid playground equipment
- Prefer tasks that can be done sitting down
- Terrified of falling even when there is no imminent danger
- Difficulty walking on uneven surfaces; afraid of stepping off a curb
- Become distressed or even aggressive if they swing, rock, or spin
- Afraid of heights; resist getting on a slide or climbing gym

- Avoid any activity where the feet leave the ground
- Resist being upside down or tilted backward
- Lose balance easily and appear clumsy

Characteristics of Preschoolers Who Are Sensory Seeking of Vestibular Input

- Constantly moving, rocking, spinning
- Love being tossed in the air
- Love intense movement; swing as high as possible; want the merry-go-round to spin faster; jump on furniture; hang upside down at every chance
- Love to spin and never get dizzy. (Note: According to the Tulsa Sunshine Center Sensory Processing Disorder Resource Center, there is a difference in the eyes of a child who gets dizzy and one who doesn't get dizzy. After spinning for about thirty seconds, the eyes of children will flutter back and forth, left to right. However, the eyes of the child who is hyposensitive to movement will stop fluttering more quickly than a typical child.)
- Rarely walk; run, hop, jump, or skip from place to place
- Like sudden or quick movements

Characteristics of Preschoolers with Poor Muscle Tone and/or Coordination

- Posture is limp or floppy; slide out of chairs
- Fatigue easily when expected to sit still for long periods
- Difficulty turning doorknobs and handles or manipulating fasteners on clothing
- Difficulty catching themselves when they fall; have a tendency to face-plant
- Poor body awareness; sit on other children, bump into them, trip, knock things over
- Difficulty with both fine and gross motor skills
- Difficulty using tools such as eating utensils, scissors, glue, combs
- Uncoordinated when it comes to learning musical games that involve specific movements

Characteristics of Children who are Sensory Seeking of Proprioceptive Stimulation

- Stomp feet when walking
- Love jumping and crashing activities
- Constantly throw their bodies around
- Crave rough-and-tumble play
- Bite, chew, or suck on clothing, fingers
- Bite other children
- Prefer to be held or hugged tightly
- Like to be wrapped tightly in blankets; will often wrap themselves up in blankets
- Ask for more blankets to be piled on during rest time
- Crave chewy foods
- Crave gum
- Pile pillows and cushions on themselves and ask for people to sit on them
- Grind teeth
- Intentionally fall on the floor
- Love to push and pull heavy objects
- Love to fill tote bags, backpacks with heavy objects
- Constantly spill things due to misjudging the weight of something or grasping too hard
- Break the points on crayons and pencils from pressing too hard, or drawing and handwriting are so light and feathery they cannot be read
- Refuse to take coat off
- Like to wear tight clothing
- Do everything with a great deal of force: slam doors, break toys, hug too hard, walk hard

Characteristics of Children with Interoceptive System Issues

- Don't recognize when they need to use the restroom; wet pants
- Chronically constipated
- Don't recognize signs of hunger or satiation; gorge on food
- Don't recognize when they are ill
- Don't feel pain

Strategies for Helping Children with Sensory Processing Issues

Creating a sensory-rich environment is important for all children, but it is essential for children with a trauma history. An environment that supports sensory integration helps children become more self-regulated. Children will always tell us what they need if adults are astute and careful observers of children.

Meeting Sensory Needs during Morning Arrival

Start the day off with "crash 'n bump" activities that specifically target proprioceptive and vestibular movements. Purvis and Cross suggest creating a circuit of activities that the children can work through for at least twenty minutes. This can also be used throughout the day when weather prevents children from going outside to play.

- Jump on a crib mattress or minitrampoline (in states where it is permitted).
- Walk on a balance beam.
- Bounce on hopper balls.
- Lie on a scooter on their tummies to knock over a tower of cardboard blocks.
- Crawl through a tunnel.
- Place a tarp over several inner tubes, and let children walk across the uneven surface.
- Stuff a duvet cover full of pieces of foam rubber to create a mountain of fluff. (Note: Many upholstery shops are happy to get rid of their old foam at no cost.)
- Spin on a Sit'N Spin or bilibo (a plastic shell that children can sit in and spin).

Meeting Sensory Needs in Group Time

Let children who struggle with sitting on other children or constantly bumping into them sit in a clothesbasket with a pillow. Bumping up against the sides of the basket tells the brain where their bodies are in space. Cozy spaces provide an enormous sense of security.

- Those with low muscle tone can sit on a T-stool, a partially inflated beach ball, or a therapy ball.

- Let children who tend to wiggle or rock back and forth sit in a rocking chair.
- Provide weighted lap pads or weighted neck buddies for children who crave deep muscle stimulation.
- Do deep muscle compressions before group time. (An occupational therapist can teach this simple procedure.)
- Provide fidgets for children to hold.
- Make "sand babies" for children to hold. (See page 244 for directions.)
- For children who constantly chew on their clothing or fingers, give them chewing gum during group time or small pieces of beef jerky.

Meeting Sensory Needs during Meal Times

Some children have a very difficult time sitting in a chair at the table and enjoying a meal. Here are some tips for helping the child with sensory needs.

- Before snack or meal time, provide a "heavy work" task that includes some kind of pushing, pulling, jumping, squishing, bouncing, rocking, pounding, or squeezing.
- Do some deep muscle compressions.
- Provide placemats to define space.
- Let the child sit on a core disk in the chair.
- Provide a weighted neck buddy or lap pad.
- Let very fidgety children stand.
- Some children with sensory needs have to feel their food before they eat it. They are not "playing" with their food. Provide lots of appropriate finger foods.
- Provide plastic cups that can't be squished if held too tightly in lieu of Styrofoam.
- Tie an exercise band, such as a TheraBand, around the front legs of the chair to give some deep muscle input.
- For children who gorge or are unable to determine hunger or satiation, create a visual cue to encourage the child to try to tune in and listen to her body. Before every snack or meal, have the child use the visual cue to indicate her level of hunger.

Meeting Sensory Needs during Nap Time

- Before nap, provide a "heavy work" task that includes some kind of pushing, pulling, jumping, squishing, bouncing, rocking, pounding, or squeezing.
- Do some deep muscle compressions.

- Use weighted blankets or heavy quilts. Do not leave these on for the duration of nap time, however. Use for no more than 20 minutes.
- Fill inexpensive gardening gloves with sand or beans. Sew or hot glue the gloves shut at the wrists. Place in the middle of a child's back.
- Provide white noise or nature sounds.
- Use aromatherapy. Lavender is known to induce relaxation.
- Use a small indoor fountain that does not hold standing water.
- Turn on a metronome and set to 80 beats a minute to simulate a heartbeat.
- Rub children's backs.
- Listen to soothing music.
- Let the child lie on a vibrating mat.
- Put a bath mat or sensory cloth at the end of the child's cot and let him rub his feet on it.

Evaluating Your Classroom

Sensory-rich environments have always been a key component of developmentally appropriate classrooms. Understanding the sensory processing system and the vestibular, proprioceptive, and interoceptive senses will allow you to take a deeper look at the sensory richness of the environment. The following checklists will help child care providers and teachers evaluate their classrooms for sensory richness.

Proprioceptive Activities

1. Provide materials for carrying or lifting objects:
   - ☐ Backpacks, fanny packs, tote bags, brief cases, small suitcases
   - ☐ Chairs or books for stacking or moving
   - ☐ A pulley system to move sand or water outside; a system to haul blocks and other items indoors
   - ☐ Buckets for hauling sand and water
   - ☐ Water hose and watering can
   - ☐ Large hollow blocks for building
2. Provide weighted clothing:
   - ☐ Vest
   - ☐ Lap pad
   - ☐ Wrist or ankle weights
   - ☐ Blanket
   - ☐ Backpack
   - ☐ Fanny pack

3. Provide equipment and materials for pushing or pulling activities:
   - [ ] Pulleys
   - [ ] Shopping carts
   - [ ] Strollers and baby carriages
   - [ ] Wagons
   - [ ] Laundry baskets
   - [ ] Tug-of-war rope
   - [ ] Brooms and mops
   - [ ] Snow shovels for snowy days
   - [ ] Rakes for gathering fallen leaves
   - [ ] Dirt and shovels for digging outside
   - [ ] Wheelbarrow
   - [ ] Scooter boards
   - [ ] TheraBand
   - [ ] Bicycles, tricycles, and Big Wheels
   - [ ] Skates and roller blades
   - [ ] Parachute games
   - [ ] Sheet or blanket for a child to sit on for you to pull around
   - [ ] Slide for climbing (yes, *up* the slide!)
   - [ ] Large box, basket, or bin for the children push each other around in
4. Provide materials for jumping or bouncing:
   - [ ] Minitrampolines
   - [ ] Mattress
   - [ ] Hoppy ball
   - [ ] Pogo stick
   - [ ] Rocking horse with springs
   - [ ] Jump rope
   - [ ] Ankle jump ropes
   - [ ] Chalk or painted hopscotch game
   - [ ] Potato sacks for races
5. Provide equipment or materials for climbing and hanging:
   - [ ] Monkey bars
   - [ ] Zip lines
   - [ ] Rock walls
   - [ ] Rocks
   - [ ] Ropes
   - [ ] Cargo nets
   - [ ] Platforms
   - [ ] Low risers
   - [ ] Lofts
   - [ ] Small slides, such as Little Tykes
   - [ ] Soft modular blocks

6. Provide materials for sandwich or "squishing" activities:
   - [ ] Floor cushions, bean-bag chairs, and pillows to "sandwich"
   - [ ] Blanket for rolling a child inside like a hot dog
   - [ ] Weighted blankets
   - [ ] Towels for firmly wrapping a child after water play
   - [ ] Giant gym or exercise ball for rolling on child
   - [ ] Ball pits and body socks
   - [ ] Deep pressure massage

7. Provide opportunities for large-muscle activities:
   - [ ] Running or crawling activities
   - [ ] Crabwalk, seal walk, other animal walks
   - [ ] Relays
   - [ ] Red Rover
   - [ ] Army crawl through tunnel

8. Provide materials for fine motor activities for upper extremities:
   - [ ] Chalkboard, eraser, and chalk for erasing and drawing
   - [ ] Paints and paper
   - [ ] Vinegar-and-water solution and paper towels for washing windows
   - [ ] Vertical surfaces, such as whiteboards or outside walls, for cleaning
   - [ ] Squeegee
   - [ ] Paint the side of the building or fence with brush or roller and water
   - [ ] Pop beads
   - [ ] Shaving cream or funny foam for making letters

9. Provide materials for resistive activities:
   - [ ] Clothespins
   - [ ] Spray bottles
   - [ ] Child-safe scissors
   - [ ] Playdough and accessories
   - [ ] Crayons for coloring on textured surfaces
   - [ ] Dot markers
   - [ ] Sponge painting
   - [ ] Paper punches
   - [ ] Spray nozzle on garden hose
   - [ ] Tweezers and tongs
   - [ ] Jars with screw-on lids for opening
   - [ ] Nutcrackers

10. Provide materials for fidgeting:
    - [ ] Textured balls
    - [ ] Silly Putty
    - [ ] Ring of textured fabric
    - [ ] Commercial fidgets
    - [ ] Large pom-poms

11. Provide materials for use on resistive surfaces:
- [ ] Sidewalk chalk
- [ ] Crayons for coloring on sandpaper, wire mesh, or paper doilies
- [ ] Brushes and dolls for brushing hair
- [ ] Sandpaper and wood
- [ ] Hammer, nails, and wood for pounding nails (if allowed)
- [ ] Golf tees, toy hammers, and Styrofoam for pounding tees

Vestibular Activities

1. Provide equipment, materials, and activities for rotary movement:
- [ ] Sit'N Spin
- [ ] Merry-go-round
- [ ] Swing the Statue game
- [ ] Pretend to be a top or a wind-up toy
- [ ] Singing games that involve turning around
- [ ] Roll down a hill
- [ ] Roll across the floor or a mat on different textures
- [ ] Roll inside a large tire or tube
- [ ] Turn somersaults on a tumbling mat

2. Provide equipment, materials, and activities for balancing:
- [ ] Walk on a balance beam
- [ ] Sit on a therapy ball and balance
- [ ] Play on or walk across a see-saw
- [ ] Bounce on a hoppy ball
- [ ] Walk on stilts
- [ ] Walk on unstable surfaces such as an air mattress, inner tubes, or a clatter bridge
- [ ] Sit on a T-stool
- [ ] Play wheelbarrow walking
- [ ] Sit on a partially inflated beach ball

3. Provide equipment, materials, and activities for swinging:
- [ ] Tire swing
- [ ] Rope swing
- [ ] Traditional swings
- [ ] Teeter totter
- [ ] Hammocks
- [ ] Swing in a sheet

4. Provide equipment for rocking:
- [ ] Rocking chairs
- [ ] Rocking horse
- [ ] Rocking boat
- [ ] Rocker boards

5. Provide equipment for bouncing:
   - ☐ Hoppy ball
   - ☐ Doorway jumper
   - ☐ Bouncy chairs
   - ☐ Therapy ball
   - ☐ Mattress or trampoline

6. Provide materials and activities for stretching:
   - ☐ Pass a ball under the legs and over the head
   - ☐ Pantomime picking apples, climbing a ladder, reaching for the sky, and so on

7. Provide materials and activities for music and creative movement:
   - ☐ Dance with scarves, streamers
   - ☐ Put paper plates under feet and "ice skate" to music
   - ☐ Dance or jump on a gathering drum
   - ☐ Walk or dance to the changing beat of a drum

Chapter 5

The Effect of Trauma on Self-Regulation

My first year out of college, I taught four-year-olds in a child care center in one of the most violent parts of Washington, DC. I was told one morning that I would be getting a new child named Scott. At about 11 a.m. I heard a blood-curdling scream in the hallway and looked out to see a little boy running toward me yelling at the top of his lungs. His mom brought up the rear, acting as if she heard nothing. They got to my door and stopped. My heart skipped a few beats. This had to be Scott.

The children were engaged in interest centers at the time, so Scott chose to play in the block area; however, it wasn't long before it was time to clean up. I gave them a five-minute warning to wrap up what they were doing and then started singing the clean-up song. Scott screamed, "I don't want to clean up!" I turned to look at him, and in a split second, he fired a block across the room, hitting me between the eyes. Blood gushed from my head onto the floor as I stood there stunned. No one had prepared me for this.

The following day Scott made his grand entrance once again. The morning was challenging, to say the least. He was at the easel as center time was ending. I gave my five-minute warning and sang my little song, and within seconds chaos broke loose. I know this dates me, but back in the early '70s we didn't have plastic. We mixed our homemade paint in glass mayonnaise jars. I heard Scott shriek, "I don't want to clean up!" I turned to see mayonnaise jars shattering against the wall, glass and paint flying everywhere. To be honest, I'm not sure what I did. I remember thinking, "This kid is going to kill me if I don't figure out how to help him." I had no idea what to do.

Out of sheer survival, I glued Scott to my side. From the moment he walked in the door, I directed his every move. "Scott, let's put your jacket in your cubby. Hang it right here." "Scott, it's time for group time. You are going to sit by me. Put your pockets right here. Put your hands in your lap, and keep your eyes on me." "Scott, would you like to do a puzzle or play Candy Land? Okay, sit right here." On and on it went. It was exhausting. But one day, the light came on. During center time, Scott went to the library center on his own accord, took a book off the shelf, and sat on the floor to read. He looked up at me and asked, "Miss Barbara, am I being good right now or am I being bad?" His question stopped me in my tracks. This was not a child who was willfully defiant; this was a child who genuinely had no clue what appropriate behavior looked or felt like. It was a watershed moment for Scott and me.

Thereafter, he would ask me through the day, "Miss Barbara, am I being good or am I being bad?" I would clap and cheer his good behavior and respond to inappropriate behavior by saying, "No, Scott. That is not okay. Let me show you what to do." As the months passed, Scott's behavior slowly began to change. By the spring, he was able to function mostly on his own. He and I had become friends. At the time, I didn't understand the dynamic of what had happened. I just knew that I had to keep this child close or I was likely to suffer bodily harm. It was out of survival, not wisdom, that I glued him to my side.

Now I understand what happened with Scott and why his behavior changed: I became Scott's external regulator. He had no capacity to regulate and control his own emotions or behavior. No amount of reasoning, sending him to time out, or giving other forms of punishment would change him. By requiring him to be within arm's length, I modeled appropriate behavior, told him when and what he was supposed to do, and when he didn't seem to understand, demonstrated the behavior and then said, "Now, you do it."

Defining Self-Regulation

When neglect, abuse, and trauma rob children of the security of a loving relationship with an invested caregiver, the capacity to self-regulate is also undermined. According to researchers, including Stephen Porges, Bruce McEwen, Elizabeth Lasley, Connie Lillas, and Janiece Turnbull, self-regulation essentially refers to how efficiently and effectively a child deals with a stressor and then recovers. It is a capacity that is created in the arms of a loving adult. Who we are and what we become largely reflects the quality of the regulatory interactions that we have with our caregivers, says Shore in his book *Affect Regulation and the Origin of Self*. Our ability to regulate ourselves in the face of stress is rooted in how well we were regulated in the first three years of life.

Stuart Shanker, author of *Self-Regulation*, points out that self-regulation differs from compliance because a child may be coerced into obedience through intimidation yet have little ability to self-regulate. Self-regulation cannot be punished into being; it comes alive in the loving dance between caregiver and child.

As previously discussed, the body is a remarkably well-orchestrated symphony of neurochemicals and electrical impulses exquisitely designed for self-protection. Many experts compare it to the acceleration and braking system of a car. When a source of stress is encountered, the body steps on the gas and revs the engine to rally the body's resources to deal with the stress. When the stressful event is effectively dealt with or goes away, the body steps on the brake to slow itself down and return to a normal state of functioning. Children who live in the context of chronic abuse, neglect and trauma are essentially trying to drive a car with one foot on the gas and the other foot on the brake. The gas pedal is always pressed to the floor because their body is never able to return to a state of equilibrium and calm before the next challenge hits them. As the braking system of the body is overridden by the gas pedal, the child increasingly has difficulty recovering from stress, and caregivers may see the following behaviors:

- The child will have an extreme emotional reaction disproportionate to the stimulus. For example, a caregiver tells a child that center time is over and she has a major temper tantrum.
- The child will have difficulty paying attention. She will struggle with sitting in group time, making transitions, and following directions.
- The child will have seemingly random temper tantrums for reasons that are difficult to understand, such as calmly playing in the block center one minute and screaming the next.

- The child is unable to calm herself down once she is stressed. For example, a child arrives at school visibly upset and crying, and Mom reports that they have had a difficult morning. The child remains irritable and cries most of the day.
- The child lives at emotional extremes. She is either extremely happy or extremely angry or sad.
- The child does not handle frustration well. For example, when she can't find a puzzle piece, she throws the puzzle on the floor and cries.

The Five Domains of Self-Regulation

Scientists who study self-regulation have created several different frameworks for understanding how it works. I find Shanker's approach helpful, that self-regulation has five components: physiological, emotional, cognitive, social, and prosocial. In reality, there is a great deal of overlap and interdependence as these components play out in daily life. The following distinctions are only to help teachers and caregivers think more deeply about self-regulation and how they can effectively nurture its development.

- **Physiological regulation** involves the sensory system and the physical sensations of the body. Being overstimulated by the sights, sounds, textures, smells, and tastes in the environment can flood a child's brain and cause dysregulated behavior. Proprioceptive, vestibular, and interoceptive sensations can also overwhelm her. Because Chapter 4 was primarily dedicated to physiological regulation, we will not discuss it in any great detail in this chapter.

- **Emotional regulation** involves the capacity to experience and enjoy positive emotions as well as the ability to manage strong or overwhelming negative feelings. Curiosity, love, joy, and perseverance fuel a child's desire to learn about the world and how it works. However, fear, anger, anxiety, and frustration can overwhelm children's ability to enjoy relationships, play, and learning. When children can't manage strong emotions with words and other appropriate strategies, those feelings likely will manifest through behaviors that are challenging to caregivers and teachers. Children who struggle in this domain will have difficulty establishing friendships with other children because their whining, crying, and emotional meltdowns tend to isolate them from others. The emotional turmoil of many maltreated children is so profound that it disrupts their ability to learn and enjoy a sense of well-being.

- **Cognitive regulation** involves the child's ability to process and remember information, maintain focused attention, think flexibly, and solve problems. When children have strong cognitive-regulation skills, they can demonstrate purposeful behavior, which means the child can inhibit her impulses, ignore distractions, sequence information, successfully switch attention, and hold several pieces of information in mind long enough to act upon them. Impulse control is perhaps one of the more difficult aspects of cognitive regulation because it involves integrating many different subskills: the ability to comply with appropriate expectations and to modulate the speed, intensity, and volume with which something is done. Children who struggle with impulse control find it very difficult to function in a group setting because they have a tendency to act upon every thought or feeling that pops into their heads. They may blurt out every answer to every question asked in group time. If someone accidently touches or bumps them, they are likely to hit that person. They approach situations like a "bull in a china shop," with an intensity that is off-putting to other children. They are likely to barge into a dramatic-play scenario, disrupt the story line, and attempt to take over the play. They may pound or shake the rhythm-band instruments with such vigor that the instruments break. They have difficulty recognizing the difference between an inside voice and an outside voice, and often the voice of a dysregulated child can be heard above the others.

At the opposite end of the continuum are the children who are so withdrawn that they disappear into the shadows. Despite their outwardly calm demeanors, they are in a state of dysregulation as severe as that of the outwardly aggressive child. Their fear overwhelms them to the point of being unable to respond appropriately to the environment. They never speak in group time, rarely make eye contact, move around the periphery of the classroom, and mostly play alone. If you try to engage them in individual conversation, their voices barely rise above a whisper—if they answer at all. It is as if they are trying to make themselves invisible. The fear inside them overwhelms their capacity to engage with the world.

- **Social regulation** involves the ability to make a friend and be a friend and depends heavily on a child's capacity to successfully read and interpret social cues. Children from hard places often misinterpret the nonverbal messages communicated by their peers. They don't pick up on cues that someone wants to play or that the theme of the play is changing. Enjoying relationships with others also requires an awareness of how one's words and actions affect other people, and they are sometimes oblivious to how their behavior affects other people. The lack of social skills further isolates them from the world around them, and they remain lost in their own aloneness. Trying to function in a group setting creates a great deal of anxiety.

- **Prosocial regulation** is the capacity to give and receive empathetic care. It requires the mental capacity to look at a situation through the eyes of another, comprehend that person's emotions, and appropriately make an empathetic response. It is an experience of feeling *with* someone, not just feeling *for* someone. When a friend arrives at school excited about his trip to Disney World, the prosocial child can express joy and interest in the child's excitement. When a friend is sad because his dog died, the prosocial child will have some understanding of his sadness and will know appropriate ways to express it. She may hug the child, pat him on the back, draw him a picture, get a tissue for him, or do some other act of kindness. Sometimes regulatory skills are referred to as "emotional intelligence." Research indicates that these key capacities are essential for a successful and productive life. They ultimately influence the ability to hold and succeed at a job, to parent, to be a marriage partner, and to make and enjoy relationships with other people. Self-regulation is the strongest predictor of well-being in all areas of life, and the foundation is established in the first three years.

The Biological Roots of Self-Regulation

The foundation for self-regulation is established before the child ever sees the light of day. In utero and during the first year of life, the architecture or neural circuitry related to self-regulation is formed. In the past, it was believed that the developing baby was safely tucked away in the womb, secluded from harm and stress and incubating in the shadowy darkness of the mother's body. We now know this is not the case. The prenatal environment is ever changing, with a variety of scents, sounds, tastes, sensations, and even dimly lit sights. *Early Development and the Brain* by Zero to Three describes the womb as a very active place in which the baby himself is constantly interacting. Ann Streissguth, author of *Fetal Alcohol Syndrome*, points out that the mom shares the air she breathes, what she eats and drinks, the emotions that she experiences, and the chemicals she encounters with the baby growing inside her.

Self-regulation begins with the first cell, which divides and the multiplication process begins. Oxygen and nutrients are the primary ingredients for healthy cell division, migration, and differentiation; therefore, anything that robs the cells of these essential elements has the potential to alter the functioning of the brain. The degree of impact can range from mild to severe, depending on factors such as timing, dosage, and the age of the mother. Smoking, alcohol, drugs, malnutrition, and toxic stress are the primary culprits that can compromise the availability of essential nutrients necessary for healthy brain development; however, none is as harmful as alcohol.

Fetal Alcohol Exposure

Alcohol has been identified as a teratogen, an agent that can interfere with the development of a fetus and cause birth defects. Alcohol exposure in utero can cause irreparable neurological damage, undermining the biological roots of a healthy regulatory system. Zero to Three points out in its DVD *Safe Babies Court Teams: Building Strong Families and Communities* that impulsivity and difficulty understanding the link between behavior and consequences are hallmarks of prenatal exposure. The National Child Traumatic Stress Network estimates that 70 percent of children in the foster-care system have at least some prenatal exposure to alcohol. Therefore, trauma-informed teachers and caregivers need to be aware of the common characteristics. If you suspect fetal alcohol spectrum disorders (FASDs), seek the help of a professional who can guide your child care facility and the family in providing help and support for the child.

Streissguth says that the impact of fetal alcohol exposure is determined by the dose, timing, and pattern of consumption. It is a myth that chronic consumption during pregnancy is the only condition that causes damage. Even moderate or sporadic drinking can have profoundly negative effects, and binge drinking is extremely toxic.

Identification of children suffering from the effects of alcohol can be tricky because there is a great deal of overlap with other traumas. According to Streissguth, a child with classic FASDs might exhibit a short stature and growth deficits; behaviors characteristic of damage to the central nervous system; and distinctive facial features, such as minor ear abnormalities, wide-set eyes, a flat nasal bridge and forehead, a smooth philtrum (the vertical groove between the nose and upper lip), and a thin upper lip. However, children can still suffer significant brain damage without the characteristic facial features and growth deficiencies.

FASD results in permanent brain damage to one degree or another, but not all children will experience mental retardation. The trauma-informed classroom is a must for these children, and an intentional focus on self-regulation is critical. The earlier there is a concerted effort to support the child with FASDs, the greater the likelihood of improved functioning.

Behavioral Characteristics of Infants and Toddlers with FASDs

- Startle easily
- Feeding and eating difficulties
- Spit up a lot
- Difficulty sucking
- Trouble gaining weight
- Motor problems
- Irritable
- Can't modulate from one mood to another

Behavioral Characteristics of Three- to Five-Year-Olds with FASDs

- Easily distracted; lack of focus
- Lack of impulse control
- Poor coordination
- Hearing abnormalities
- Difficulty with cause and effect
- Difficulty with self-regulation

Self-Regulation in Infancy and Toddlerhood

During infancy, the primary regulatory domains that need to be addressed are physiological and emotional. When a baby is born she has the capacity to experience basic emotions such as anger, joy, and fear. When the baby experiences gas, the physical pain may be accompanied by fear or anger; playful interactions with family members may elicit feelings of joy and contentment. But even these happy moments can exceed the child's capacity to self-regulate. The child may experience too much interaction and become overstimulated, which may escalate into a frenzied state. Her capacity to regulate her emotions is overwhelmed, and what started out as playful and enjoyable becomes dysregulating and uncomfortable.

The time frame between eighteen and thirty-six months is a critical period of development, especially for self-regulation. The increasing mobility of the toddler and her drive to master and explore the world require increased attention to not only the physiological and emotional aspects of functioning but also to cognitive regulation. Inquisitive toddlers will pull things out of drawers, make messes, climb on furniture and shelves, and remain on the go. Their insatiable curiosity is a normal stage of development and should not be interpreted as "bad" or challenging behavior. It is critical for caregivers to effectively guide and support the curious child's exploration of the world.

The process of learning to self-regulate can only happen in the context of a relationship. Babies cannot learn to self-regulate on their own, through technology, or through maturation alone. It only develops in the context of a warm, sensitive relationship with another invested human being. It is the result of being consistently regulated by another more organized brain.

About the most a baby can do to self-regulate is to get a fist into her mouth to suck, to look away from an overwhelming stimulus, or to go to sleep. She is totally dependent on the adults around her to bring her back into a state of calm by meeting her physical needs or by comforting her. When the needs of a baby are consistently met in a timely manner with sensitive care, the regulatory systems of the brain repeatedly fire. As the cycle of regulation, dysregulation, affectionate care, and reregulation plays out minute by minute, day after day, the regulatory connections in the brain become more complex, stronger, and faster. In just a few months, the well-nurtured infant can calm down at the mere sound of mom's voice because the regulatory system activates when the brain makes the association between the voice and the past history of being regulated.

> Babies cannot learn to self-regulate on their own, through technology, or through maturation alone. It only develops in the context of a warm, sensitive relationship with another invested human being.

But when no one pays attention to the baby's cues and no one can serve as the baby's external regulator, the child remains in an increasingly elevated state of physical discomfort and emotional distress. The cries of the baby will typically become more intense and the movements increasingly agitated until she exhausts herself and falls into a fitful sleep. The infant's body remains in an elevated state of neurochemical alarm. When this is a consistent pattern, the biological structures of the brain related to regulatory capacities will form inefficiently.

The dance of attunement between an infant and a caregiver is possible through an invisible channel of communication that Digby Tantam, author of *Can the World Afford Autistic Spectrum Disorder?*, calls the *interbrain*. It resembles "emotional radar," a connection between the organized brain of the adult and the unorganized brain of the baby. The adult reads the baby's facial expressions, body language, movements, and sounds to discern the baby's needs.

However, not only does the adult read the cues of the infant, but the child also begins to read the cues of the caregiver. This is how the baby learns to interpret the world. For example, Mom and eighteen-month-old Eleanor are out shopping when they see a family friend. The friend leans down and greets Eleanor, who has never met this lady and is guarded. Apprehension is evident on Eleanor's face as she anxiously looks to check out her mom's reaction. Mom and her friend calmly chit-chat for a few moments while Eleanor intently watches. Eleanor's demeanor changes. When the friend addresses her once again, she smiles and reaches out to touch her face. By observing her mom's reaction to this stranger, she can determine that this person is safe. This is called *social referencing*. If Eleanor's mom became alarmed or agitated, the toddler would have followed suit. However, when parents or caregivers are checked out or preoccupied because of drugs, alcohol, or stress, the baby is left to figure things out on her own.

Let's consider another child, three-year-old Kevin. Kevin and his mom live with her boyfriend. She is asleep on the couch in a drunken stupor while Kevin watches TV. In midafternoon, someone starts pounding on the door. The loud noise startles Kevin, and fear floods his brain. He runs to his mom, but she remains asleep. Kevin stands there, frozen. After a few minutes of pounding, the man starts kicking the door and shouting, "Open the door, you !@##$%^! You need to pay up!" Kevin's heart is racing and his breathing is shallow. His mom finally opens her eyes and, without acknowledging Kevin, staggers to the door, opens it, and yells, "He ain't here, you #@##$%^, so get out of here." She slams the door shut, staggers back to the couch, and closes her eyes. In just a few minutes, she is sound asleep.

Kevin's fear is never acknowledged and no one comforts him, which leaves him in a state of confusion. The loud pounding, kicking, and yelling communicated a sense of danger to him, but his mom's reaction did not validate his perception. Her failure to acknowledge Kevin's fear causes him to doubt the truth of his experience. His inner reality and her response are contradictory. He is left to cope with his fear and confusion alone.

This is the kind of dilemma that children from hard places face time and again. No one interprets the world and helps them make sense of daily life. When a child experiences a feeling in a particular context and another person confirms it through words or actions, it becomes a shared reality. The child begins to make connections between life events and particular internal emotions and ideas. But if a child experiences an emotion and no one confirms or contradicts her reality, she does not know how to make sense of the situation and will not make accurate cause-and-effect associations. If a child is left in her aloneness day in and day out, she lives in world of chronic internal chaos and confusion.

Another dynamic to this critical partnership between a caregiver and an infant or toddler is the adult giving the language to a child's inner experiences. For example, sixteen-month-old Krista somehow gets hold of a pencil. She is toddling about the room when her mother notices the potentially dangerous instrument in her hands. Her mom offers Krista a toy and says, "Here, I'll trade you. Put the pencil in my hand, and you can have the toy." Krista pulls her hand back and shakes her head no. She turns away from her mom as if she is going to run. Her mom takes the pencil from her, and Krista has a visceral reaction, throwing herself on the floor. She begins to scream at the top of her lungs. She has no tools to express her anger and frustration, so she expresses her emotion through her body. Her mom offers her the toy, but she continues to thrash. Her mom picks her up, holds her close, and says, "I see your mad face! You are really mad that I took the pencil. Here. You can have the rattle." She shakes the toy, and Krista reluctantly takes it as her cries begin to subside. "There. That's better. The toy is safe for you to play with. Oh, now I see your happy face!"

In this interaction, her mom validates Krista's desire to play with the pencil and the anger she feels at having it taken away. She gives Krista a tool to express her reality: The word *mad* is a symbolic tool that represents the internal feeling. Over time, as Krista and her mom have many more similar interactions, Krista will become less dependent on visceral reactions to express her inner life and will become more adept at using words.

When parents and caregivers are unavailable to label the child's inner experiences and emotions with words, the child is left with no tools. She continues to have visceral reactions long past the age at which such behavior typically gives way to language and other means of expression. Emotion easily overwhelms children from hard places, and they have few resources to manage.

A toddler once wanted me to push her in a doll stroller. I pushed her for a few minutes varying the speed as we zoomed around the room. After a few minutes, I stopped. She immediately began to thrash and yell in protest. I knew that this particular child knew some sign language and had some verbal vocabulary. I stooped down to look her in the face and calmly said, "Give me a word." I demonstrated the sign for *please* and said the word. She immediately calmed down and said, "Please," with the accompanying sign. I started pushing her again and I turned it into a game. I made frequent stops and each time said, "Give me a word." She would grin and give me a verbal "Please" with the accompanying sign. Playful interactions such as these help children to understand that they can effectively use words to get their needs met.

Adults who care for infants and toddlers with a trauma history must be highly attuned to their emotional and physiological state. The dance of attunement is critical to building the regulatory capacities of the brain. The caregiver should mirror the emotion that the child is feeling through body language and facial expressions and purposefully use a word to identify the emotion. If appropriate, she can then use some form of touch or rhythmic movement to bring the child back into a state of calm.

Some infants and toddlers have a flight response to stress and may become lethargic and withdrawn instead of aggressive or agitated. An untrained caregiver might mistakenly assume that the child is okay because she isn't crying, but an infant or toddler who often seems checked out or lethargic is cause for concern. This baby needs an attuned response and comforting interactions from her caregivers as much as the agitated child. She may need to be fed or taken on a walk. The caregiver might quietly play with her on the floor or roll a beach ball back and forth. Do not overwhelm the baby with fast movements, a high energy level, or a loud voice; instead, slowly increase the level and intensity of interaction as the child's arousal state increases.

Characteristics of Maltreated Infants and Toddlers

Because infants and toddlers don't have the physical ability to run away from frightening people and circumstances or to aggressively fight back, the trauma is stored in the body, resulting in the disorganization and disruption of the sensory systems and biological rhythms. Maltreated infants and toddlers display disruptions such as:

- Long periods of inconsolable crying
- Lack of response to the caregiver's attempts to soothe

- Flailing limbs and uncoordinated movement
- Muscular rigidity
- Agitation and restlessness
- Lack of appetite or excessive eating
- Difficulty falling asleep
- Restless sleep
- Night terrors
- Constipation or diarrhea
- Numbing of emotion
- Subdued demeanor
- Unresponsiveness to stimulation
- Meltdowns and temper tantrums

Perry said in his 2013 webinar, *Neurosequential Model of Education*, caring for a baby with a history of trauma becomes even more challenging in group settings. A child care center is a busy place. At any given moment, a little person needs the attention of the adults in the room. Consistently being fully present for the needs of babies in such a way that caregivers can attune to the baby's cues and help her regulate is no easy task. It is demanding on all levels—physically, emotionally, and mentally. This is why, in a trauma-informed environment, ratios matter so much.

Strategies for Soothing Infants and Toddlers

Visual
Calm infants and toddlers through visual means by:
- Dimming the lights
- Reducing clutter on the walls
- Using a partition around the child's crib or stroller
- Using a light machine that projects stars on the ceiling
- Providing small enclosures where toddlers can "hide"

Auditory
Calm infants and toddlers through auditory means by:
- Humming or singing
- Talking in a soothing voice
- Chanting in a rhythmical manner
- Playing instrumental music
- Playing white noise
- Playing nature sounds

Tactile

Calm infants and toddlers through touch by:

- Patting or rubbing the back
- Swaddling
- Stroking
- Providing textured blankets
- Providing deep muscle compressions
- Massaging

Olfactory

Calm infants and toddlers through smell by:

- Using a diffuser with essential oils
- Spraying lavender oil on the sheets

Vestibular

Calm infants and toddlers through rhythmic movement by:

- Rocking
- Swinging
- Bouncing
- Swaying
- Walking
- Riding in a stroller

Self-Regulation and Three- to Five-Year-Olds

Kevin was born to a drug-addicted mother with no permanent residence or place to call home. She lived with a string of boyfriends who inevitably tired of her and turned her out on the streets until she found her next stopover. She loved her baby, but she loved the drug-induced highs even more. She was an easy target for unscrupulous men who used and abused her. She did the best she could for her baby and threw a blanket over the crib when the beatings began.

When Kevin was three years old, neighbors reportedly found him sleeping on the sidewalk in front of the apartment building on several occasions. He was taken into state custody and put in a foster home. His foster mother reported that he had multiple temper tantrums throughout the day both at home and in child care. He would thrash on the floor, yell, kick, and scream if anyone said no to his incessant demands. Any change in schedule would throw him into a frenzy, and he violently resisted any transition. Getting him out of the house to go to child care and coaxing him in off the playground were the biggest challenges of the day.

It is not unusual for children from hard places to have emotional meltdowns into later childhood that look much like those of a two-year-old. As we have learned, abuse and neglect in the earliest years of life give children few tools to deal with their emotions. As children move into the preschool years, we continue to help them regulate the physiological, emotional, and cognitive domains, but as they become increasingly social, more attention is given to the social and prosocial aspects. Let's take a look at emotional regulation of the three- to five-year-old.

Identifying Emotions

The capacity to appropriately manage strong emotion begins with the ability to identify and name emotions. If a child can name it, she can more likely control it. Here are some strategies to help children learn to identify emotion.

- **Label your own emotions throughout the day, and describe the causes of your emotional state.** A caregiver who had a flat tire on her way to work one morning used her experience as an opportunity to model self-regulation. By sitting in the rocking chair and verbalizing her feelings, she demonstrated how she was calming herself. She gave language to her emotions.

- **Describe the emotional state of individual children throughout the day.** For example, if a child reluctantly comes through the door in the morning with tears in his eyes, describe what you see, and then hang the language on the emotion: "Johnny, the tears and the frown on your face tell me that you are sad. Have you had a difficult morning?" The question invites the child to talk about it, but it is not uncommon for children to simply shrug or ignore the adult. As time passes and the children grow more comfortable with the caregivers or teachers, most will begin to open up and share their stories.

- **Explore the cause-and-effect relationship between an event and an emotion.** Children from hard places often have no idea where emotions come from. To them, emotions just seem to bubble up from within for no reason. Tear pictures of faces from magazines. Ask children to describe what they think the person in the picture is feeling. Then ask them to tell you what they think happened before the picture was taken. Ask what they think happened after the picture was taken. Being able to link an event to an emotion is difficult for children from hard places because their understanding of cause-and-effect relationships is typically weak.

- **Make a feeling wheel or feeling die.** Spin the spinner or roll the die and have children tell a story about a time they experienced the feeling indicated on the wheel or die.

- **Establish a morning ritual in which children check in when they arrive.** Provide a way for children to indicate their emotional states.

- **Listen to different genres of music and ask children to identify how the music makes them feel.** Have the children draw a picture of how the music makes them feel. Give them streamers, scarves, or lengths of construction tape, and ask them to move and dance to the music according to how it makes them feel.

- **Read books that talk about emotions.** As you read a story, have children identify the emotion that they believe the characters in the story are feeling. They could use a feeling chart, feeling faces, or a feeling die.

- **Give children instant or digital cameras and have them take pictures of things that make them happy.** Making associations between an event and the feeling of happiness is difficult for children from hard places. It is easier for them to identify feelings of fear and anger than to identify happiness and link it to an event.

- **Sing songs and do fingerplays that talk about emotions.** Hundreds of appropriate songs and fingerplays are available online.

- **Put emotion charts in all of your interest centers.** As children experience strong emotion, have them identify the feeling on the chart. When children become dysregulated, it is difficult for them to process words. They need picture cues to help them process.

- **Trace the bodies of children on large butcher paper.** Talk about where they feel certain emotions in their body, and color those particular parts or use symbols to indicate. For example, often children describe feeling fear in their stomachs. Some say it feels like butterflies; others may say that it just feels funny. The children could put butterfly stickers on their tummies.

■ **Create a "fear-o-meter" or "mad-o-meter" indicating different signs and symptoms of these emotions.** When children exhibit these feelings, ask them to show you where they are on the meter. Start with the four basic ones—happy, sad, mad, and afraid—and as children grow in their understanding, other emotions can be added to the list and they can think of synonyms for *mad*, *sad*, *happy*, and *afraid*.

Remember: All emotions are legitimate. It is okay to be angry or sad. It is okay to be happy or afraid. Children should never be punished or shamed for feeling strong emotion—even negative ones. Brain research indicates that we actually have little control over the initial experience of emotion that we feel. The stress response reacts so quickly that emotion basically overtakes us; however, we *do* have control over what we do with the emotion.

A trauma-informed classroom recognizes that children from hard places have many unresolved emotions that bubble up at unexpected times. It is not always possible to pinpoint until after the fact what exactly triggers the emotion. It could be a smell, a sound, a tone of voice, or a sensation. The therapeutic classroom is a place where children know they are safe and can express their emotions without adults coming unglued or getting angry. They know that the adults in the space will take care of them and keep them safe.

As children ride the emotional roller coaster throughout the day, talk about the emotions they experience. Make comments such as, "Anna, it's okay to be mad that Joey knocked over your block structure, but let's figure out how we are going to handle it." Point out the emotions that characters in stories are feeling. When a character expresses a negative emotion, say something like, "Lilly is mad that Mr. Slinger took her purse. Is it okay for Lilly to be mad?" "Is it okay for Lilly to stick her tongue out at Mr. Slinger? Is it okay for Lilly to say unkind things to Mr. Slinger?" "What can Lilly do to handle her mad appropriately?"

From time to time, there will be legitimate reasons for adults to be mad in the classroom. Talk to children about your feelings and the cause for them. Model appropriate ways of dealing with anger. Help children learn that they are responsible for managing their emotions appropriately. They can't control their initial emotional response to a situation, but they can control what they do with the feeling.

A trauma-informed classroom recognizes that children from hard places have many unresolved emotions that bubble up at unexpected times. It is a place where children know they are safe and can express their emotions without adults coming unglued or getting angry.

Strategies for Managing Strong Emotions

Approach the emotionally tough moments of life as problems to be solved, and teach children strategies for managing strong emotion. Following are some strategies that help children manage their feelings in appropriate ways. Talk about these strategies in large group, small group, and throughout the day when children are calm. Make visual cues to put on the wall or on rings that children can carry in their pockets or hook onto their belts. Coach them through emotional moments, and help them apply the strategies in real-life situations.

- **Deep breathing:** Breathing deeply and purposefully activates neurohormones that inhibit the stress response of the body and promote relaxation. It is sometimes difficult for children to grasp the concept of breathing slowly and deeply. Here are some strategies to help:
  - **Cooling the soup:** Show children how to cup their hands and make a pretend bowl of soup. Tell them to smell the delicious chicken noodle soup. Model how to take a long, deep breath as you smell your pretend bowl. Then ask the children to cool it off because it is too hot to eat at the moment. Demonstrate to the children how to cool it off by blowing slowly on the soup. Rhythmically smell and cool the soup several times. Note: This idea is from Purvis and Cross in their *TBRI Professional Training Program.*
  - **Smelling the flowers and blowing out the candle:** Have the children cross their arms over their chests. Pretend that in one hand they have a bouquet of flowers, and in the other hand they have a birthday candle. Demonstrate how to smell the flowers and then blow out the birthday candle. Smell the flower and blow out the candle several times.
  - **Blowing pinwheels:** Give children pinwheels to blow.
  - **Blowing up a "balloon":** Pretend to be a balloon, and make yourself big by making a pretend bubble around yourself.
  - **Blowing bubbles:** Give the children commercially purchased or homemade bubble solution with a bubble wand. Or, put a tiny amount of nontoxic baby wash in a cup of water. Cut a small *V*-shaped notch one inch from the end of a straw. By cutting this notch, the child will only be able to blow air through the straw and not suck the water up. Invite the child to blow bubbles. Be sure the cup is sitting on a tray to contain the bubbles.
    - **Blowing a cotton ball:** Have children try to keep a cotton ball on the table while they blow it back and forth with a straw or a party horn.
- **Make a magic mustache:** Show children how to crook the pointer finger and press it on the phitrium (that little dent) under the nose. This is a pressure point that triggers the release of calming neurochemicals. Note:

This idea is from Purvis and Cross in their *TBRI Professional Training Program*.

- **Listen to soothing music.** Provide headphones in a quiet part of the room where children can listen and relax.
- **Work at the water or sensory table.** Demonstrate how soothing it is to run your fingers through water, sand, or birdseed. Similarly, play with clay or playdough.
- **Draw a picture**. It can help children to draw a picture of what they are afraid of or upset about.
- **Have some quiet time.** Encourage children to go to a quiet corner and read a book, snuggle with a stuffed animal, or hold a transitional object.
- **Take a walk with an adult.**
- **Push the wall.** Have children go to a nearby wall and pretend they are trying to knock it over.
- **Do chair push-ups.** Have children sit on a chair or on the floor and place their hands flat against the surface on either side of their legs. Demonstrate how they can lift their bottoms off the chair by using their arms to push themselves up. Hold for a count of ten.
- **Get a drink or a snack.** Children who have been exposed to alcohol in utero dehydrate more quickly than typical children. It is also important to keep blood sugars stable.
- **Ask for a hug.**
- **Rock in a rocking chair.**
- **Rock a sand baby.***
- **Swing.**

Foster children, in particular, struggle with the concept that they can feel two different emotions at the same time. They often experience a great deal of inner turmoil navigating and understanding their feelings toward their biological family and their foster family. They struggle with being mad at biological parents for the choices that they made, yet they still love them. They may inwardly love and appreciate their foster family but feel that doing so is a betrayal of their biological parents. This inner struggle can be overwhelming and very confusing to sort out. These children need to know that they can ask for help when they feel overwhelmed.

Many children from hard places have been left to fend for themselves and can be very street smart and adept at taking care of themselves in the practical realities of life, but emotionally most of them are about half of their chronological age. For example, a four-year-old may know how to open a can of soup and heat it on the stove or in the microwave yet will have a temper tantrum like a two-year-old when she can't be the waitress in the restaurant

* Instructions for making a sand baby are on page 244.

set up in the dramatic-play corner. The skewed development of the children confuses them as much as it does the adults who care for them. Remember, when children are most unlovable, that is when they need our love the most.

Cognitive Regulation

Cognitive regulation has a direct effect on a child's ability to learn and experience academic success. *Working memory*, the ability to process and retain information long enough to use it, is one aspect of cognitive regulation. For example, when I ask for a phone number, working memory enables me to remember it long enough to actually dial it. Children who are lacking in this basic capacity will find it hard to function in a group of children. Johnny will not be able to remember a two-part direction. You tell him to get his coat and line up to go outside, but you find him with his coat slung over his shoulder playing with the blocks. During interest-center time, you find him walking around the room carrying a pair of scissors because he forgets basic procedures and routines. He struggles with counting and often doesn't remember the names of other children in his group.

There is a biological component to working memory. Chronically elevated levels of cortisol in the first years of life can damage the hippocampus, which is associated with memory impairments. As you remember from Chapter 2, cortisol is one of the primary stress hormones produced by the body. Research by Charles Nelson, Nathan Fox, and Charles Zeanah with institutionalized children in Romania, described in their book *Romania's Abandoned Children*, indicates that memory did not improve with intervention; therefore, it remains unclear how much working memory can be repaired in a child who has experienced extreme neglect. Another reason that a child with a trauma history struggles with memory is that many of his memories of trauma may remain below consciousness and function as implicit memory. Therefore, many of the implicit memories are not integrated and then intrude upon his explicit memory and cause confusion.

In light of the uncertainty, working memory needs to be approached from two angles with children from hard places: provide opportunities for children to engage in activities that exercise working memory, and teach compensatory skills for children who struggle with tasks involving memory.

Strategies to Exercise Working Memory

- **Make or buy simple matching games.**
- **Play games that involve verbal memory.** For example, pretend you are going on a trip and each child decides what he will take, but before he can identify his item, he has to repeat—in order—the items named by the other children before him. For example, "I'm going on vacation, and I'm

going to take a suitcase." The next child says, "I'm going on vacation, and I'm going to take a suitcase and a bathing suit." The next child names the first two items and adds a third.

- **Play a flannel-board matching game.** Make individual flannel boards for each child. Cut out a pumpkin from orange felt for each child and a set of small geometric shapes cut from black felt to be used to create facial features. Make a pumpkin face with the felt shapes on a flannel board, and give the children ten seconds to look at it. Cover the board and then ask the children to re-create what they saw. After a designated time period, uncover the original face and let the children compare. The children can take turns being "it" and making pumpkin faces. Other objects can be used, such as snowmen, Christmas trees, people, and so on.
- **Guess what is missing.** Place ten to twelve objects on a tray, and give children twenty seconds to look at them. Have the children close their eyes, and remove one of the objects. Have them guess what object is missing.

Strategies for Compensatory Skills

If a child consistently can't follow a two-step direction, provide visual cues. For example, a teacher in a pre-K classroom has a child who consistently forgets things. He forgets to get his milk at lunch, forgets his coat and hat when they go out to recess, and aimlessly wanders around the room during interest-center time unless prompted to find an activity. She could give him picture cards to keep in his pocket, reminding him of the items he needs in different situations. Or, a chart can be posted by the door, reminding children of what they need to take outside. When children aimlessly wander, prepare a center-time chart with pictures identifying the different activities, and have the child make two choices. He puts pictures of his first and second choice in his pocket or they are attached to a lanyard, and then he is directed to go to his first activity. When he is finished with the first choice, he looks at the picture in his pocket or on his lanyard and goes to the next thing. When he is finished with the second activity, he reports back to the teacher.

- Provide graphic organizers for children to process information.
- Use KWL charts, graphs, rebus charts, and photographs to help children process information.
- Teach concepts and skills in a variety of ways that use multiple learning modalities. For example, when children are learning their address, sing it to them. Have them paint a picture of their home and put the addresses on it. Have children deliver mail to the houses by identifying addresses.
- Use *lots* of repetition. It sometimes takes many, many repetitions for a child to master information.

Strategies for Sustained Attention

Research indicate that a child's capacity for focused attention is the number one predictor of success in school. A key aspect of this capacity is the ability to ignore unimportant stimuli and give full attention to the task at hand. The early childhood setting is a busy place with multiple forms of stimulation bombarding a child's brain every second. Children who can't ignore unimportant stimuli easily become overwhelmed and find it very difficult to function and benefit from the learning environment. Sensory-integration issues can also undermine the development of focused attention. If sensory issues go unaddressed, focused attention will be difficult to develop.

Abuse, neglect, and trauma also undermine the development of focused attention because children live in a state of hypervigilance, where they are primed to pay attention to *everything*, which is a primitive survival mechanism. The child is unable to ignore distractions and is highly attuned to every sound, every movement, and every variation in the classroom. This makes perfect sense in a threatening environment. The sound of the key in the lock may indicate that Dad is home and the abuse is about to begin. The stumbling footsteps on the stairs may mean Mom is drunk and is about to go into a screaming rage. This hypervigilance wreaks havoc on a child's ability to learn in the child care or school setting.

Two key elements in fostering focused and sustained attention are a play-based environment and choice. When children are given the freedom to make choices in an open-ended play environment, they choose to play with things that are of interest to them. They quickly realize when something doesn't satisfy their curiosity, and they move on to something else. When interest is high, children will sustain focused attention for long periods of time. Adults need to be astute observers of children to identify each child's interests and abilities, so they can provide materials and activities to meet individual needs.

I once knew a two-year-old who brought a thirty-two-piece cardboard puzzle to the center. She loved the single-object, knobbed toddler puzzles we had, but I was curious to see what she would do with the more complex puzzle. She spent most of her day tediously taking the puzzle apart and putting it back together. By the end of the day, she could put the puzzle together in a matter of minutes. Interest, choice, and opportunity came together, and this child demonstrated a capacity for sustained attention well beyond her years.

Strategies for Sequencing Information

When children live in chaotic and unpredictable environments, their ability to sequence information and events is often nonexistent. For the concepts of *past*, *present*, and *future* or *beginning*, *middle*, and *end* to make sense to children, they must first have a predictable environment. If a child lives in chaos, there is no past and there is no future. There is only now.

If a child lives in chaos, there is no past and there is no future. There is only now.

A child's ability to sequence thoughts also enables him to plan for the future. Children have difficulty conceiving of what comes next. A key factor in a healing environment is predictability—predictable schedule, predictable limits, predictable people, and predictable procedures. Other ways to help children develop this concept include the following:

- **Cooking:** Cooking involves planning and following a sequence. Providing opportunities for children to participate in making snacks and meals gives them experience with following a sequence of directions. When the sequence is not followed, there is usually a natural and logical consequence—the recipe doesn't taste or look just right. Use rebus charts and pictures for children to follow recipes. Allowing children to make mistakes without fear of punishment is critical. Use mistakes in following a recipe as a problem-solving opportunity to figure out what went wrong.

- **First/then charts:** When a child is having trouble remembering routines and procedures, create charts that illustrate what he does first before he does the second thing. For example, "First, we wash our hands, then we eat lunch." "First, we put on a smock, then we paint at the easel."

- **Photo sequencing:** Take pictures of an activity as it unfolds, and have the children arrange the pictures in sequential order. For example, as you carve a jack-o-lantern, take pictures of the different steps and have the children put the pictures in order. Take pictures of a particular tree as it begins to change in autumn, and have children put them in sequential order.

- **Dramatic play, block play, and art:** Participating in each of these interest areas involves a great deal of planning. In dramatic play, children plan the theme of their play, the roles they take on, and the props they will need. A similar process takes place in blocks. Art experiences give children the opportunity to plan how to use the paper, what materials they are going to use, and envision the final product.

- **Beginning-middle-end stories:** Give children three objects, and help them create a story using the concepts of *beginning*, *middle*, and *end*. For example, a child might have a yo-yo, a plastic tiger, and a car. The story could go something like this:

One day Rachel and her family got in their car to go to the zoo. At the zoo, Rachel saw many different animals. Her favorite was the tiger. As they were leaving the zoo, they stopped to look at the gift shop. Rachel bought a yo-yo to play with.

- **All grown up:** Bring pictures of yourself taken at different stages of your life for children to sequence from youngest to oldest. They love seeing pictures of teachers and caregivers when they were young!

Cognitive Flexibility

Cognitive flexibility means that children are able to adapt their behavior to different settings. They understand that during group time they are expected to be attentive and use an inside voice. When they are outside, they can be active and loud. Transitions are not overwhelming or upsetting because these children can shift their attention and behavior from one thing to the next. When they make a mistake, they are able to fix it, and encountering a challenge does not cause them to come unglued. They are able to think outside the box and problem solve.

Children from hard places have a tendency to be rigid and inflexible. They struggle with transitions and unexpected change and insist on things being done in a certain way. The slightest change in schedule or in procedures can send them into an emotional meltdown. They are often diagnosed with oppositional defiant disorder when really it is fear that drives them to be inflexible. Their noncompliance is not rebellion and self-will but a symptom of their fear of the unknown.

> Children from hard places have a tendency to be rigid and inflexible. They are often diagnosed with oppositional defiant disorder when really it is fear that drives them to be this way.

An environment of safety and predictability is once again a critical element in a trauma-informed classroom. When children feel safe, they can relax control. They will never do so if they feel threatened. Caregivers and teachers should not force, coerce, or punish children who are afraid. Some clues indicating fear are dilated pupils, shallow breathing, clinched jaw, and/or shoulders drawn up tight.

- **Offer to help:** Offer to help the child with the expectations, and carry out the activity alongside her. Encourage even the slightest steps toward meeting the expectations.
- **Take small steps:** Break the activity down, if possible, into small, manageable steps. Set a realistic expectation for the child to accomplish just one or two. For example, if children are having difficulty remembering what to do at the paint easel, you might take photos depicting the following steps:
  - Put on a smock,
  - Attach the paper to the easel.

- Write your name at the top of the paper.
- Dip the paintbrush into the container.
- Wipe the drips on the side of the container.
- Paint the picture.
- Hang it up to dry on the rack.

Strategies for Developing Behavioral Self-Regulation

Impulse control and behavioral regulation are considered part of cognitive regulation because it takes thinking to control one's actions. Behavioral regulation is a complex concept that has many facets for children to master. Children are a work in progress, and developmentally appropriate expectations are important. Keep in mind that children from hard places often perform at a level much younger than their chronological age; take this into consideration when setting goals and expectations for individual children. We will look at some of the basic components and strategies to develop this capacity.

Set clear, simple rules. The early childhood classroom is, in a sense, a microsociety, and any organized group of people needs rules to govern and guide behavior. Choose no more than three or four simple rules for children to follow. Children have a sense of ownership when they are given the opportunity to help identify the rules, or you can choose some from established programs. For example, in their book *Theraplay: Helping Parents and Children Build Better Relationships through Attachment Play*, Phyllis Booth and Ann Jernberg define *Theraplay* as a form of therapy (group or individual) that uses play to enhance attachment relationships. In their group sessions, they use the following guiding principles that can also work well in early childhood settings:

- **No hurts.** Physical and emotional safety are essential to the mental health of all children. Explain to them that there are inside hurts and outside hurts. An inside hurt is one that hurts our heart or our feelings. For example, calling someone names can hurt that person's feelings. An outside hurt is one that hurts the body, such as kicking, hitting, slapping, and pinching.
- **Stick together.** Functioning in a group setting requires a great deal of sticking together. For example, if a child gets up during group time and starts turning somersaults, you can remind her to stick together and come back to the group. If a child plays in the block center when he is supposed to line up to go outside, he can be reminded to stick together.

- **Have fun.** The goal is for everyone to have a pleasant and enjoyable experience. Talk to the children about the factors that make a child care setting fun, and then talk to them about what makes it not fun.

Have them discuss and/or make pictures or charts that illustrate what the rules look like and sound like. For example, children might find or draw pictures of children sharing or taking turns to show "no hurts." Words to describe what that would sound like might include, "No one is crying or yelling," and "Children use good words to get what they need."

Rules for Miss Barbara's Bears

Rule	Looks Like	Sounds Like
No hurts	- Children share materials. - Children use gentle touch. - Children do not hit, kick, spit, or bite. - Children give each other compliments.	- Children say kind things. - Children do not yell at each other. - No one says, "You can't play with us." - No one makes fun of others.
Stick together	- Children follow the rules. - Children help each other.	- Children ask for help. - Children ask others if they need help. - Children invite other children to play.
Have fun	- Children paint and create art. - Children build with blocks. - Children engage in dramatic play.	- Children laugh. - Children make plans. - Children share ideas.

Following the rules seems like a simple and basic concept, but it presents challenges for children from hard places. It is not uncommon for maltreated children to be diagnosed with oppositional defiant disorder. Why is it so hard for harmed children to follow basic classroom rules?

Children who have a fear-based orientation to life and relationships often have a strong need to control the environment and those around them. Purvis and Cross assert that maltreated children's fear is so pervasive and so deep that they believe they will die if they lose control. Therefore, they attempt to control everything and everybody in their path. Following someone else's rules and complying with someone else's requests cause a deep sense of vulnerability. To deal with their fear, such children may become very bossy and manipulative, possibly disguising it as "helpfulness." It is sometimes challenging to distinguish between manipulation and a genuine need.

I once knew a child who constantly monitored the movements of everyone in the room. She played the role of policeman, reporting to me every minor infraction that played out in the room. She also knew about every need. If someone needed a tissue, she jumped to get one. If someone needed scissors, she scrambled to retrieve them. During group time, she wanted to hold the book or lead whatever activity we were doing. My initial reaction was, "Oh, what a helpful child!" But within a few hours, I realized her behavior was driven by a powerful need to stay in control. She could not relax and just enjoy the day but instead had to constantly stay on guard and struggled to remain in charge.

The roots of this inordinate need for control can go back to the powerlessness that many maltreated children feel in the first years of life. Think about the enormous amount of control that a well-nurtured baby has over his caregivers: His cry causes people to respond to him and meet his needs. He can make things happen in the world by effectively getting the attention of others to attend to his needs.

But consider the neglected or maltreated baby: His legitimate cries are ignored or met with indifference, violence, or harshness, rendering him powerless. Children who are denied legitimate power in the first years of life will eventually usurp power to get their needs met and to feel safe. So how do we engage their cooperation and help them learn to follow rules of the classroom?

Strategies for Teaching Behavioral Control

- **Do-overs:** One of the primary goals of a healing environment is to replace children's maladaptive behaviors with appropriate ones. It is not effective to simply tell children to stop doing something. We must always replace the inappropriate behavior with an acceptable one. A powerful tool to accomplish this goal is the do-over, an idea from *The Connected Child* by Purvis and Cross.

  When a child behaves inappropriately, calmly ask him to try it again. Say something like, "It's not okay to grab the markers from your friend. Let's try that again with respect." The child is required to redo the situation and use appropriate words to get his needs met. Before asking for a redo, however, make sure the child actually knows the appropriate way to behave. You might say something like, "It's not okay to grab the crayons from your neighbor. This is how you ask with respect: 'Susie, may I please share the crayons with you?'"

  The rationale for do-overs is based on Hebb's Axiom: Neurons that fire together, wire together. When adults require children to demonstrate and practice appropriate behavior, they strengthen the connections in the brain related to that particular behavior. By using do-overs consistently, the connections in the brain become stronger and faster, making it more likely that the child will be able to access appropriate behaviors. I have had caregivers report dramatic results in their classrooms by using this one simple strategy.

- **Behavioral rehearsal.** Working one-on-one with the child, have him practice the appropriate behavior at a time when he isn't distracted by other children. Before the others arrive in the morning, during outdoor play, or late in the afternoon, have the child practice the behavior you want to instill. Make this interaction playful and encouraging. Most children enjoy this one-on-one attention from adults.

  For example, I had a child who struggled in group time. Not only did he blurt out answers, but he lunged forward and flopped on the floor, which created havoc. I asked Jack's mom to bring him in early for a few weeks so we could do a behavioral rehearsal before the rest of the children arrived. Jack and I pretended to be in group time. I walked him through his visual cues and read a few pages from a book. I asked a few questions about the book and asked, "Jack, what are you going to do? Let's practice raising your hand."

The flopping on the floor stopped, but Jack continued to struggle with raising his hand and blurting all the answers to questions. Finally, I gave him four tickets and explained that in group time he would have four opportunities to answer a question. Each time he answered a question, he would give me a ticket. When he was out of tickets, he needed to let other children answer. This gave him a tangible reminder of the expectations and was, in a sense, providing external regulation. This strategy clicked with Jack, and his behavior in group time began to dramatically improve.

- **Role play.** Talk about situations that children struggle with on a daily basis. For example, if you notice that children fight over easel painting in the art center, bring it to their attention during group time and present it as a problem to solve. Brainstorm solutions and have children act out what they will say and how they will act when they want a turn to paint.

- **Puppets.** Sometimes children feel more comfortable practicing appropriate behaviors with a puppet rather than role playing. Have them practice what to say and do in different scenarios. Ask them to show you what it looks like when someone is disrespectful and what it looks like when someone handles the situation appropriately.

- **Scripted stories.** Write short, simple stories to introduce a problem-solving session with the children. For example, children struggle with taking turns at the water table. A simple story might say something like the following:

The children in Mrs. Brown's room love playing at the water table. They like it so much that sometimes they all want to play at the same time. But when everyone crowds around the table, there is not enough room for everyone to enjoy it. Yesterday, someone stepped on Johnny's toes. It hurt. Johnny cried. Susie grabbed the funnel away from Joey because she said he was taking too long. Joey got mad, yelled, and pushed Susie away. Susie tripped over Cody's foot and fell down. No one had fun at the water table.

Mrs. Brown asked, "What can we do to make playing at the water table more enjoyable?" Susie suggested they make a sign-up sheet. Every morning six people could sign up to play. Johnny suggested they use a timer. Each person could play at the table for fifteen minutes, and then it would be the next person's turn. Emily suggested that they get some dishpans to fill with water. The dishpans could be set on another table for children to enjoy. The water table is not the only place for water.

The children implemented their solutions. On Monday they tried the sign-up sheet. On Tuesday, they tried using the timer. On Wednesday, they tried using the dishpans. The class decided they liked the dishpans the best because more people could play in the water. Now the children in Mrs. Brown's class are happy and there is less fighting at the water table.

When writing scripted stories, use fictional characters and not the children themselves to avoid embarrassing a child. Illustrate the stories with drawings or magazine pictures, or use some of the programs available on the Internet. If you have a child who continues to struggle with the situation, pull him aside each day and review the story and the solutions. Encourage him to ask for help if he gets frustrated.

■ **Visual cues.** The study "Addressing Challenging Behaviors in Head Start: A Closer Look at Program Policies and Procedures," by Amanda Quesenberry, Mary Louise Hemmeter, and Michaelene Ostrosky, found that children with behavioral challenges often need visual cues to help them learn appropriate behaviors. When children become dysregulated, it is very difficult for them to access language and remember the narrative that tells them what to do in a given situation. For example, if Damon struggles with group time, I will create visual cues to remind him of the expectations. I'll give him four pictures on four index cards: eyes, hands, ears, and mouth. For a period of six weeks, whenever Damon comes to group time, I am going to show Damon the cards one by one and verbalize the "script."

TEACHER: Damon, what are your eyes going to do in group time?

DAMON: My eyes are going to look at the book or the person speaking.

TEACHER: Damon, what are your hands going to do?

DAMON: I will keep my hands to myself and not bother people.

TEACHER: Damon, what will your ears do?

DAMON: My ears will be listening to who is talking.

TEACHER: Damon, what is your mouth going to do?

DAMON: My mouth is going to be quiet unless it is my turn to talk.

This ritual is based on Vygotsky's belief that children who demonstrate challenging behavior have not internalized the social script or internal narrative that guides their behavior. Before the script is internalized, it must first be externalized, which is why I ask Damon to speak the expectations out loud every time he comes to group time. After four to six weeks of consistently doing this, I will move to the next level of intervention that provides less scaffolding and hand Damon the four cards when he comes to group time and say, "Damon, take a look at your cards and remind yourself of what you will do in group time." If Damon succeeds, I will celebrate and continue to have him look silently at his cards for four to six weeks. If he does not succeed at sitting in group time, I will have him externalize the script for a few days and try again.

The last step is to just say to Damon as he comes to group time, "Damon, think about the four things you are going to remember in group time." If he succeeds, I will celebrate. If he does not, I will use the cards a few more days and try again. The goal is to reach the point where Damon needs no visual or verbal cues to follow through.

Not all strategies will work with all children. Adults have to think like detectives and carefully observe the child to determine which strategies are likely to work. It's a "guess and go" type of thing—you make your best guess and go with it. If it doesn't work, you try something else.

Handling Noncompliance

So what do you do when children refuse to comply? Remember, your capacity to influence a child's behavior is directly proportional to the strength of the relationship you have with that child. When behavior becomes an issue, the first question is not, "How can I change this behavior?" The first question is, "How can I strengthen my relationship with this child?"

However, the reality of classroom life is that a caregiver has to deal with the behavior at the moment, regardless of the strength of the relationship. When you work with maltreated children, expect noncompliance. You must remember that you are bumping up against the child's history—it isn't about you.

Give Choices

Developmentally appropriate practice advocates empowering children by giving them many choices throughout the day. During interest center time, children are free to choose who and what they will play with. They determine what interest center they will play in and how long they will play. On the playground, they choose how and with whom they will spend their time.

Choices can also be given in those moments when a child struggles to comply with the rules. For example, I was in a classroom when it was time for the children to move to the large-motor room. Aaron was given a warning that a transition was imminent, but when he was told it was time to go he shouted, "No! I'm staying here." I deliberately did not engage his words. I simply responded by asking, "Would you rather hop like a bunny or jump like a frog?" He looked at me quizzically for a moment, then jumped and "ribbeted" like a frog to the play area.

In another situation, the children participated in a water battle on the playground. When it was time to go indoors, the teacher told the children to put their water tubes in the plastic tub. A five-year-old put the water tube behind

When behavior becomes an issue, the first question is not, "How can I change this behavior?" The first question is, "How can I strengthen my relationship with this child?"

her back as if to hide it. The caregiver simply said, "Would you rather put it in my hand or put it in the tub?" The child complied and put it in the tub.

Ask for a Compromise

Helping children to verbalize their needs, preferences, and interests is a goal of any early childhood program. Children who have suffered maltreatment have been given the message that their opinions and needs don't matter. Teaching children to ask for a compromise when their needs and desires are in conflict with the stated expectations is a way of sharing power, engaging cooperation, and helping children recover their voice.

For example, Casey loved to build complex structures in the block area. The rule was to clean up the blocks each day after interest-center time. Casey had a difficult time demolishing his structures, despite the fact that he had the option of taking a photograph of the structure to preserve his work. On occasion, Casey became distraught over having to put away the blocks to the point of throwing a fit. He would cry inconsolably and throw himself on the floor.

Casey's teacher wanted him to learn to use his words rather than behavior to express himself, so she worked with him and taught him how to ask for a compromise. They practiced through role play and with puppets. When he created a structure that he wanted to leave up for some reason, he would say to his teacher, "May I please ask for a compromise?" She would respond with something like, "Sure, what do you have in mind?"

"May I please leave my block structure up until this afternoon so that I can finish working on it?" If at all possible, his teacher would grant his request. Sometimes she had to say no because space was limited and the area was needed for another activity. In the early stages, however, the teacher said yes to Casey at times when it was inconvenient because she wanted him to learn that he would be heard and his thoughts and opinions mattered. As time went on, Casey was able to accept no when the situation warranted it.

Teaching children to ask for a compromise is a powerful strategy in engaging cooperation. Children learn that their words have power and when they use appropriate language, people can understand what they need and help them. In the early stages of learning to ask for a compromise, the adult will say yes to things that, down the road, will be no. As children gradually come to the understanding that words are powerful, their capacity to accept no will begin to increase. The basic principle is that when a child has a bucket of yeses, he will gradually be able to accept legitimate nos.

Learning how to say no to a child takes some thought. When a situation arises where you have to say no, first acknowledge the legitimacy of the child's desire. For example, it is time to go in from the playground. You get within 36 inches of David and give him a warning. Ask him look at his visual schedule and tell you what is going to happen next. You come back to David, look him in the eye while holding his hands, and tell him it is time to go inside. He looks at you and says, "No. I want to stay out and play." Acknowledge his desire by saying something like, "I know you really love to play outside. You had fun today going down the slide, and it is hard to stop doing something that is so fun. But it is time to go inside. Would you rather hold my hand and walk in with me, or would you like to pull the library wagon inside? Which do you choose?"

In this scenario, the teacher acknowledged David's love of the outdoors and the fun that he had on the slide. She validated the fact that it is hard to stop doing something that is so fun. She denied his request to remain outside, but she gave him two yeses when she offered two options: hold her hand or pull the book wagon. Whenever possible, give two yeses whenever you have to say no.

The reality of life, however, is there will be times when it isn't possible or even desirable to offer choices, give a compromise, or give two yeses. The answer must be no. In this instance, Purvis and Cross suggest to quickly follow up your no with the comment, "Thanks for accepting no," before the child has the chance of protesting.

What about Time Out?

Time out is one of the most widely used forms of discipline and punishment in child care centers and schools today. Children are sent to a designated spot in the room to supposedly think about their behavior and how they can do better next time. But have you noticed that once they are out of time out, they generally turn around and do the same thing next time? Have you also noticed that the same children who were sitting in time out in kindergarten are still sitting in time out in fifth grade? Little has changed in the intervening years.

Time out stops inappropriate behavior for the moment and may give the adult a brief break from the child, but it does nothing to change the child from the inside out over the long term. Purvis and Cross assert that time out is particularly ineffective with children with attachment issues, as it further disconnects and psychologically isolates a child who is already emotionally disconnected and isolated. These children have experienced very little emotional attunement and genuine warmth with any kind of attachment figure. Their out-of-control and confusing behaviors result from a lack of emotional connection to a more organized and stable adult who can provide appropriate levels of support and guidance in learning how to manage their emotions and behavior. Sending them to time out will not provide the support and emotional connection they need to learn new ways of behavior and functioning in the world.

Time out also sends the unspoken message of conditional love and acceptance. It communicates to children, "You can only be in my presence and enjoy my love and acceptance if you can get your act together and behave in appropriate ways." Children who have experienced abuse and neglect already have a deep core of shame and rejection. Time out only confirms their sense of being somehow flawed and expects an already dysregulated child to self-regulate. Inappropriate behavior arises from an inability to self-regulate. Aggressive behavior is an inability to control strong emotions in a socially acceptable way. Back talk or "sass" is an inability to express anger and frustration in an appropriate manner. An aggressive or angry child who acts out needs help from a more organized and self-regulated adult to help her calm down and learn new ways of expressing herself. Sending a child to time out essentially relegates her to remain in a dysregulated state.

> The underlying message we want them to hear is that we will love them through their unlovely behavior. Rather than abandon them, we will hang in there with them and help them find new ways of behaving.

A fundamental principle to remember in dealing with children from hard places is that we need to bring them close rather than push them away when they display inappropriate behavior. The underlying message we want them to hear is that we will love them through their unlovely behavior. Rather than abandon them, we will hang in there with them and help them find new ways of behaving. We bring them close physically and psychologically to teach them rather than punish them.

Strategies for Teaching Impulse Control

Learning to control one's impulses is a life skill that all children need, but it is particularly challenging for children from hard places. A child who is not able to control his impulses reacts to every thought or emotion that pops into his head. He sees a toy he wants and, without considering the wants and wishes of the child playing with it, rips it out of the child's hands. Another child touches "his" tricycle, and he immediately punches that child without really understanding her intentions. Remember, hypervigilant children *react* to their environment rather than *respond*. Impulse control can be developed through games and activities that require children to resist their natural inclinations. Here are some games and activities that children enjoy playing:

- Red Rover, London Bridge Is Falling Down, Duck Duck Goose, Go In and Out the Windows: These games require children to wait their turn, walk or sit in a circle, and use gentle touch.

- Do This, Do That: This game is similar to Simon Says. When the adult says, "Do this," the children follow the direction. When the adult says, "Do that," the children do not follow the direction.

- Red Light, Green Light and Mother May I? These games also require children to wait their turn and to listen carefully to instructions.

- Water fights: Playing with water is very enticing for most young children. You can use commercially purchased water guns or squeeze bottles. However, modify the rules of the game slightly to require children to inhibit their excitement and behavior. Before they squirt someone, they must first ask permission. If the person says no, then they cannot squirt the person. If they squirt without permission, they are "frozen" until someone unfreezes them with a hug, high five, or a handshake.

- Snowball fights: "Snowball" fights can be played with soft bath balls, Nerf balls, wads of newspaper, or rolled-up socks. Use rules similar to the water fight: children must ask permission before throwing a "snowball" at another child.

- Singing: Singing songs that require children to clap at certain times develops behavioral control. An example would be the song "Bingo."

- Hand-clapping games: Play hand-clapping games such as Miss Mary Mack. Simplify the hand motions for young children.

- Feel the beat: Have children play rhythm-band instruments to the beat of music. They can also clap, march, or jump to the beat. Play a rhythm on a gathering drum, and ask children to jump on the drum to the beat of the music.

- Call and response: Sing call-and-response songs such as, "Did You Feed My Cow?" Ella Jenkins is a well-known and beloved musician who has recorded many call-and-response songs for young children.

- Listen for the word: Write simple stories that require children to listen for certain words that require them to do a certain movement. For example, I like to use this following story of Mrs. Down. As you read this story aloud, have the children stand up every time they hear the word *up* and sit down every time they hear the word *down*.

    One summer morning, Mrs. Down woke up. The shades were pulled down, so she jumped out of bed and raised up the shade. It was a bright sunny day. "I think I will go downtown to do a little shopping," she said. She got all dressed up and went downstairs to eat a little breakfast. She made some eggs sunny-side up and ate a piece of toast. When Mrs. Down was finished, she went upstairs to get her purse. She hurried out the door to her car. She opened the door and sat down in the seat. She looked up and down the street. There were no cars, so she backed out of her driveway and drove up the street. When she arrived downtown, she parked her car and walked up the street to the store. Mrs. Down walked up and down the aisles looking for things she needed. When her cart was filled up, she decided it was time to go home, so she paid for her things. When she stepped outside, rain was falling down from the sky. She was always prepared for such things, so she reached into her purse and pulled out her umbrella and raised it up. She walked down the street to her car. She opened the trunk, picked up her bags, and set them down in her car.

She drove up the street back to her house. When Mrs. Down got home, the rain had let up, so she got her bags and hurried inside. She decided she was tired, so she sat down in her favorite chair and went to sleep.

- One, Two, Three, Pop: Children sit in a circle. Point to a child who then says, "One." The next child in the circle says, "Two." The third child says, "Three." The fourth child says, "Pop!" and stands up. Continue counting around until everyone is standing. This is also a good activity to transition children to another part of the room or the next experience.
- Freeze dance: Have children move to music with scarves or streamers. When the music stops, they "freeze."
- Talking stick: When children have difficulty blurting out answers in group time, use a talking stick to indicate who should be talking. The stick or object is passed from child to child, and only the child with the stick has permission to talk.

Strategies for Teaching Behavioral Modulation

Behavioral modulation means that a child can control the volume, the intensity, and the speed of her behavior.

- **Voice modulation:** Children from hard places who live in a state of hypervigilance sometimes have their volume control set at one level—loud. If you stand outside the door of their classroom, their voices can often be heard above the rest of the children, even though they are usually unaware of the loudness of their voices. Sometimes, adults try to out-shout them. Generally, when we are trying to get children's attention in a nonemergency situation, a soft voice works more effectively than a louder voice. Get within arm's length of the child, make eye contact, and softly say, "Jennifer, let's use our inside voice." However, we must first make sure that Jennifer knows what an inside voice sounds like. There are playful ways that we can do this.
  - Sing favorite songs in a variety of voices—great big "dinosaur" voices, tiny little "mouse" voices, or medium-sized voices.

- Read stories that lend themselves to speaking with different volumes. For example, *Goldilocks and The Three Bears* or *Three Billy Goats Gruff* have small, medium, and large characters that can speak in soft, medium, and loud voices.
- Sing songs and perform fingerplays that employ different levels of volume. For example, songs such as "John Jacob Jingleheimer Schmidt" and the familiar chant "Peanut Butter and Jelly" use fluctuating volumes.

Remember, too, that some children from hard places are very withdrawn and seem to try to make themselves invisible. They speak only when spoken to, and when they do it is almost a whisper. It is critical for these children to feel safe in the presence of adults. Chastising a child for barely speaking above a whisper or saying something like, "The cat got your tongue?" shames children and only sends them deeper inside themselves. Spend one-on-one time with the withdrawn child and talk about things that are important to her. The safer she feels in your presence, the more likely she will be to raise the volume of her voice. Sometimes, when children do not feel safe, they resort to baby-like voices that are high pitched and squeaky. Very gently point it out to them by saying something like, "Your voice tells me that you feel anxious. Let's take a deep breath (breathe with the child) and try that again." Some other strategies to try:

- Give the child a puppet. Sometimes speaking through a puppet will help the child feel safe enough to speak at a normal volume.
- Give the child a pretend microphone.
- Sing songs and fingerplays that involve variable levels of volume.
- Invite the child to tell a story and record it. Let her listen to herself and challenge her tell the story again until she can clearly hear all of the words. This needs to be playfully done and not forced. If the child resists, then honor the child's no.

- **Modulating intensity of behavior:** Hypervigilant children often approach everything they do at ninety miles an hour. They walk at a trot or run every place they go. They have a tendency to be rough, knock things over, and bump into things and people. When you ask for a high five, they slap your hand so hard it hurts. When they give you a hug, they nearly knock you over.

In these moments it is important to ask for a "do-over" and to walk them through the appropriate behavior. But there are also activities that can help build awareness of the intensity of behavior.

- High fives: Practice giving soft, medium, and hard high fives.
- Parachute storm: Gather children around a parachute. Pretend that a storm is coming and the wind is beginning to gently blow across the sea. Have the children gently shake the parachute. The rain begins to fall and the wind gets a little stronger. Have the children shake the

parachute harder. Thunder and lightning begin, and waves begin to crash on the shore. Have them shake the parachute very intensely.

- Hear the music: Give children rhythm sticks, drums, or a variety of rhythm instruments. Have the children play music that demonstrates different volumes of sound—soft, medium, and loud.

- Move to the music: Play music and have the children walk in circle using movements of different intensities: tiptoe, stomp, march, walk, and so on.

- Bounce the ball: Pair the children, and give each pair a bath towel and a bath ball, fidget, or small rubber ball. Have the partners work together to gently bounce the ball up and down on the towel. Try a big bounce.

- Obstacle course: Create an obstacle course that alternates gross and fine motor activities. For example, children can crawl through a tunnel and then put cotton balls in a jar using tweezers. They can bounce on a crib mattress, then string beads on yarn.

- **Changing the speed of behavior**: Hypervigilant children also tend to move quickly. There are activities that can help them build awareness of the speed of their behavior.

  - Play games such as Motor Boat, Motor Boat. Children join hands in a circle and chant together:

    Motor boat, motor boat, go so slow. (Walk slowly around the circle with an exaggerated motion.)

    Motor boat, motor boat, go so fast. (Go a little faster.)

    Motor boat, motor boat, step on the gas. (Go as fast as is reasonable for the age of the group.)

Usually what happens at this point is the children start laughing and fall in a heap together. Other songs can be adapted in this way.

- Play Hot Potato. Pass an object around a circle. When the adult says, "Cold potato," the children pass the object slowly. When the adult says, "Hot potato," the children pass the object quickly.

- Slow and fast: Call out different actions or movements and have the children do them in slow and fast motion.

Chapter 6

The Effect of Trauma on Social Skills

Roger was one of the most challenging children I have ever encountered. He had little capacity for self-regulation, and biting other people was pretty much the only strategy he had for solving conflict. Needless to say, he had no friends—the children were terrified of him. When he entered the block center, everyone left. If he approached a particular area of the playground, the other children cleared out. Roger's home life was chaotic. We never knew from day to day who was going to pick him up from childcare. When someone came to take him home, he would frantically run around the classroom hide under tables and jump over chairs. It was a daily game of chase to get him out the door. Roger was the only child of a very young single mom who reportedly lived with a revolving door of men in an environment of domestic violence. I unsuccessfully tried every strategy I could think of to stop Roger's biting, but as a rookie teacher, my tools were minimal. Finally, much to my surprise, another child bit him back. In shock, Roger ran to me exclaiming, "It hurts, it hurts! Teacher, put your hand right there and feel the hurt." It was a light-bulb moment for Roger. I responded, "Yes, Roger, I know it hurts. Biting hurts people. That's what it feels like when you bite other people."

The next day, Roger came in with two big apples. He slowly walked toward me, staring down at the floor, and offered me the apples. He said, "I promise never to bite again." And he didn't. It did not take long for the other children to realize that Roger had finally surrendered his weapon. Instead of biting, he would just sit and cry when he was upset. Other children slowly started interacting with him. They no longer left the block center when he came to play. They allowed him to play chase with them on the playground. Obviously, Roger's issues were not over—we had to help him learn to deal with conflict—but he was making small steps toward understanding how to be and make a friend.

When children live in relational chaos where relationships with caregivers are characterized by mistrust, unresponsiveness, and violence, the resulting internal working model is one that tells them relationships are not safe and satisfying. This same belief system is applied to peer relationships. Basic relational skills are not modeled in the home, so the children have no idea how to develop friendships.

Research indicates that peer relationships are important to healthy growth and development across the life span. Researchers William Bukowski and Lorrie Sippola have found that the ability to have and enjoy peer relationships in the early years of life predicts later success in intellectual growth, self-esteem, mental health, and school performance. Research also indicates that the ability to make friends in the preschool years carries over into adolescence and enables teens to enjoy peer relationships. Researchers Alan Sroufe, Byron Egeland, and Elizabeth Carlson observe that children who struggle with social skills in the preschool years continue to struggle in adolescence. Other studies, such as that done by Jeffrey Parker and Steven Asher, have shown that children who are not well liked in school do not do as well academically and are more likely to drop out of school in adolescence. The evidence is convincing that social skills are critical to all children but are even more important for children with a trauma history.

Children are born innately social. According to Dave Riley, Robert San Juan, Joan Klinkner, and Ann Ramminger in *Social and Emotional Development*, babies prefer the human voice to all other sounds in the environment and, by six weeks of age, show a preference for human interaction over other nonhuman forms of engagement. However, for the neglected or harmed baby, this natural inclination is derailed by the toxic effects of trauma. The child quickly learns that relationships are not satisfying, and the baby resorts to different forms of avoidance and shutdown.

Social Regulation

The first forms of human communication are nonverbal. There is a dance of communication that takes place between caregivers and children. Babies communicate through crying, vocalizing, facial expressions, and movements. Unfortunately the messages communicated by babies living in neglectful and traumatic conditions are ignored, misinterpreted, or in the worst-case scenario, met with violence. It is not uncommon for the incessant cries of a baby to lead to abuse.

When caregivers are addicted to substances or living in the depths of depression, the vocalizations and initiations of the baby are often met with little eye contact or animated body language. The child has limited opportunity to "read" and respond to nonverbal forms of communication. Therefore, children from hard places often struggle with knowing how to read nonverbal cues. They commonly misinterpret the body language, facial expressions, and behaviors of other children and adults. An accidental bump from another child is misconstrued as an intentional push and a shoving match begins. A child scrunches up his face when he eats a sour grape at snack time, and the child sitting across from him shouts, "He's lookin' at me!" To an adult who is not trauma informed, this statement sounds ridiculous, and she may dismiss the child's complaints or even punish him for tattling. But when the interbrain connection is malfunctioning, children struggle to accurately interpret the intentions and nonverbal cues of others. Sending children to time out for tattling, or telling the child it doesn't matter are not going to bring this essential capacity online.

When a child misreads another child's body language or facial expression, adults need to take the time to help the child adjust his perception. Help the child recognize that sometimes people do things on purpose, and sometimes children do things by accident. Talk about circumstances that may cause children to bump into one another: too many people at the cubbies at the same time; people pushing and shoving trying to be first; children slinging their coats over their head to put them on. Brainstorm solutions to the problem.

When children misread the nonverbal cues of another, ask them to look at the other person and describe what makes them think the other person is angry. Help the child identify the many reasons why someone might frown, scowl, or look upset. Maybe someone else stepped on her toe. Maybe she is hungry or tired. Maybe she has a headache. If possible, ask the other child what she is feeling. Learning to read social cues will not be a quick process, but with intention and consistency children can make great progress.

It is important to note that before a child can successfully read the social cues of another child and identify the expressed emotion, he must first be able to identify his own emotions. A child who is not able to identify his own emotions will most certainly not be able to identify the emotions of another. The strategies discussed in the previous chapter will help with this.

Concrete Strategies for Developing Social-Regulation Skills

- Talk to children about where they feel different emotions in their body. For example, in group time, talk about what people look like when they are happy, sad, mad, or scared. Make a chart of the different characteristics

- Have children paint or draw feelings faces that portray different emotions.

- Give children paper dolls and have them identify parts of their body where they feel various emotions. For example, a child may say he feels butterflies in his tummy when he is scared. Another child may say he feels the "mad" in his hands and wants to hurt people.

- Play charades. Whisper an emotion in a child's ear and have him act it out. The other children guess what he is feeling.

- When children get into conflicts, direct their attention to the face of the other child. For example, when Joey and Cody start arguing in the block center because Joey pulled some blocks that he wanted out of the foundation of Cody's building, direct Joey to look at Cody's face and say something like, "Joey, look at Cody's face. What is his face telling you? Does he like it when you take his blocks?"

- Have children solve conflicts in front of a mirror, which draws their attention to faces.

- Allow children to engage in rough-and-tumble play. Researchers including Anthony Pellegrini and Sergio Pellis and Vivian Pellis have found that it is a primary way that children, especially boys, learn to read social cues. With this form of play, children constantly have to monitor when their play partners enjoy the play and when they do not; when they have pushed a little too hard or when it is okay; when the other person has had enough and when they are coming back for more. Rough-and-tumble play is often frowned upon in early childhood settings but is very valuable with regard to self-regulation.

- While reading stories, pause to ask the children what they think the characters in the story are feeling. Give them pictures of feeling faces to show.

Empathy

Developmental psychologists have long debated the age at which children can understand and experience what another person is feeling. Until the 1970s, it was generally accepted that children are developmentally incapable of taking the perspective of another until they are seven years old. More recent research, according to Ann Epstein, author of *Me, You, Us: Social-Emotional Learning in Preschool*, indicates otherwise. The consensus is that there are different kinds of perspective taking, but experts disagree about what to call and how to describe the different components. It is my opinion based on reading and my own personal experience that there are at least three different kinds of perspective taking.

- *Perceptual perspective taking* is the ability of the child to imagine and comprehend what another person is seeing or hearing.
- *Conceptual or cognitive perspective taking* is the ability to imagine and understand what someone is thinking and wanting.
- *Emotional perspective taking* is the ability to imagine and comprehend what another is feeling.

Research and anecdotal experience indicates that babies and toddlers can demonstrate empathetic behaviors. It is not uncommon in group settings for babies to begin crying in unison when they hear the cry of another. A mobile infant might stand close to a crying baby and anxiously look at the caregiver. Toddlers have been observed to pat, share a blanket or other transitional object, or even hug a crying child. Researcher Carolyn Zahn-Waxler and colleagues have found that the roots of empathy begin in the dance of attunement that takes place between a caregiver and a baby. When an infant cries and a caregiver reflects the baby's sadness in her own face and tone of voice, the baby feels understood. Knowing what empathetic care looks like and feels like lays the foundation for the growing baby to eventually be able to express empathetic care to another. A child cannot feel and express empathy to another unless he has first felt and had empathetic care administered to him. Sometimes children from hard places are viewed as being calloused and uncaring toward other children. They may grab a toy or hit someone and then walk away as if nothing happened. They may even laugh when another gets hurt. Their behavior can seem off-putting to adults, and sometimes they are even punished for this behavior. Rejection and punishment only serves to deepen the child's sense of disconnection and alienation. Helping the child who has had little opportunity to experience empathetic care is no easy task. Some children have become so emotionally shut down that receiving empathy from others heightens their sense of vulnerability and fear. They may resist your overtures or even become aggressive. This is particularly true for the avoidant child. Many will overtly retreat from receiving help or refuse your offer to comfort.

In my early days of teaching, I discovered the power of an adhesive bandage, such as a Band-Aid. A Band-Aid could fix everything from a scrape to a headache to a tummy ache. I passed them out prolifically. I believe the "magic" was because a Band-Aid is a tangible symbol of empathy and communicates "I acknowledge the reality of your pain."

A way to integrate nurturing touch and empathetic interactions into everyday classroom life, the *check in* is a simple ritual that can become part of the daily routine. Although used by a number of programs, this activity is taken from the Alert Program as described in *How Does Your Engine Run?* by Mary Sue Williams and Sherry Shellenberger. Mornings are sometimes difficult for families, and getting everyone out of the house can be an ordeal. This is especially true for children in foster care. Transitions are rarely easy for them. Mornings can also be hard for children living in neglectful conditions or domestic violence. It is not uncommon for them to be expected to get themselves up and ready for the day. Therefore, children might be in a highly aroused emotional state when they arrive.

The check in acknowledges strong feelings and helps children self-regulate before they begin their day. As children arrive, ask them if they have any inside or outside hurts today. An outside hurt is a physical wound such as a bruise, scratch, or cut. An inside hurt can be a hurtful word, an unkind action, a hateful tone of voice, or a disrespectful facial expression—things that children often describe as hurting their hearts.

If a child identifies an inside or outside hurt, ask the child if she would like a Band-Aid. This communicates to the child, "I get you." Place the bandage over the child's physical or invisible hurt. If she tells you about multiple hurts, give her multiple bandages. You also could use baby lotion or cotton balls to acknowledge the hurt.

Be sensitive to opportunities to dig deeper with the child. In their article "Restoring Safety and Hope: From Victim to Survivor," Caelan Kuban and William Steele identify some questions to ask when children indicate hurt.

- Is the hurt still here?
- When it happened, where did you feel the hurt the most in your body?
- How small or big is your hurt?
- Does the hurt ever go away?
- Is there something you do to make the hurt go away?
- Is there something or someone who makes it come back?
- How long has the hurt been there?
- What happened that caused the hurt?
- Have you ever told anyone about your hurt? What did that person say?

This simple ritual helps children develop awareness of their own internal state and learn to accept comfort from another.

Once the children are familiar with the check-in routine, you might try it in a group setting. Children can ask each other about their inside and outside hurts and can put Band-Aids on each other. Note: Teach children to seek adult help if there really is blood.

When you observe a child responding in a calloused or inappropriate way to another child's pain or distress, gently pull the child aside and explain why the other child is upset, and help him think of one thing he can do to comfort the other child. It might be getting him a drink of water or a tissue or retrieving the child's blanket or transitional object.

Turn Taking

The roots of taking turns start in the first year of life in common reciprocal interactions between a caregiver and a child. Mom and baby roll a beach ball back and forth and play peekaboo or patty-cake. In these simple games, children experience the pleasure of social interactions and the basic process of taking turns—I roll the ball, then you roll it back; I hide my face with a blanket and you look for me. However, when infants experience abuse and neglect, these simple interactions are few and far between. For these children, social-skill development is often significantly younger than their chronological age. It is common to see, for example, a five-year-old with the social skills of a two-year-old. It can be confusing to the adults who work with these children to see a child in a five-year-old body acting much younger.

Keeping in mind the basic principle that healing is about recovering what was lost, caregivers need to become a child's play partner and engage in these basic forms of play, regardless of the child's age. Whether the child is eighteen months or five years old, recovering social skills begins with play that supports taking turns.

Engage the child in simple activities that involve a volley—throwing or kicking a ball back and forth, tossing a bean bag, or filling up a pail with sand as a turn-taking activity. Play games that involve mimicking or looking for each other. Simple board games such as Candy Land or Hi Ho! Cherry-O also help teach how to take turns. Once the child becomes proficient at these simple forms of play with the adult caregiver or teacher, add another child to the activity, and let them play with your supervision.

Healing is about recovering what was lost. Caregivers need to become a child's play partner and engage in these basic forms of play, regardless of the child's age.

It is important to recognize the difference between taking turns and sharing. Sometimes adults use these two terms interchangeably, which can confuse children who are just learning these skills. For example, I don't take turns with a cookie; I share a cookie. *Sharing* means that I can give a portion to you and a portion to me simultaneously. I can share playdough, but I can't share a bike. I can share the scraps of fabric we are using to make a collage, but I take turns with the paintbrush.

Although basic experiences with turn taking begin in the first year of life, we don't expect children to be able to take turns with any consistency until age three, and even then, the skill is only beginning to emerge. Obviously, children who have had plenty of experiences with turn-taking play will have a better understanding of this skill than those who have had little opportunity for reciprocal interactions. When I see a child who consistently grabs things from other people and insists on everything being "mine," I realize the child needs to have more experiences with turn-taking play with an adult play partner.

Once another child is introduced into the play, it is important to think about and integrate strategies typically used for younger children to deal with turn-taking dilemmas. For example, we deal with conflict between toddlers primarily with distraction. Timmy grabs the toy phone away from Sam. The adult sees a set of toy keys lying nearby and says, "Timmy, give Sam back his phone, then get the keys and go start the car." Distraction also may work with older children who are very young developmentally.

When children have lots of experiences with turn-taking play and begin to increasingly engage with other children, distraction will not always work. The caregiver or teacher will need to introduce new strategies for taking turns and to help children solve social problems. Remember that conflicts among children are opportunities to teach, not punish.

One day, I watched a three-year-old take a phone away from another child. (Both of these children had a significant trauma history.) He grabbed the phone and said, "Gimme that." A scuffle ensued. I was sitting on the floor nearby, so I reached out and put one child on each knee. I said, "Don, we don't grab toys from other people. This is what you say, 'Khalil, may I please have a turn with the phone?'" I instructed Don to repeat what I just said. When he asked Khalil for a turn, Khalil said exactly what most children are going to say: "No!"

I told Don what to say next. "Don, this is what you say when someone says no. You say, 'When you are finished with the phone, will you let me know so that I can have a turn?'" I instructed Don to look at Khalil and repeat what I just said. I lucked out on this one, as Khalil handed the phone to Don and they both went off to play. This isn't always going to be the case. If Khalil protests and announces that he is going to keep the phone all day, then a problem-solving conversation will need to take place: "We have one phone and two children who want to play. We need to figure out a solution to our problem."

In the earliest stages, the adult will have to guide the children through some solutions. For example:

- The teacher can help Don find a way to make a pretend phone. It could be a block or his hands.
- Set a timer to determine when Khalil's turn is over.
- Don can think of another way to communicate. He could use a walkie-talkie, a megaphone, or a special telephone built into a watch, or he could "write" a letter.

The goal is to help children see conflict as a problem to solve and not as an opportunity to fight. Creating visual cues for common sharing scenarios can help children who struggle. Children from hard places have a quick trigger and can go into a meltdown in a matter of seconds. It is difficult for children to process language when they are distressed. A picture cue can trigger a thought that would never be heard through language.

When in conflict mode, children's emotions can run very high. Before problem solving can begin, allow children to calm down first. We bring children back into regulation by bringing them close, not by pushing them away. Once again, through the interbrain and full presence of a more organized brain, we help children regroup. Had Don gone into meltdown mode when I told him he had to ask for the phone politely, I would have said something like, "I know you really like playing with the phone, and it's really hard when someone else is playing with it." By calmly making this statement, I acknowledge his desire to play with the phone and his frustration at not being able to. I am activating the connection between my brain and his. Hopefully, my more organized brain will at least slightly calm his dysregulated state. Then I could hug him, rock him, offer him a drink of water, or suggest some other way to help him calm down. Once he returned to a frame of mind where he could think and talk, we would problem solve and find a solution to our dilemma.

Children from hard places struggle with ownership. When children have lost so much, they often have strong attachments to things, which makes it difficult for them to take turns and share. They are not selfish; they are children who have been robbed of life's most basic experiences. Social skills will not appear overnight and will require a great deal of patience and support from adults.

Sharing

The process of learning to share has some similarities with taking turns and will need a great deal of coaching by adults. Children from hard places often hoard things or take more than their fair share, leading some adults to label them self-centered and greedy. When children live with a scarcity mentality, it leads to behavior that looks like greed but is really motivated by a fear of not having enough. Many hoard things because they have no concept of a future. Their thinking is, "I get what I can get when I can get it."

Like taking turns, the conversation about sharing and some beginning expectations about the ability to share should take place around three years of age. It is appropriate to set children up for both sharing and turn-taking experiences. Plan activities where children have to share materials or take turns using equipment. Brainstorm strategies that children can use while waiting for their turn. We can't simply tell children, "Wait your turn." We have to give them strategies to successfully accomplish this. Point out when you notice children successfully sharing and taking turns throughout the day: "I saw you were patiently waiting for your turn on the swing. That was some good waiting! You did it!"

Joining in Play

One of the primary reasons that children are excluded from play and struggle to participate in activities with others is that they do not know how to join an existing theme of play. They hijack the theme and attempt to redirect it to suit their own agenda. For example, Casey and Jasmine are in the block center creating a train station. They have spent most of the morning building a town and carefully encircling it with a train track. Amy, dressed like a princess, suddenly runs through the middle of the train station, scattering the blocks everywhere, and announces, "I'm the princess, and I'm going to build a fairy princess castle!"

Casey yells, "Stop!" and starts to cry. Jasmine screams, "Get out of here! You can't play!" This is a daily event with Amy. She has no idea how to join an existing theme of play. Sending Amy to time out or having her sit on the bench during outdoor play will not change her behavior or teach her new skills. For that to happen, the adult must become her play partner and coach her in an actual play scenario. For example, the children have created a pizza parlor in the dramatic play center. Amy stands on the sidelines, watching. She has a clown wig on and has been trying to get children to play "parade" with her all morning, but no one has joined her. Her teacher knows that she is about to crash the scene and disrupt the pizza parlor. She might engage Amy like this:

TEACHER: Hey, Amy, I'm hungry. Would you like to join me for a pizza? What kind of pizza do you like? Pepperoni? cheese? sausage?

AMY: Sausage.

TEACHER: Great. Me, too. What kind of crust do you like? Thin or thick?

AMY: I like thick crust.

TEACHER: Are you really, really hungry, or are you just a little bit hungry?

AMY: I'm really hungry.

TEACHER: Okay, let's sit down at the table and order a pizza. Tell the waitress that we want a large, thick-crust sausage pizza. By the way, what do you want to drink? Sprite or water?

In this scenario, the teacher coaches the child as to what to say and do in the context of the theme. Day after day, she will be the child's play partner until she sees an indication that the child is beginning to internalize the process. This may take four to six weeks or even longer, depending upon the social-emotional maturity of the child.

Once the child has gained some skills and requires only a minimal amount of prompting from the adult, the teacher can step back and coach the child from the sidelines. This means that she is no longer the child's play partner but carefully monitors what the child does and offers suggestions when the child gets stuck. For example, the teacher hears a commotion in the dramatic play center and hears someone shriek, "No! You can't do that." She sees Amy crawling around on the floor among the patients in the "doctor's office." After briefly listening to the conversation, she determines that Amy has abandoned her role as the doctor and is acting like a dog.

The teacher might say something like, "Amy, I hear a sick baby crying. He needs you to check his temperature and give him a shot to help him feel better." With external coaching, the adult offers suggestions to help get the child integrated back into the theme of play. If the child refuses and continues to attempt to hijack the play toward another theme, the play will either come to a standstill or the arguing and protesting will escalate. The adult should then intervene and give Amy two choices. "Amy, would you like to continue being the doctor and help the sick babies, or would you like to do something different, such as being the receptionist or a mommy with a sick child? Give me some words."

If Amy continues to ignore the teacher, then she would give Amy two legitimate choices. "Amy, you can choose to be a doctor or a mommy, or we can help you find something else to do in another center that you would enjoy. Which do you choose?" If Amy refuses to answer, the teacher would take her by the hand and lead her to a quiet place to talk, read, or engage in some other quiet activity to give her time to regain some internal regulation. The important thing is for the teacher to remain connected to Amy until she has transitioned successfully into another role or activity and not just send her away to do something else.

Conflict Resolution

Imagine a world where everyone was skilled at conflict resolution! An inability to solve conflict factors into most of the world's pain—war, divorce, prejudice, race relations, work conflicts, and family feuds. Children who experience domestic violence particularly struggle with conflict resolution because the only examples they have seen are aggression and violence. Perry commented in a 2014 webinar titled *Neurosequential Model of Therapeutics* that children are not always good listeners, but they are always good imitators. The only solution many children have to settle conflict is violence because it is all they know.

Teaching conflict-resolution skills is a key component of a trauma-informed environment. At the heart of conflict resolution is the capacity for cognitive or conceptual perspective taking, meaning that the child is able to imagine and understand the wants and thoughts of another. Once again, if the child has never been in a relationship where his wants and thoughts were validated and accepted, it will be very hard for him to imagine and accept the thoughts wishes of another. Adults can begin to intentionally teach cognitive perspective-taking strategies to children at around three years of age.

For example, a pair of "wings" was donated to the classroom. Emily put them on and began "flying" around the room saying she was Tinker Bell. Tanya grabbed the wings and started yanking on them, trying to pull the elastic off of Emily's arms. A squabble erupted, with both girls yelling, "It's not fair!" The natural inclination for some adults is to take the wings away and say something like, "If you two can't play together and get along, then we will put the wings up until you can learn how to play nice." This strategy teaches the girls nothing about solving conflict.

Instead, the caregiver or teacher could sit down with the children and walk them through the conflict-resolution process. It would go something like this:

TEACHER: We have a problem! There is one set of wings and two girls who want to play with them. Emily, tell Tonya what you are feeling right now.

EMILY: I'm mad because you pulled on my wings and you can't play.

TEACHER: Tonya, tell Emily what you are feeling right now.

TONYA: It's not fair. I want to play.

TEACHER: Both of you are unhappy with each other because you both want to play with the wings. What do you think we need to do?

EMILY: I think she should go away because I had them first.

TEACHER: Tonya, what do you think about that?

Conflict in the classroom can be overwhelming for children who grow up in the context of domestic violence and may initiate a freeze response for some. They may cower in the corner of the classroom or go hide under a table. Empowering children by giving them tools to deal with conflict can help them learn to not be overwhelmed by fear.

The Center on the Social and Emotional Foundations for Early Learning (CSEFEL) has a wonderful website with lots of free resources. On that website you will find a scripted story called, "Tucker the Turtle Takes Time to Tuck and Think" and a pattern for a paper-plate turtle puppet. Read the story during group time, and children can role play the steps for conflict resolution described in the story. Children can use the puppet as a visual reminder of what to do.

I have also used conflict bracelets as a visual reminder of what to do. String six beads on a chenille wire in the following order, and explain to the children what each bead means.

- First, string one red bead. Red means, "Stop."
- Next, thread one blue bead. Blue means, "Take a deep breath."
- String three green beads. Touch each green bead—one-two-three—and take a breath for each bead.
- Add a purple bead. The purple bead signifies, "Make a good choice." Brainstorm with children about good choices for different scenarios.

Saying Sorry

In my first year of teaching, I required children to say they were sorry after a conflict. I quickly realized the flaw of my thinking when a little boy hit another child and shrugged it off by saying, "Sorry." When I approached him to talk about the incident, he quickly shouted, "But I said, 'I'm sorry!'" The truth is that most of the time an adult tells a child to do this, the child really isn't sorry. He is just sorry he got caught! But it is important to teach children to make amends when they hurt someone physically or emotionally. During group time conversations and in moments of calm and quiet, talk to children about the importance of "making it better." Brainstorm strategies for repairing ruptures in relationships. Make picture cues to put on the wall or on a ring for easy access. Here are some common strategies typically mentioned by children:

- Give a hug.
- Draw a picture.
- Make a card.
- Share a snack.
- Push the other child on the swing.
- Play a game with the other child.
- Share a favorite toy.
- Invite the other child to play.

Chapter 7

The Effect of Trauma on Developmental Processes and Learning

Abuse and neglect disrupt normal developmental processes and compromise a child's capacity to learn and function in a caregiving or school setting. Understanding the implications for development and learning is critical to a therapeutic environment. Trauma-informed teachers must identify the developmental milestones that were only partially met or completely missed altogether and work with the child to achieve these milestones. This is why an understanding of child development is critical.

Curiosity

In his article "Curiosity: The Fuel of Development" Perry describes curiosity as the fuel for learning; however, he observes that curiosity is often stifled in a child with a history of maltreatment. Children who have the benefit of a secure attachment relationship with a warm and responsive caregiver have the internal security from which to launch out and explore their world. A child with secure-base behavior knows that if she gets into a situation where she doesn't know what to do, she can call on her caregivers for help, and the caregivers will respond.

Secure-base behavior can be observed between young parents and their children in parks and on playgrounds. The parents may sit on a bench talking among themselves as they keep an eye on the children. Periodically, a young child will stop and look back at his parent on the bench and seek to make eye contact, or he may even run back and touch the parent on the leg only to run off again and play. The child balances the competing needs for closeness and exploration.

It functions much the same way in a child care environment. When children have loving relationships with caregivers and teachers, they can invest their emotional energies into learning and play rather than merely coping. They do not fear trying new things or asking for help. They approach life with gusto, and the drive to master their world is apparent. A child approaches the new slide on the playground and his apprehension is visible. He glances over at his teacher or caregiver, who smiles and gives a nod. He pauses a moment and then robustly climbs up the slide. His security tank has been filled, and he has the courage to explore because of the trusting relationship he has with his caregiver.

Maltreatment robs children of this most basic need. There is no closeness; therefore, there is no safety in exploration. They have no security of knowing that a loving caregiver will be consistently there for them and therefore navigate the world alone. Only a relationship with a warm and responsive caregiver will provide the secure base that a child needs to venture out and explore the world with confidence.

When adults try to renew the curious spark in a maltreated child, they must be attuned to the child's particular interests and provide experiences where the child will succeed. In the initial stages, harmed children often pull inward and reluctantly engage. They may compensate for their lack of confidence by dismissing things as boring or too babyish. They will act nonchalant, as if uninterested in what is going on, but it is fear that paralyzes them.

Invite the child to be your play partner. Allow him to be as dependent as he needs to be to gain confidence, learn new skills, use new tools, or learn new rules. His life experiences are typically very limited and his exposure to typical childhood experiences often minimal. For example, I regularly meet children who have never cut with scissors or played with playdough. Gently nudge the child toward greater independence as his confidence and curiosity grows.

Autonomy

In their study "How Home Gets to School: Parental Control Strategies that Predict School Readiness," Aimée Walker and David MacPhee found that a child's sense of autonomy is a strong predictor of academic success and adjustment to school. Children who have a healthy sense of autonomy have stronger social skills, an inclination to master their world, stronger self-regulation skills, and overall competence. Psychologist Erik Erikson identified autonomy as the second developmental task, and it typically refers to the toddler's realization that he is a separate person with his own desires and abilities. A healthy toddler has a strong drive to do things for himself without help from other people. Children who successfully negotiate this stage of development generally acquire a strong sense of self, a healthy independence, and the ability to comply with reasonable consistency to the appropriate expectations of family and school.

One of the first indications of this emerging drive is the toddler's use of the word no. Understand that the no of the toddler is a declaration of independence and not the no of defiance. It indicates the child's growing awareness of himself as a separate individual with his own desires, interests, preferences, dislikes, opinions, and aversions. Neufeld and Maté assert that when a toddler says no, it indicates that his will conflicts with the desires, expectations, and wishes of significant others, and his awareness of himself as a separate other is starting to take shape. In healthy development, this period is but a fleeting moment in the developmental process, and the child emerges at age three with a healthy awareness of his ability to think and do things for himself. He also can inhibit his responses, modify his actions, or comply with requests with the support and guidance of adults.

Unfortunately, for children who experience relational trauma, the lack of a safe and secure attachment figure thwarts the healthy development of autonomy. They cannot come close to someone and move away to develop a sense of self or resist someone to feel a sense of independence. There is no one to bump up against to test the limits and understand boundaries, no consistent and safe attachment figure to help a child define himself.

Not only is there no one to break away from to establish boundaries of self, but the no of the toddler often provokes abuse. This stage of development evokes some of the highest rates of abuse, because unstable parents take the toddler's no personally and retaliate with violence.

The implications are profound. Children lacking in autonomy will struggle in the child care or classroom environment. Their ability to self-regulate and navigate group settings is compromised. They will demonstrate higher levels of aggressive behavior, have fewer social relationships, and lack success managing transitions in the environment. They will demonstrate less curiosity about their world and will experience less satisfaction and enjoyment in learning. Without an awareness of "self," they live in an undifferentiated world of internal chaos where emotions seem to come from nowhere.

Once again, a warm responsive relationship with an invested caregiver is a prerequisite for the development of autonomy—no shortcuts. Once the relationship is established, the child care environment or classroom needs to be a place for children to safely test the limits and discover the power of *no*. Also, remember that maltreated children may be chronologically older when they enter this stage than a typical child. A four-year-old with a history of trauma may not have a sense of autonomy. As relationships form in the classroom and the child begins to feel safe, *no* may become the four-year-old's favorite word. The trauma-informed adult needs to recognize that this child is recovering what he lost and not become unnerved or irritated by the child's negativity. This challenge with maltreated children continues in all domains of development.

A developmentally appropriate classroom creates many opportunities for children to development autonomy.

- Let children look at themselves in mirrors. Talk about similarities and differences among children and the fact that each child is uniquely made.
- Take children's interests and questions seriously. Incorporate them into the daily curriculum.
- Give children age-appropriate responsibilities for the care of their classroom. Let them get their own cot ready for nap, help pick up cots, put materials away, transport materials to and from the outdoor environment, water the plants, and care for animals. Provide child-sized cleaning tools.

- Give children choices of activities.
- Allow children to pursue individual interests through project work.
- Help children to set goals for learning. Celebrate their accomplishments. For example, if a child struggles with cutting, you might say, "Let's help you this week on your cutting skills." The teacher would scaffold the experience by first giving him scrap paper to tear in half, because cutting involves the ability to manage a piece of paper in both hands. The next day, the teacher may provide narrow strips of paper for the child to snip. After the child masters snipping, then he gets paper with straight lines to cut. Eventually he advances to cutting curved lines. Celebrate each successful step.
- Allow children to assume appropriate responsibility for self-care. Teach them self-help skills. Provide low racks for hanging coats and jackets. Provide small pitchers for children to pour their own juice.
- Create *All about Me* books for each child.
- Provide unbreakable hand mirrors and full-length mirrors to help children develop a concept of self. Make self-portraits.

Object Permanence and Object Constancy

Object permanence means the child can hold an image of an object in his mind even when it is out of sight. Before seven or eight months of age, if a ball rolls behind a couch and the child can no longer see it, he will immediately turn his attention to something else because he no longer believes the ball exists. However, a dramatic shift in a child's cognitive capacities occurs at this stage and becomes apparent when the baby begins to search for objects no longer within his sight. The child's looking indicates that he can hold an image of an unseen object in mind and has achieved the capacity for object permanence.

This is one of the reasons that separation anxiety begins to take hold around seven or eight months of age. The infant now knows that when a parent or caregiver is out of sight, she still exists. Other behaviors begin to appear when object permanency begins to develop. Infants take great delight in playing peekaboo. The adult comes and goes, to the baby's delight. Children also begin to play "throw and retrieve," a game that sometimes exasperates caregivers. The infant suddenly enjoys throwing things off the tray of his high chair and watching the adult pick them up—over and over again—as he practices his newfound capacity.

However, when life is a state of chaos both physically and emotionally, object permanence is delayed or significantly altered. In homes that stay in a state of total disarray with no organization or consistency, a child's toys and belongings may regularly disappear in the mess of clutter, making it difficult for him to develop object permanency. No one will play peekaboo or "throw and retrieve." For object permanence to fully develop, there must be consistency to the environment.

The development of object permanence matters to language development as well, because babies begin to label individual objects in their environment when they realize that objects in the environment are separate from them and have a reality of their own.

Object permanence eventually allows the child to develop *object constancy*. This refers to the capacity of the child to hold the image of a comforting caregiver in mind. In healthy relationships, caregivers go away and come back. Mom may go into the bedroom to make the bed, but the toddler knows that if he pinches his finger in the drawer, he can seek her out for comfort or she will reappear at the sound of his cries. The child can hold a comforting image of his mom in mind and does not come unglued with short absences.

Also, even good parents have good days and bad days. Sometimes they are distressed or upset, interfering with their capacity to fully respond to the needs of their children. However, when there is "good enough" care, the child recognizes that the stressed-out mom is the same mom who is usually comforting. The child can carry a consistent image of a nurturing mom in his mind that offers some comfort.

Unfortunately, maltreated children live in such an unpredictable and inconsistent world that they typically fail to develop this fundamental capacity. Adults may disappear at all hours and times of the day or night. I am continually amazed and brokenhearted at the reports I hear of small children being taken into custody because a neighbor found them wandering the streets looking for an absent parent.

Those in the foster system live with a profound sense of uncertainty. One child I know continually asks her foster mom, "Who is going to be mommy?" Others have experienced multiple placements. I asked an eleven-year-old who has been in the system since she was two how many placements she has had. She replied, "I don't know. There are too many to count."

Children living in an environment of abuse and domestic violence never know from one moment to the next what face of Mom or Dad they will see. One minute Dad might be fun loving and nice and moments later might be a raging drunk. These circumstances make it virtually impossible for young children to develop a sense of object constancy and carry an image of a comforting caregiver in mind.

This is one of the reasons why children from hard places have a difficult time separating in the morning. They don't have the assurance that the parent or guardian who goes away will come back. Their chaotic world leaves them without an anchor to calm their anxious souls. They often become very agitated when other parents begin to arrive at the end of the day to pick children up from care. They may stand at the door and anxiously peer down the hall. Being the last one picked up can be very disconcerting, even for a typical child. The inability to hold the comforting image of a caregiver in mind saps children's emotional energy that should be invested in learning. Their inner resources are used to merely cope and survive the day.

Separation rituals can help develop the capacity for object permanence and bring a measure of comfort to children.

- Frame pictures of a child's family or primary attachment figures to display in the classroom. It is important to recognize that even when children come from homes of domestic violence or abuse, there is often some form of attachment to someone in the home.

- Allow a child to carry a photo of a safe person in his pocket.

- Read *The Kissing Hand* by Audrey Penn. Create a kissing hand by gluing a felt heart on a dark sport sock. When the parent or guardian leaves in the morning, he or she can leave a kiss on the kissing hand. The child can keep it in his pocket and during nap time, which is often a difficult time for a child, he can put it on his hand while he rests. Note: This idea is from the Center on the Social and Emotional Foundations for Early Learning.

- Read *The Kiss Box* by Bonnie Verburg. Get a small decorative box from a dollar store and use it to collect "kisses." The child can keep it in his cubby.

- Have the parent or guardian make a photo album of pictures taken at her place of business. Allow the child to see different aspects of the parent's work. Suggest that parents and guardians take children to see their places of business.

- Suggest that parents and guardians put notes in the child's backpack, lunchbox, or pocket. This lets the child know that the adult holds him in mind when they are separated.

- When caregivers and teachers know they are going to be absent from the classroom or center, discuss your absence with the children. Leave a picture behind for the children to see. Tell them that you will be thinking about them and leave a note for the substitute to read to the children.

- Provide cozy spots in the hallway or the classroom for parents and guardians to say goodbye.

Body Integrity

Object constancy and the ability to hold within the mind a coherent image of a comforting caregiver who is sometimes tired, sometimes frustrated, and sometimes happy also plays into a child's capacity for body integrity. *Body integrity* means that the child is able to think of himself as a coherent whole. Children who struggle with body integrity may become very upset when they hurt themselves even mildly because they believe they have lost a body part. They become distressed when they see a doll with a missing leg because they believe the same could happen to them. They sometimes struggle with constipation because losing their poop means they are losing a part of themselves. They cry when they get a haircut, lose a tooth, or have their fingernails cut.

Lack of body integrity can cause children to become preoccupied in the learning environment. When they fall on the playground, they worry excessively about their body. When other children are hurt or the legs of a doll get broken, they obsess over the possibility of it happening to them. They may resist going to the bathroom and to the point of being very uncomfortable and extremely constipated. If the teacher comes to school with a haircut, it can be scary and unnerving. For these children, the world is not a stable place where the wholeness of things can be counted on.

When children from hard places fall down and get hurt, it helps the child who struggles with body integrity to look in a mirror as the adult playfully says, "Yep. All your parts are here. Arms, legs, tummy, head, fingers, toes, ears. You're all here."

Inability to Work with Symbols

From time to time I volunteer in the local shelter for children who have been brought into state custody after maltreatment. The children's inability to use symbols always strikes me. I was sitting on the floor one day when a three-year-old child walked by. He picked up a toy cell phone lying on the floor and tossed it into my lap. I put it to my ear and said, "Hello, Dougie. How are you today?" He looked at me quizzically and said, "I don't have a phone. I can't play." I gave him the plastic phone and said, "Watch this." I made a pretend phone with my hand and finger and said, "See my pretend phone. Watch this." I put my hand to my ear as if using a phone and said, "Hello, Dougie. How are you today?" He just stood there with a confused look on his face for several seconds, threw down his phone, and moved on to do something else.

A few minutes later, the same thing happened with a five-year-old. However, this time, when I showed him my pretend phone and initiated a verbal volley, he "got it." He suddenly smiled and began to engage in a conversation using our phones.

When children live in a supportive and consistent environment and can develop object permanence and object constancy, their capacity to symbolically represent their world increases. As they grow and develop, they begin to use visible symbols to represent the images they carry in their minds, in a sense, giving us a window into their thinking.

For example, a child who has the capacity to hold an image of a comforting caregiver in mind may use what we call a *transitional object* to bring comfort. A teddy bear or a blanket brings comfort in times of distress. A special bracelet or necklace may symbolize the relationship that they have with a parent or caregiver and bring a measure of consolation.

The child may build with blocks, draw pictures, create sculptures, and dramatize imaginary worlds that live in her mind. These tools become windows into a child's thinking and are symbols of her reality. The capacity to use the symbol systems common to children's play lays the foundation for children to understand and use the more complex symbol system that we call the alphabet.

On the other hand, children who have an inconsistent awareness of object constancy or permanency will typically not be able to use transitional objects. (A blanket keeps them warm; it doesn't bring emotional comfort.) Therefore, their capacity to self-soothe is compromised. Their capacity to play likely will be limited because so much of open-ended play depends on using symbols—a block serves as a telephone or a cardboard box serves as a computer.

Strategies for Supporting Symbolic Thinking

A trauma-informed environment is rich in the use of symbols and symbolic play.

- Open-ended art materials give children opportunities to explore drawing, painting, and sculpting.
- Blocks and construction materials allow children to construct what they see in their world.
- Doll houses and figurines give children the opportunity to create oral stories that represent their understandings.
- Dramatic play gives them tools to enact life experiences and use symbols: a paper plate becomes a steering wheel, a block becomes a telephone, and a box becomes a computer keyboard.

These important avenues allow children to express their understanding of the world in symbols. As they grow in their capacity to use symbolic tools, they have the foundation to allow them to develop an understanding of the alphabet, a very complex symbol system.

Language Delay

One of the most serious consequences of maltreatment early in life is a delay in language. We learned in Chapter 4 on sensory integration that movement and sound are intricately related, and a lack of movement may play a part in a child's language delay.

But there are also more obvious reasons for this delay. Children learn to talk out of a desire to communicate with the people that they love. Without loving relationships, they have no motivation to communicate. When Mom and Dad are passed out on the couch from substance abuse, the child has no one to talk to; therefore, vocabulary and language learning are minimal. Language is the conduit of thinking. When language is off-line, a child loses more than the number of vocabulary words. A lack of language means that the capacity to think in flexible and complex ways is also limited. I have met foster children who do not have even the most basic understandings of how the world works. A principal shared a story about a four-year-old foster child in her program. He had had a meltdown in class, so she was walking him to her office. She calmly kept repeating to him, "When you are calm, we will go have lunch." After several minutes of this he finally stopped, looked at her, and asked, "What's lunch?"

Maltreated children also interpret words very literally. For example, I commented one day that I was going to run to the store to get some art supplies for the children. A little girl looked at me and asked, "Don't you have a car?" The literal use of words, such as *run*, is very common among children from hard places.

Creating an environment that gives children lots to talk about is critical. The world of a maltreated child is often very small. When I worked in the inner city of Washington, DC, I knew children who had never crossed the Anacostia River to see the Capitol building, the Smithsonian museum, or the Washington monument that was only seven miles away. Their "world" was the drug-infested, violence-ridden square mile that defined their neighborhood.

Language is also related to IQ. Children with a rich language background and conceptual understandings of the world have higher IQs than children who do not have this background or understanding. Many people don't realize that IQ isn't static. Children are born with a biologically predetermined potential, but the richness or poverty of the child's life experience will determine whether or not he reaches that potential. A language-rich environment is a critical factor in a trauma-informed classroom.

Strategies for Supporting Language Development

- Provide a variety of loose parts, nonspecific items that can be used for a variety of purposes. For example, yogurt cups, tongue depressors, hair rollers, clothespins, sponges, coffee cans, and lengths of fabric are open-ended materials that children can use to create a variety of things. The yogurt cups can become tables in a dollhouse made from blocks; the clothespins and tongue depressors can be made into airplanes and windmills; the lengths of fabric become a train on a wedding dress, a river for the block structure, or a blanket in the dramatic play center. Loose parts motivate a great deal of conversation about the many uses for the objects.
- Sing lots of songs and do fingerplays.
- Create many opportunities for children to compare and contrast objects and experiences.
- Provide rich dramatic-play experiences. Be sure to provide adequate background knowledge. The life experiences of children with a trauma history are typically minimal. If you set up a fruit stand, make sure they know what it is and know the names of the different fruits and vegetables.
- Read all day long.
- Talk to children about things that matter to them.
- Provide interesting science displays with objects that typically aren't encountered in everyday life. For example, set up a display of unusual kitchen gadgets, pulleys, gears, pendulums, or natural items.

Sequence of Time

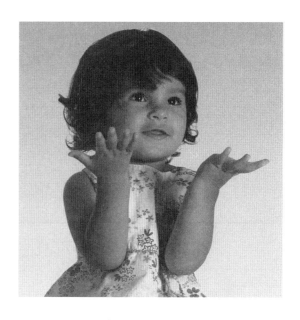

Children need predictability for an understanding of the concept of time to emerge. When life is unpredictable and chaotic, there is no understanding of the past and no concept of the future. All a child has is the now. Children will struggle with sequencing events accurately and grasping the passage of time. The concepts of *beginning*, *middle*, and *end* will be compromised, and they will be unable to tell their own stories with any coherence.

Strategies for Supporting Understanding of Time

- **Documentation board:** A common tool used in a developmentally appropriate classroom, a documentation board is a display of photographs and artifacts attractively displayed to document children's learning. For example, a group of four-year-olds have been doing a worm investigation. They have read books on worms, learned songs and fingerplays, created a worm farm, observed worms with magnifying glasses, drew pictures of what they learned about worms, created class books, and dug for worms out on the playground. Their caregiver took pictures of the children engaged in the many facets of this project and attached them to a science display board. Also displayed were the pictures and diagrams that children had drawn, illustrating what they had learned. Under the photos, she wrote captions, explaining what the children learned in each activity. The children loved to revisit their experiences and talk about what they learned and what they would like to learn in the future.

- **KWL chart:** KWL charts are also a way to help children develop an understanding of past and present. For example, when the worm investigation was introduced, a KWL chart was created to launch the project. The *K* stands for, "What do I already *know* about the topic?" The children brainstormed and listed their knowledge. The *W* stands for, "What do I *wonder* about?" The children identified the things they would like to know about worms. The teacher listed their questions on the chart. Then, they read an informational book about worms. Afterward, they addressed the last section of the chart, the *L*. The teacher asked them what they *learned* about worms from reading the book. They reviewed their new understandings and compared them with the questions they generated.

- **Portfolio:** A portfolio of children's work is also a good way to document change over time. Children can revisit their work and their progress over and over again through their portfolios.

Because children from hard places often have learning delays, some people assume that they can't learn. They can—they just need a different kind of environment that understands their history and where they are developmentally, then gives them the time and support to recover what they have lost. Maltreated children can learn, but they must be allowed to learn in their own time, in their own way, and with teachers and caregivers who understand developmental processes and trauma.

Chapter 8

Implications for the Physical Environment

There is a trend in early childhood education, due in part to the influence of Reggio Emilia schools, toward creating homelike environments for young children. I have heard it stated in conferences from time to time that environments for traumatized children need to be homelike to help them feel safe. It is important to recognize, however, that a homelike environment will not automatically cause a maltreated child to feel safe. The home is often the most violent place in a child's life and where some children are literally incubated in violence and abuse, both in person and through the media. Safety is not found in a place. Safety is first and foremost found in the context of a warm, nurturing, and protective relationship.

However, it is important to create thoughtful environments with traumatized children's needs in mind. Many foster children have had disturbing experiences in hospitals, police departments, children's shelters, and welfare agencies, and most of these places are very sterile and institutional. The presence of toys and teddy bears is an attempt to make these places appeal to children, but it is difficult to neutralize the institutional look and feel.

A homelike environment in the best sense contains many ingredients that create an emotionally safe place. There are soft elements that beckon children to relax, calm down, and enjoy a sensory-rich experience. Overstuffed chairs, pillows, afghans, natural items, cozy corners, pleasant aromas, and a variety of materials contribute to a sense of safety and well-being.

> Safety is not found in a place. Safety is first and foremost found in the context of a warm, nurturing, and protective relationship.

Organization of Space

Spaces send messages to both children and adults about how to behave. For example, think about the unspoken messages you receive upon entering a cathedral versus an amusement park, or a room lined with books and overstuffed furniture versus a room with a desk, stiff-backed chairs, copy machines, and computers. The design of a space influences children: Long hallways and aisles beckon children to run; open spaces invite children to turn cartwheels and engage in gross motor play. Environments with open shelves and accessible materials encourage children to explore; whereas, environments with materials stored high on shelves or out of reach in closets send a "hands off" message.

Be mindful of the messages that the environment communicates from the moment a child walks into the child care center or school. Look at the space through the eyes of a traumatized child. Despite our best efforts, the environment will inevitably have elements that may trigger memories within the child, but we have no way of knowing that except by astutely observing the child's behavior. When patterns of dysregulated behavior reoccur, carefully take note of the spaces and places where meltdowns and difficulties happen.

Every environment has a sensory load composed of the sights, sounds, and smells that immediately affect the senses. Because it is not unusual for traumatized children to have sensory issues, create an environment that has a low-to-moderate sensory load. It is commonly stated that early childhood environments should be stimulating places for children, and somewhere along the line this statement has been interpreted to mean brightly colored walls covered with posters, charts, and busy bulletin boards; patterned rugs or floors; cluttered furniture; toys with flashing lights and annoying sounds; and brightly colored plastic tubs overflowing with toys. This high sensory load may trigger the fight, flight, or freeze response in a traumatized child.

An environment with a low sensory load typically has neutral colors and carefully organized materials and equipment on shelves in natural baskets or neutral-colored containers. Floor coverings have subtle colors or patterns that do not distract, and there are pleasant odors and calming, rhythmic sounds. The primary source of stimulation is provided through engagement with sensory-rich materials.

Arrangement of Furniture

Finding just the right room arrangement can be a process. The arrangement of the furniture needs to be especially mindful of traffic patterns. Children with vestibular issues have balance problems and easily trip over the legs of the furniture or over other children in highly congested areas. Those who have difficulty with motor planning will be prone to bumping into other children or the furniture itself, so allow plenty of space for children to move easily about the room.

Keep in mind that foster children, in particular, are easily jolted by change. Their environments have typically been very unpredictable and chaotic, and any change in the placement of furniture can trigger fear and uncertainty. Make as few changes in the physical environment as possible and, when it is necessary to change, orient the child by warning him the day before that things will be different when he comes in and by explaining why. Upon his arrival, take a tour of the classroom, pointing out any changes, and show the child how to use and operate any new pieces of furniture or equipment that were introduced.

Square Footage

Another factor to consider is the actual square footage of the space and the ratio of square footage to the number of children. Most states have minimum standards for child care centers that include a required minimum of square footage per child in each classroom. Remember that minimum standards are just that— requirements for a minimal environment that addresses the basic necessities.

Research indicates that density of people is a critical factor in predicting the potential and frequency of aggression and violence. According to Lorraine Maxwell, author of "Multiple Effects of Home and Day Care Crowding," the more people you put in a given space, the greater the likelihood of aggressive behavior. For traumatized children, who often misinterpret body language, an accidental bump or brush with another person can be construed as an aggressive act and can trigger a shoving match. We set children up to fail when we put them in crowded classrooms.

This also has implications for the number of children placed in a given space. Minimum requirements for child-to-adult ratios vary from state to state. If at all possible, follow the ratios recommended by the NAEYC, available at http://www.naeyc.org/policy/advocacy/ProgramFacts#Ratios. One adult will have difficulty as the sole external regulator for a large group of children. The more individualized attention and care, the greater the likelihood of healing.

Spaces for Large Motor Play

Provide indoor space for active play, because it is critical for children from hard places to have plenty of opportunity for large motor activity. Purvis and Cross recommend that children with a trauma history have gross motor activity for at least twenty minutes every two hours. When planning the layout of the classroom, consider this need. It is always better for children to run and play outside, but this is not always possible. When space is limited, the large group area and the gross motor area may serve a dual purpose with some minimal adjustment.

Some child care centers provide a rough-and-tumble play area to accommodate children's need for deep-muscle stimulation and play. Tumbling mats, modular soft blocks, body pillows, and large pieces of foam rubber can create such an area. A teacher of three-year-olds reported to me that the rough-and-tumble play area significantly reduced aggressive play in her classroom during the winter months. I observed in her classroom on several occasions and never saw the play in this center get out of hand and become directed at other children. The children wrestled with the pillows and rolled around on the floor with the modular blocks and pieces of foam.

Noise Levels

A busy place, the early childhood classroom will inevitably have noise. There has long been a misguided notion that learning happens in quiet environments, but learning is an interactive and active experience, and I often speak of the busy hum of children playing and learning. There is a vast difference between the sound of a chaotic and out-of-control environment and an intentionally planned and purposeful learning environment of play. In chaotic environments, you will hear the sounds of both children and adults yelling, children constantly crying, equipment clattering to the floor, and children arguing. Sometimes, loud children's music drones in the background.

In a play-based, intentional learning environment, you will hear the murmur of conversation between children and adults and among the children themselves. You will hear an occasional cry and perhaps a loud exclamation as an initial reaction of a child to a distressing event, but you won't hear chronic and consistent wailing. You will hear happy sounds of children laughing, giggling, singing, and chanting. There will be the usual clunking and clanging of blocks toppling and wheeled toys rolling, but it will not be an overwhelming cacophony of noise created in an unorganized environment. Music is used with intentionality, not as background clatter.

But even in the most organized and intentional environments, children will need to seek times of solitude and quiet, especially children who have been harmed. When children live in threatening environments, they become finely attuned to the sounds of the environment, because certain sounds can predict harm. It is not unusual for the constant noise of a busy classroom to overwhelm a maltreated child.

Quiet Spaces

Children need spaces that allow them to retreat from the constant noise of a busy classroom to enjoy moments of solitude and quiet. A blanket or sheet thrown over a table; a crib mattress in a corner with pillows, small blankets and stuffed animals; or a large appliance box are inexpensive ways to accommodate children's needs to rest and relax. Small pup tents or lofts also provide spaces for solitude but are obviously more expensive. Head phones, ear plugs, and personal CD players with headphones help children who are auditorially overstimulated come back into regulation. CDs of nature sounds, classical guitar, piano, and harp music as well as Native American drumming can soothe.

Pleasant Aromas

In the early childhood literature, you often find comments about making sure the environment has pleasing smells. Our brains process smells faster than any other sensory stimulation, so a child's reaction to a particular smell can be instantaneous. A mom once reported taking her foster daughter to a nail salon as part of an enjoyable girls' day out. The second the child stepped in the door, she ran to a salon chair and began to violently spin and laugh hysterically. It was later learned that this child's abuse took place at a nail salon, and the smell triggered this strange reaction.

Identifying soothing aromas for the children in your care can be tricky because what soothes one child may trigger another. For example, the scent of lavender is usually considered a calming smell and one that triggers a relaxation response. However, if the person who abused a child used a lavender-scented bath and body wash, you can bet that lavender will not have the typical effect on that child.

It is not uncommon for aromas associated with food to be a trigger for harmed children. Many maltreated children have experienced starvation or have been denied access to food as a form of punishment. The smell of food can trigger the fight, flight, or freeze response and can instigate challenging behaviors. This becomes especially difficult in classrooms located near the kitchen or where children eat in their rooms. The aroma of food can linger for hours after lunch or breakfast and can have a negative effect on a child's behavior and feeling of safety. Even though best practice recommends that children eat in their rooms rather than go to large cafeterias for meals, an exception may be necessary if a child is sensitive to the aromas of food.

Organization of Materials

In developmentally appropriate classrooms, the room is divided into smaller spaces commonly called *interest centers*. An interest center consists of a grouping of materials carefully chosen to evoke a particular kind of play. Typical interest centers include art, dramatic play, science, math, manipulatives, library, writing, music, blocks, and woodworking. Materials within the interest centers are usually stored on open shelving units where children have the opportunity to freely choose activities during periods of child-initiated play.

Designing environments with the element of choice in mind is particularly important for traumatized children because this is one of the ways we fill their buckets with yeses and give them a voice. When children have the opportunity to make choices and pursue activities of personal interest, this affirms and acknowledges the child. Therefore, carefully choose materials and activities that reflect the interests and needs of the children.

A well-organized classroom is necessary. Store materials in baskets or containers labeled with both pictures and words. You want to communicate the messages that everything has a place and materials are used then put back in their places. Not only does this help with organization, but it also helps children develop object permanence. Predictability must exist before a child can establish the permanency of objects. An organized and labeled environment helps facilitate this critical concept.

Because traumatized children typically have limited life experiences, you need to model and teach proper use and care of materials. Ordinary materials such as glue, scissors, playdough, and markers are often foreign to them. Nothing should be put on the shelves before adults model then allow children to practice appropriate use of the materials. Take scissors, for example. First, demonstrate in a large or small group how to safely pick up and carry a pair of scissors with the points down. Model how to pass a pair of scissors to another child by grasping the pointed end and handing them off with the handles placed in the palm of the other child. Model how to open and shut the scissors, how to hold the paper and scissors together to cut, and how to put the scissors back on the shelf in their proper container. Provide 1-inch strips of scrap paper for guided practice before giving children the freedom to use scissors without supervision.

As children learn to use a variety of tools and materials, their buckets are being filled with *yes*—"Yes, I believe you are capable." "Yes, you are worth the time and energy that is required for me to help you learn." "Yes, I trust you to use the materials appropriately." The child's sense of competence and confidence grows.

Equipping the Room to Foster Independence

Another way we fill children's buckets with yeses is to equip the room in a way that allows them as much independence as possible. I often hear reports of maltreated children being inappropriately restrained in cribs, playpens, or car seats. Not only does this fill a child's bucket with nos, but it thwarts the child's internal drive to master her world, compromises physical coordination and development, and undermines a child's belief in the world as a safe place.

Obviously, as we seek to foster children's independence, each child's skill level must be taken into consideration and level of confidence respected. Children grow when we give them manageable challenges, not overwhelming challenges.

Also, different children will perceive experiences differently. What may feel unsafe and restraining to one child may feel safe and containing to another. The child who has been left for long hours in a car seat may experience swinging in an infant swing as restraining and struggle to be set free. On the other hand, a crying child may experience the infant swing as containing and may be calmed by the experience. Some children may perceive being wrapped in a blanket as restrictive; others may experience it as comforting. Watch children's reactions to different activities, movements, and experiences and adjust accordingly.

Strategies for Fostering Independence

- Provide child-sized table and chairs.
- Place toddler stairs next to changing tables.
- Provide child-sized whisk brooms, dust pans, and mops for cleanup.
- Provide child-sized sinks and water fountains.
- If child-sized water fountains are not available, provide small pitchers and cups for those who can pour their own drinks.
- Provide child-sized hooks or cubbies for personal items.
- Provide child-sized shelving units and water displays.

Outdoor Spaces that Heal

Most playgrounds in schoolyards and at child care centers across America have changed very little in the past decades: primary-colored pieces of tubular steel and plastic anchored in a sea of rubber. Very few moveable parts or open-ended pieces exist that children can manipulate and reconfigure in new and interesting ways. Greenery, if any, is limited to whatever may spontaneously emerge around the edges of the designated space. Some would argue that the sterile, child-proof playgrounds of today appear designed and built to meet adults' need to create a safe world rather than a child's need to explore and discover.

Natural Spaces Are Healing Spaces

Creating a healing environment for traumatized children means that we need to think differently about outdoor environments. A growing body of research confirms the restorative and healing powers of natural or green environments for the young and old alike. Before industrialization, most children grew up on farms and had vast wooded areas and open fields in which to play. Once industrialization took over, children gravitated to vacant lots, undeveloped wooded areas, or other uninhabited spaces. They climbed trees, created secret places among bushes, hid in tall grass, rolled down hills, climbed on rocks, dammed moving water, made mud pies, and jumped in piles of leaves. Natural spaces, or "naturescapes" as they are sometimes called, are green places of beauty and enchantment consisting of more wild features than man-made, where children can intimately interact with nature, experience a sense of wonder, and reconfigure parts and pieces. Giant boulders that children can climb become lookout towers and ships. Bushes and shrubs are configured in such a way that allows children to have places to be alone. Balance beams are made from fallen logs and huts are created out of willow branches growing over a wire frame. Mud kitchens and mud pits provide a rich sensory experience. Gardens, bird houses, worm farms, and insect hotels give children the opportunity to observe and care for the natural world. Natural playscapes are places where children can just be rather than achieve.

Some argue that natural playgrounds are far too costly and dangerous to be practical. The evidence suggests otherwise. In his article "If You Go Down to the Woods Today," Tim Gill cites an example from Germany. Freiburg, Germany, has built more than forty natural playscapes in their town and reports that the cost is about half of what would be spent on traditional play spaces, mainly due to the high cost of tubular steel. As for the safety factor, Janny Scott, in an article in the *New York Times* titled "When Child's Play Is Too Simple," quotes playground expert Dr. Joe Frost's assertion that children's play is more sustained with fewer injuries and behavior problems on playgrounds that are "broad, expansive, and designed for all of the developmental needs of children."

Richard Louv, author of *Last Child in the Woods*, cites Nancy Wells, an assistant professor of design and environmental analysis at Cornell University, who reports that the benefits of natural environments are strongest for vulnerable children. Exposure to natural spaces has been shown to normalize heart rate and blood pressure and to relieve muscle tension, according to Stephen Kaplan, author of the article "The Restorative Benefits of Nature." This is especially important for children with a trauma history because their heart rates and blood pressure tend to be elevated. Nancy Wells and Gary Evans, authors of "Nearby Nature: A Buffer of Life Stress among Rural Children," found that access to nature reduces conduct disorders, anxiety, and depression in children. Children with a history of trauma are likely to display symptoms of sensory processing disorder, and there is nothing more sensory rich than the natural world. The typical playground made of tubular steel and rubber ground cover offers minimal sensory input as compared to a naturescape.

Natural Environments and Attention

Andrea Taylor, Frances Kuo, and William Sullivan, in their article "Coping with ADD: The Surprising Connection to Green Play Settings," have documented the positive effect of natural environments on children diagnosed with ADD or ADHD. They found that even a twenty-minute walk in a natural environment works as effectively as an extended-release dose of methylphenidate, a drug commonly used for the treatment of ADHD. After taking a walk in a park, children have a greater capacity for focused attention and concentration. Focused attention has been shown to be the primary predictive factor of success in school.

In the *Monitor on Psychology*, Stephen Kaplan suggests in his article "The Restorative Benefits of Nature" that natural environments increase a child's ability to concentrate, differentiating between directed attention and fascination. When children exercise directed attention, they make a conscious effort to stay on task, remain focused, and screen out extraneous stimuli.

Children must use directed attention every day in early care and learning settings. Although a necessary and important aspect of daily living and functioning, it is nonetheless exhausting over long periods of time. Louv claims too much directed attention leads to impulsive behavior, agitation, irritation, and lack of concentration. Fascination, on the other hand, is the spontaneous captivation of attention and focus. It is not something a child makes herself do but is elicited by the intrinsically intriguing nature of the object or experience. For example, adults generally don't have to cajole, encourage, or nag most children to watch a spider spin a web or observe a butterfly sip nectar from a flower. The intriguing nature of the experiences pulls children in and captures not only their minds but their hearts. Kaplan points out that fascination has restorative powers for children and renews their cognitive capacities; whereas, directed attention tends to exhaust the energies of the child.

Healing environments strive to create surroundings that fascinate and encourage a sense of wonder. These spaces beckon children to explore and play in a sensory-rich world. A healing environment also recognizes the importance of time. A thirty-minute time slot once or twice a day is not enough for complex play and rich exploration to emerge. Anything that can be done indoors can be done outdoors; therefore, healing environments view the outdoor playspace as an extension of the classroom and allow children to enjoy long periods of time in a natural setting.

Creativity and Imagination

Relational trauma impairs children's language development and their capacity to manipulate symbols, which, in turn, stifle children's capacity to engage in fantasy or pretend play. Children from hard places, therefore, need many opportunities to develop their capacity for this form of engagement.

Natural environments, as opposed to traditional playgrounds, have been shown to motivate and inspire pretend or fantasy play. According to Elaine Weitzman and Janice Greenberg, authors of *Learning Language and Loving It*, pretend or dramatic play is the most language-rich form of play that children engage in, and it fosters the development of the most complex forms of language. Natural environments have been shown to inspire greater capacity for creativity and imagination. In his article "How Not to Cheat Children: The Theory of

Loose Parts," Simon Nicholson, a British architect, writes that the degree of inventiveness and creativity and the possibility of discovery in an environment are directly proportional to the number and kind of variables. The natural world is made up of many, many loose parts. Leaves, sticks, twigs, logs, insects, grasses, sand, rocks, pebbles, acorns, and the many other elements of nature are a gold mine of loose parts that inspire creativity and imagination.

Elements for Natural Outdoor Spaces

- Provide places for shade:
    - Plant a variety of trees.
    - Set up inexpensive canopies or tents purchased from discount and home-improvement stores.
    - Build a gazebo or pergola.
    - Plant vines at the base of the pergola supports to grow over the top to create shade.
- Provide places for solitude:
    - Plant bushes and shrubs in clusters to create "secret" places for children to hide.
    - Create lean-tos or teepees out of sticks or bamboo.
    - Provide large cardboard boxes for forts and hideouts.
    - Mount a retractable clothesline on the side of the building, and allow children to attach sheets and lengths of fabric with clothespins to create tents.
    - Create a sunflower house by planting sunflower seeds in a circle.
    - Hang mosquito netting from trees to create the illusion of an enclosed space.
    - Provide a variety of loose parts, such as crates, barrels, scraps of lumber, planks, large boxes, lengths of fabric, mosquito netting, shower curtains, PVC pipe, tarps, limbs, tree cookies (slices of tree trunks), and large sheets of cardboard, for children to use to create their own cozy spaces.
- Provide a gathering space:
    - Provide picnic tables or patio furniture where children can eat or play games.
    - Blankets, logs, tree stumps or creates provide places for children to gather and talk.
- Provide storage:
    - Build a shed.
    - Provide benches with built-in storage.
- Provide places to climb:
    - Provide a rock pile or large boulders.
    - Create mounds of grass-covered dirt for children to climb and roll down.

- Embed the body of a slide in the side of a hill for children to slide down.
- Check with local licensing standards regarding climbing walls and tree forts.
- Build a low wall between 24 and 36 inches tall for children to walk on and jump off.
- Provide places for sand, mud, and water exploration:
  - Create a mud pit and/or a large sand area that has access to water.
  - Create watercourses for moving water using lengths of vinyl guttering and PVC pipe.
  - Install a rain barrel for use in watering plants.
  - Provide hoses, water pumps, watering cans, and buckets for moving water.
  - Create a mud kitchen with an old table, pie pans, cookie sheets, muffin tins, and other kitchen gadgets.
- Provide an art space:
  - Set up an art pavilion under a canopy. Provide card tables, picnic tables or large stumps for work areas, and keep art supplies on a rolling cart for easy transport.
  - Mount a sheet of Plexiglas to a fence between two landscape timbers mounted upright in the ground. Use tempera paint or window markers to create designs. Provide a hose or a spray bottle of water to erase pictures with a squeegee.
  - Paint a wooden table or sheet of plywood with chalk paint for outdoor chalk art.
  - Weave strips of fabric through chain-link or wooden fencing.
  - Mount chicken wire on a wooden frame and weave grasses and other natural materials.
  - Create a mural wall for children to engage in cooperative endeavors.
- Provide construction space:
  - Provide materials for building forts: sawhorses, planks, cardboard boxes, sheets and blankets hung over retractable clothes lines, crates, and scraps of lumber.
  - Cut PVC pipe to different lengths, and provide an assortment of connectors. After creating a frame, children can hang sheets or lengths of fabric over the pipe to create an enclosed space.
- Provide an outdoor library:
  - Set up canopies and tents for reading. Provide lawn chairs. Use a wagon to transport books.
  - Build a gazebo and plant bushes and flowers around it to create a lovely space to read.

- Provide a dramatic-play space:
  - Set up a puppet theater made from a large cardboard box.
  - Create a stage or amphitheater for creative dramatics and performances.
  - Provide prop boxes that support outdoor themes that can be enacted on the playground: firefighter, police, fast-food restaurant, gas station, car wash, farm, racetrack, beach, picnic, camping, fishing, and so on.
  - Build a playhouse, log cabin, or other stationary structure for pretend play.
- Provide a science-exploration space:
  - Create garden plots, raised beds, hanging pots, and container gardens. Grow fruits and vegetables that can be used for snack or shared with a food bank.
  - If your center allows, raise chickens, rabbits, ducks, or other barnyard animals and pets.
  - Create a compost pile.
  - Do worm composting. (Instructions are available on the Internet.)
  - Set up birdhouses and birdbaths for bird watching. Provide binoculars and cameras for documenting and viewing.
  - Make and fly kites.
  - Create a worm or roly-poly (pillbug) farm in a galvanized tub.
  - Collect insects found on the playground.
  - Provide a rain gauge, sundial, or rain barrel.
  - Build or purchase a small, inexpensive greenhouse or cold frame for growing plants.
- Provide a music area:
  - Make wind chimes from lengths of pipe.
  - Cut large plastic barrels to varying heights, making sure that children can reach the top with drum mallets. Mount them upside down on landscape timbers using bolts. The variety of heights will create different tones when children strike them with mallets. Cut thick dowel rods and attach tennis balls to the ends to create mallets.
  - Suspend a variety of pots, pans, cookie sheets, and cake pans from a swing-set frame. Provide a variety of mallets for children to experiment with the sounds.
  - Add wind harps to the outdoor environment. The wind blowing through appropriately configured strings creates different tonal qualities. Check the Internet for commercially made wind harps and instructions for making your own.

Chapter 9

Organization of Time

When children live in chaotic and unpredictable environments, their ability to sequence information and events is often nonexistent. For the concepts of *past*, *present*, and *future* or *beginning*, *middle*, and *end* to make sense to children, they must first have a predictable environment.

Overall Principles

How we structure the day will have a huge impact on children's sense of safety and on their behavior. There are some key principles to keep in mind when scheduling the day with children from hard places.

Set a Leisurely Pace

Children are not meant to be hurried, so the day should move at a leisurely pace, not a frantic rush to get through to the next activity. Author Ann Voskamp writes in her book *A Thousand Gifts*, "Hurry empties the soul." Although true of both children and adults, this statement holds special significance for maltreated children. A frenzied pace can tax even the most highly self-regulated child and can completely undo a child who has suffered maltreatment and trauma.

Provide Predictability

The daily schedule should be predictable and consistent. Our brains don't like surprises. According to an issue brief from the U. S. Department of Health and Human Services titled *Understanding the Effects of Maltreatment on Brain Development*, "prolonged, severe, or unpredictable stress—including abuse and neglect" is far more toxic than stress that is predictable and/or moderate. When abuse is unpredictable, the brain and body remain in a state of chronic hypervigilance. Environments that lack structure and routine are stressful for all children but even more so for those with a history of maltreatment. Stable and predictable routines allow children to relax and feel safe.

Children from hard places commonly have emotional outbursts and meltdowns that make it challenging for caregivers and teachers to maintain the flow of daily activities. This is why it is critical to have at least two adults in any early childhood environment that serves maltreated children. One adult can help a child manage his behavior while the other teacher maintains the flow of the activities. Children need to see that classroom life will go on in a predictable fashion and their behavior will not overpower and disrupt it.

Provide Visual Cues

Research, such as that by Jennifer Ganz and Margaret Flores, Carmen Rasmussen, Gill Thompson, and Karen Hyche and Vickie Maertz, with children diagnosed with autism, ADD/ADHD, sensory processing disorder, fetal alcohol exposure, communication difficulties, and problem behaviors shows these children can benefit from the use of visual cues. Visual schedules provide a sense of predictability as the child can easily see what is going to happen next. Many are not able to process information quickly, and visual cues remain present after words are spoken. Visual cues reduce the need for wordy directions

and give the children another sensory avenue to process instructions. Pictures can be simple stick figures drawn on cards, actual photographs of the children in the classroom engaged in the various activities, or pictures found online. Display the cards in sequential order in a place where the children have access and can manipulate the cards. Each time you are about to make a transition, ask children who struggle with transitions to check the visual schedule and point to the activity that will come next. A child can keep a personalized ring of small 2-inch x 2-inch cards in his pocket or attached to a belt.

Allow Lots of Time for Child-Directed Activities

The daily schedule reveals a great deal about a caregiver or teacher's beliefs regarding how children learn and what it means to teach children. The traditional "sage on stage" approach, where the adult deposits knowledge into children's heads much like we deposit money in the bank, is a *transactional model* of teaching and learning. The underlying belief is that children only learn when the adult is in control and instructing the children. Play is seen as incidental, a break from the real business of learning.

Usually these sorts of early childhood environments present difficulties for children from hard places. Children are expected to sit for long periods of time listening to a teacher talk. There is typically a strong and single-minded focus on academics and little focus on social and emotional development. Maltreated children usually don't fare well in such a context.

Child-initiated activities, such as interest-center time and outdoor play, should make up the bulk of the day. Interest-center time is sometimes referred to as free play, and adults often view it as down time. However, they should use interest-center time and outdoor play as primary teaching opportunities. Caregivers and teachers should be actively involved, asking questions, making written observations, coaching, playing, and interacting with children.

Offer Short Teacher-Directed Activities

Throughout the day, plan short group times for children to come together in large and small groups for adult-planned activities and instruction. Design these experiences with specific needs and children in mind. Be purposeful and engage children's interest and curiosity. Include shared reading and writing, games, musical experiences, or discussions.

Minimize the Number of Transitions

The daily schedule in an early childhood program typically has multiple transitions throughout the day. A significant amount of coming and going and moving between and among activities and places within the classroom and building takes place. Transitions are especially challenging for children who have suffered maltreatment and for those in foster care. Children from hard places have experienced significant loss in their lives—loss of attachment relationships, loss of their homes, loss of familiar schools and child care centers, loss of friends and family, and a loss of identity.

Transitions also involve loss. To move from one activity to another, a child must let go of something to obtain something else. For example, a child must let go of the joy and satisfaction of playing in the blocks to go outside to play. But children who have lost so much feel this daily "losing" more profoundly than those who have been well-nurtured. Heather Forbes and Bryan Post, authors of *Beyond Consequences, Logic,* and *Control,* report that these seemingly minor losses of everyday living can seem like matters of life and death to a traumatized child.

Other reasons also make transitions difficult for children who have suffered maltreatment and loss. Individuals who live in uncertainty and chaos often become inflexible and rigid in their approach to life. A child who feels that his life is out of control may become very controlling in his approach to relationships and events in an attempt to reduce the feelings of chaos and disorder. Therefore, transitioning from one activity to another threatens the child who wants to remain in control and call the shots.

Maltreated children also struggle with situations where they have to figure out the "script" for themselves. For example, teachers and caregivers often simply tell children to clean up. The open-endedness of "cleaning up" can confuse a child who needs concrete and specific instructions. Transitions also require a lot of negotiation and interaction with other children—skills that are difficult for traumatized children to navigate. Lining up to go outside seems simple enough, but is not so for many children. Jockeying for a place in line, issues of proximity and spatial awareness, children brushing up against each other—all of these can cause a child to have a meltdown.

It is, therefore, important for teachers and caregivers to carefully examine the daily schedule and eliminate as many transitions as possible. Avoid chopping the day up into twenty-to-thirty-minute segments. Provide long blocks of time of one to two hours for child-initiated activities, such as interest-center time and outdoor play. Not only does this cut down on the number of transitions, but it also allows plenty of time for complex play and creativity to emerge. It gives children the opportunity to explore their inner lives and time to pursue their interests and ideas without feeling rushed.

Provide Lots of Outdoor Play

Gross motor activity is especially important for traumatized children, because vigorous play has a calming effect on the regulatory system. It raises serotonin levels, increases deep breathing, and develops muscle tone. As mentioned earlier, Purvis and Cross recommend that children from hard places need gross motor activity at least every two hours for a minimum of twenty minutes.

Best practice calls for a minimum of 20 percent of the time in care or in school to be spent in outdoor play. For example, a child in care for ten hours a day should play outside for at least two hours. Keep weather considerations in mind, of course, but anything that can be done indoors also can be done outdoors with a little modification.

Managing Transitions and Routines

The daily schedule in any early childhood setting is punctuated by routines and transitions that can present challenges for all children but especially for children from hard places. Established routines that are consistently carried out bring predictability to the environment and help children feel safe. Thoughtfully think through the daily routines to eliminate unnecessary confusion and chaos so that children can proceed as smoothly as possible.

Adults often give directions to children and assume they know how to carry out the instructions. Never assume that children know what you expect. Teach and model the processes so children know exactly what is expected. Here are some steps to keep in mind.

- **Model the routine.** When introducing children to "how we do things," show them—don't just tell them. Actually demonstrate the process of showing them how to take off their jackets and hang them up in the cubbies. Think out loud as you walk through the steps, and explain the process as you model: "I'm walking into the classroom. Now I look for my cubby. Oh, there it is. I know where it is because I see my picture and my name. Now I take off my coat. I'm careful not to sling it around and hit someone with the zipper. Now I hang it up on the hook. Oops, it fell down. There we go. It's on the hook."
- **Have children model the routine.** Once you have explained and modeled, ask two or three children to demonstrate the process as you provide commentary. "Look, Latoya's walking into the room. She's looking for her cubby. She finds her picture and her name. She takes her coat off, being careful not to sling it around. She puts it on the hook."
- **Give guided practice.** You might have the children pantomime a process if appropriate. Throughout the day, in small groups, have children practice.
- **Observe the children in action.** As children learn new routines, adults need to stand by and coach as children get stuck.

Breaking Routine Tasks into Smaller Steps

Traumatized children sometimes struggle with short-term memory. Breaking routine tasks into smaller steps and creating visual cues for each step can help children learn and assimilate established procedures. Take, for example, the daily routine of hand washing. Photograph the following actions, and mount them in order above the sink.

- Turn on the faucet and wet your hands.
- Put soap on your hands.
- Rub your hands together, and sing "Happy Birthday" two times.
- Put your hands under the water and rinse the soap off.
- Turn the water off.
- Get a paper towel and dry your hands.

Guiding Children through Transitions

Proximity is key during transitions. Don't lob words across the room at the child, but get within 36 inches, make eye contact, and if possible, hold the child's hands or put a hand on her shoulder. This engages multiple sensory modalities—vision, touch, and hearing. Give the child a warning that a change is coming by saying something like, "In ten minutes it will be time to clean up and come to circle time. Is there something that you want to finish up before it is time to put your things away?"

Conventional time carries very little meaning to young children, so they need to mark time in a way that makes sense to them. An hourglass gives children a visual cue of the passing of time, for example, and there are timers on the market specifically designed for this purpose.

Once the designated time has passed, go to the child once again and tell her it is now time to clean up and go to group time. Point out the coming activity on the visual schedule on the wall or on the child's personal ring of cues. Be very specific in identifying exactly what the child needs to do during this time, but do not give more than two directions at once. Traumatized children often struggle with working memory and find it difficult to remember directions. For example, if she is making a collage, you might say, "Put your collage on the drying rack, and then put the glue bottles on the shelf. Check back with me when you are finished." When that has been accomplished, she checks back and you give her the next set of instructions.

If you have a child who simply cannot manage transitions, you or another adult will need to act as the child's external regulator. This means that you stay by the child's side and coach her step by step through the transitions. You may even need to model each step in the process. Being the external regulator for a very dysregulated child is exhausting, but the child needs that kind of coaching to help her develop the regulatory skills to function successfully. Transitions are very busy times in a classroom, and many things need adult attention, but it is especially important to pay attention to the needs of children from hard places.

Allow children to use transitional objects when going from one activity to the next. Transitional objects, such as stuffed animals, can help the child feel safe and secure and can offer comfort for the minor losses a child experiences during a transition. Be sure to build in adequate time for transitions in the daily schedule. A common mistake is to underestimate the amount of time they take.

Entry into Care

Foster and maltreated children often experience multiple moves in any given year and may enter a program at any point in time. Becoming acclimated to a new environment is difficult for most children but even more so for children from hard places. Combine this with what Neufeld and Maté refer to as an orientation void, and it becomes important that a child's first introduction to a particular setting be positive and emotionally safe.

If at all possible, introduce children from hard places to the environment on an individual basis. At the beginning of the year, assign time slots so each child is introduced to the adults and the environment on an individual basis. If a child enrolls during the school year, ask the parent or guardian to bring the child before or after the day begins or ends or during outdoor play. This way, adults can give undivided attention to the child.

It is critical that caregivers and teachers be mindful of their demeanor when introducing a child to the environment. You likely will become the child's primary orienting factor, and he will continue to look to you for guidance and direction as long as he feels safe in your presence. Here are some things to consider and explain to the child.

- **Be at eye level or below when you introduce yourself.** Perry, in his 2014 webinar *Neurosequential Model of Therapeutics*, stated that maltreated children find giving an upward eye gaze very threatening. Reducing your size reduces the threat. If your knees are bad, sit in a child-sized chair.

- **Don't assume the child is comfortable with touch.** Don't immediately hug or embrace the child. Let the child warm up to you, and as the child leaves you might ask, "Can I give you a high five, a handshake, or a hug?" If the child says no, say something like, "That's okay. Maybe another day."

On the other hand, some children are indiscriminately affectionate. Sexually and physically abused children have had their boundaries violated, and they often have difficulty recognizing the physical boundaries of others. Sometimes they will immediately jump into your lap or even climb on your back if you stoop down. Calmly ask the child to stand in front of you, then say something like, "In our classroom, we ask permission to hug or touch other people. When you ask me for a hug, a handshake, or a high five, I will always give you one. I will always ask your permission to hug or touch you, too. If you say no, I will honor your request and not touch." Establishing these boundaries from the very beginning is critical. It is much harder to enforce physical boundaries if they have been violated for several days than it is to establish the boundaries from the start.

- **Walk the child through the morning routine.** As you orient the child to the classroom, say something like, "Let me show you how we do things around here." Don't say, "These are the rules." Show him where to put his belongings, transitional object, backpack, and so on. Point out the visual schedule, and let him know what comes next. Show him where to find the carpet squares, fidgets, cots, snacks, and so on. Give the child his own visual schedule to keep in his pocket to reference throughout the day. Let the child know that it's okay to ask for help if he doesn't know what to do. Reassure him that everyone forgets sometimes and you are here to help each other. When a child asks for help, honor his request. We undermine any amount of trust the child may have in us when we refuse to help or say something like, "Why weren't you listening?" From time to time, ask competent other children to show the new child "how we do things."

Children who have suffered significant maltreatment have a smaller hippocampus in their brains, which affects short-term memory. Keep an eye on the child and show him how to do things throughout the day. For example, if the child chooses the block center during interest-center time, demonstrate how to remove blocks from the shelf one at a time. Show him the "no-building zone" and where to start building his structure. Show him how to dismantle his structure block by block instead of kicking or knocking it over.

- **Make the child feel a part of the group.** Add the child's name to birthday charts, helper charts, and so on. At the end of the day, affirm to the child how happy you are that he is with you.

Arrival in the Mornings

Separations from caregivers can easily upset foster children who have experienced traumatic separations from biological parents and multiple placements. Many foster children were abruptly removed from their homes by police officers or social workers in the midst of a violent or traumatic family crisis. They may have been taken to a child welfare office, a residential treatment facility, a police station, or a medical facility. They may experience several different moves until a long-term foster or kinship placement can be found.

Not only do these children experience the loss of a parent or caregiver, but they also typically are removed with only the clothes on their backs. Familiar toys, blankets, stuffed animals, and pets remain behind, so children are suddenly thrust into settings with unfamiliar sights, sounds, and smells. Any separation can trigger memories of these traumatic events and cause the child to become dysregulated and to display maladaptive behavior.

Mornings can be difficult for all children but even more so for children from hard places. Many arrive at school in a dysregulated state after rushing through the morning, often without feeding, diapering, or dressing. But even with the best of nurturing care, transitions and separation are often difficult. What happens in the first five minutes upon arrival at child care or school will set the tone for the day. Here are some things to keep in mind:

- **Be aware of environmental triggers that may set a child off.** For example, sometimes entry ways to buildings have tile floors that amplify sound. As adults and children come and go in the morning, the noise and activity level can overwhelm children with sensory issues. Because of the highly individual variables of emotional triggers, the only way adults can figure out those of a particular child is to carefully observe her behavior.

- **Be ready to greet the children as they arrive.** As children enter the room each morning, they need to know that someone is anticipating their arrival. Have your room in order and your supplies for the day ready so you can give your full attention to the children as they arrive. If there is more than one adult in the room, the same person should greet a particular child each day.

- **Reduce your power by getting down to eye level or lower to greet the children.** If a child avoids eye contact, gently brush your index finger under her chin. Most children will at least momentarily make eye contact. If she does, say something like, "Thanks for letting me see those pretty eyes." If the child does not respond to the finger under the chin, say something silly like, "Did you bring your purple eyes to school today?" Comment if she makes eye contact. If not, drop it and try again later in the day. Never force a child to look at you.

Some children feel so threatened by eye contact that they may actually push your face away and scream, "Don't look at me!" You could offer the child sunglasses to "hide" behind. Or, you can put your open hands over your face and look at the child through your fingers. Ask the child if she feels comfortable looking at you "through the fence."

- **Establish rituals for greeting.** For example, you might create a silly handshake, hug, chant, or song. I once watched the director of the lab school at Oklahoma State University greet the children each morning. Every child had a particular way that he or she entered the room. The director took the time to know each child and determine what made each child feel welcome. One child wanted a hug; another wanted a handshake. One went into her office each morning for a piece of candy. It was obvious that each child felt important and wanted. They bounded into the center looking for Ms. Sheeran.

- **Allow children time to feel safe.** Don't immediately snatch babies out of the arms of caregivers or foster parents or immediately take a child by the hand and lead him into the room. Babies especially will need the opportunity to *social reference* the attachment figure that brings them to school. This means that upon seeing the caregiver or teacher the baby will look at the parent, guardian, or foster parent to check that person's facial expression. If a baby sees fear on the parent or guardian's face, the child will withdraw from the teacher. If the baby sees openness and calm, the child will understand that is a safe person. It may take a few minutes for the child to warm up to you.

- **Subtly mirror the child's body language or activity.** If, for example, the child is excited and comes jumping into the room, your body language should be very animated and more exaggerated than usual. If a child comes into the room crying and trying to bury his head in mom's leg, you will want to be more subdued. Match your energy level to the child's.

- **Keep a basket of small trinkets to offer a child who struggles.** Sadly, many infants and children have moved around so much that they have not had time or can't develop an attachment relationship with a foster parent or guardian. These children may have a very difficult time with morning separations since they're unable to use attachment figures to help them feel safe. Often, maltreated children who lack a secure attachment relationship with an adult feel more comfortable with things than with people. Offering a trinket to a child can deflect the intensity of personal interaction and help the child feel safe. Simply say something like, "Susie, would you like to pick something out of my basket to play with?"

- **Acknowledge the child's feelings.** If a child comes into the room hiding behind mom's leg and pulling back, say something like, "Are you having a hard time this morning? Are you wanting to stay with Mom?" Or, if a child comes prancing into the room obviously happy and excited, say something like, "Wow, your smile, bright eyes, and dancing feet tell me that you are really happy today!"

Have some kind of check-in system that facilitates children's growing understanding of their feelings and emotional states. Provide a way for them to assess their own inner states and indicate them on a chart. This will help both children and adults discern strategies for helping self-regulation.

When children enter the room already upset, offer some kind of somatosensory strategy for calming. This will vary from child to child: One child may need to go to the water table to play; another might need to go to the quiet corner to listen to soft music; and another may need to bounce on a therapy ball to self-soothe. Allow children to leisurely ease into the routines and activities of the day.

Some children benefit by carrying a picture of his caregivers in his pocket or placing a photo in his cubby. Framed pictures of families displayed in the classroom can also help children hold an image of a comforting caregiver in his mind.

When we give children a voice for expressing their emotions and help them find strategies for dealing with strong feelings, we lay the foundation for a lifetime of self-control.

- **Acknowledge the parent's or guardian's feelings.** Caregivers and teachers need to recognize and embrace the fact that the family members and guardians often need as much coaching and support as the children on how to navigate the morning routine. Sometimes foster and adoptive parents of a maltreated child are afraid of traumatizing the child even more. They often display high levels of anxiety in their tone of voice and body language. They may cling to the child and ask if she is okay. Some will linger for a long time in the classroom. Acknowledge that these parents have the best of intentions and truly do want to do the right thing.

Address the parent's concerns out of earshot of the child. Explain the difference between manageable and unmanageable challenges. A *manageable challenge* pushes children to their leading edge of capabilities but they can deal with and overcome it with support and encouragement. Children grow by bumping up against manageable challenges and overcoming them. An *unmanageable challenge* is one in which the child cannot cope, even with adult support and encouragement, and it undermines her sense of competence and confidence. Abuse and significant neglect are unmanageable challenges. This is why it is important to know the children well and know where their leading edges of challenge and capabilities lie.

> When we give children a voice for expressing their emotions and help them find strategies for dealing with strong feelings, we lay the foundation for a lifetime of self-control.

Reassure the parent that you will call if the child does not quickly settle down and adjust. My rule of thumb is to call if the child cries inconsolably for thirty minutes. I have never had to call, but that doesn't mean it can't happen. One of the benefits of technology is the ability to snap a picture of a child once she is calm and engaged and to email or text it to the parent. In years past, I have called parents once the child settled down and have described what the child was doing. This simple act had enormous benefit in building relationships with parents.

There may be cases where children have experienced so much trauma that separation is extremely difficult and retraumatizing. In such situations, work with the child's therapist and other support professionals. The child might need to begin by staying for only fifteen or twenty minutes at a time until she starts to feel safe. Early childhood professionals and mental health providers need to work together as a team to develop a plan for the child.

Morning-Routine Tips for Parents and Guardians

- Avoid rushing children in the morning. Allow plenty of time for morning routines.

- On the way to school or child care, talk to the children about what they will do that day. Point out the child's favorite activities.

- If the child is walking, begin the separation process at the car by holding her hand when walking in together.

- Some children may benefit from quiet time with a parent. Overstuffed chairs and love seats in the classroom give parents a place to read a story, sing a song, or quietly talk to a child before leaving. Other children benefit more from a quick goodbye.

- Rituals help. I often use the "Goodbye" chant that children love:

  See ya later, alligator.

  After while, crocodile.

  Be sweet, parakeet.

  Give a hug, ladybug.

  Out the door, dinosaur.

  So long, King Kong.

  "Bye-bye," said the fly.

  Be back soon, raccoon.

- Know the children and what works best for them.

Nap Time

Nap time is a great opportunity to provide individualized attention and nurturing, but it can be a challenging time for children who have suffered maltreatment. Abuse, especially sexual abuse, often happens at night when children are supposedly sleeping in bed. Even a child who has no conscious memory of abuse can suddenly feel unsafe when the shades drawn and the lights turned off. Feelings of vulnerability can overwhelm the child and cause him to become dysregulated.

Also, domestic violence commonly breaks out at bedtime, and children hear frightening sounds of shouting, physical violence, and furniture being shoved around while they cower in bed. Bad things happen in the dark, and quiet means things are about to explode. Intrusive and unwanted thoughts march across the internal screen of a child's mind.

Maltreated children find feeling vulnerable intolerable. They cope with their fears by creating chaos with running, jumping, yelling, and disrupting other children. Maltreated children often cope with feelings of vulnerability through aggressive behavior because aggression feels more tolerable than vulnerability. Trauma-informed teachers and caregivers can look through the lens of compassion and understanding instead of frustration and anger. The teacher will need to think carefully and find ways to help the child feel safe and relax. Here are some strategies to try:

- Put the child's cot near a trusted adult.
- Give the child control regarding where he wants his cot.
- Allow children to take their shoes and socks off before they lie down. Do not take shoes, socks, or any item of clothing off of a child after he lies down. This has the possibility of causing an explosive fear reaction.
- Put a table lamp or night-light near the child.
- Let children take books or quiet activities to their cots to play with for ten to fifteen minutes before they are required to rest on their cots.
- Give the child an iPod or headphones, and let him listen to music.
- Allow children to use transitional objects, such as special blankets or stuffed animals, during nap time.
- Allow the child to have a weighted blanket.
- Fill a gardening glove with rice or dried corn, and sew the opening shut. Put the weighted glove on the child's back.

- Give children flashlights and let them "dance" on the ceiling to music for several minutes before being expected to rest quietly.
- Be very aware of a child's reaction to touch. Some teachers soothe children by rubbing or scratching their backs, which may trigger a fear response in a maltreated child.
- Create a cozy corner by hanging netting from the ceiling on a large plastic hoop. The netting can drape over the child's cot to create the illusion of a cozy and private corner.
- Some children may be so threatened that they cannot bear to lie down on a cot. Let the child rest on a beanbag chair, rocking chair, or simply sit in a chair and do quiet activities.

I know—I can hear some of you saying, "But if we let one child do it, all of the other children will want to do it." One of the key concepts to visit every day with children is that we all get what we need but not necessarily what we want. When we talk about this day in and day out with children, pointing out the many ways that we are all alike and different, children will accept the idea of needs and wants without a great deal of trouble.

I once taught a Sunday school class for five-year-olds at my church. On average, I had around twenty-five children with one other person helping. A very diverse group, it included a child with autism, a child with Down syndrome, and several children with significantly challenging behaviors. The child with autism struggled to sit through story time without becoming disruptive. There happened to be a very large pillow in the room, and as long as Carrie sat on that pillow, she could focus and remain a part of the group. But every week, one little guy named Roger would ask, "How come I don't get a pillow?" And every week I gave the same response: "Roger, you don't need a pillow. You have already learned to sit in group time. We are helping Carrie learn how to be in group time. She is still learning, so I need you to help us out and show her how." Once I explained it, Roger was content to sit without a pillow.

Snack Time

Many maltreated children have anxiety that is often triggered by food-related issues. Starvation in utero touches children at the most primitive of levels. I once knew a family who had adopted twin boys at birth. The children were born to a very young teen mom, who admitted to significant alcohol ingestion while pregnant. This very nurturing, loving family took the twins home from the hospital and gave them all the food they wanted and needed. But as the children grew, one of the twins acted as if he had been starved. He hoarded food, hiding it in his closet and under his mattress, and gorged on snacks. He incessantly

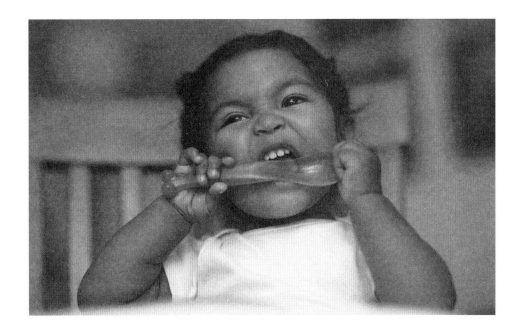

asked for food throughout the day. His behavior was similar to a child who had experienced significant food scarcity in the first years of life.

Children who suffer neglect often have experienced starvation of one degree or another, and abused children commonly have food withheld from them as a punishment for behavior. A basic necessity of life, food taps into our primal need for survival. Unfortunately, adults often misinterpret the confusing behavior triggered by food.

The basic goal in dealing with food issues of maltreated children is to take away the fear regarding availability. One way to do this is to make healthy snacks always available—granola bars, fruit, cheese sticks, turkey rollups, peanut butter and crackers, or nuts appeal to most children. Let them self-select snacks throughout the day as they decide they need to. This strategy eliminates the need for yet another transition into a group snack time event, helps keep sugar levels stable, and helps children learn to read their own internal cues that indicate hunger.

For self-selected snack times to succeed, you need to thoughtfully plan the process. Let the children follow visual recipes that indicate the steps of preparation. Using measuring cups and spoons or using a prescribed number of carrot or celery sticks, for example, can help with gorging issues. Self-selected snack can also help children develop internal awareness by providing visual cues. Try posting a cartoon-like character cut from tagboard, and indicate different levels of hunger on the poster with different levels of color. For example, label them as *not hungry at all*, *a little bit hungry*, *hungry*, *very hungry*, and *famished*. Or, employ humor and label the colors as *hungry as a bird*, *hungry as a mouse, hungry as a dog, hungry as a horse*, and *hungry as an elephant*. Before eating, ask the child to pause, read the message her body is sending, and move a clothespin to the level that matches her hunger. Helping all children learn to listen to the messages of their body teaches them an important life skill.

There will always be children who want seconds or who will try to take more than the amount designated in the recipe—especially those who have a tendency to gorge. That is why it is important to have a visual recipe that the children follow. Instead of saying, "No, you can only have three celery sticks," the caregiver can point to the recipe and say, "The recipe says only three celery sticks and three tablespoons of peanut butter." It deflects from the issue becoming a power struggle with the teacher and makes it an issue with the recipe. When children ask for more after eating, make it a routine practice to require them to wait twenty minutes. Nutritionists indicate that it takes the body twenty minutes to process food and communicate the degree of satiation back to the brain. Use a visual timer to track the twenty-minute waiting period. Then the child can come back, do an internal check, and have more if she desires.

When children take food, do not view it as a moral issue and label it as stealing. Taking food is a survival issue for a maltreated child and indicates that the child does not yet feel safe with regard to the availability of food. This child may need to carry a granola bar in her pocket when she goes out to the playground or have a snack by her cot. It takes a great deal of patience to help a child recover from the primitive fear of food scarcity.

Using the Restroom

It is not uncommon for maltreated children to struggle with toileting issues for many reasons. There is a direct relationship between the stress response and the "gut." In fact, research by Michael Gershon, author of *The Second Brain: A Groundbreaking New Understanding of Nervous Disorders of the Stomach and Intestine*, indicates that the "gut" is the second brain. Children who have experienced abuse and neglect often struggle with potty training. This will require a great deal of patience and understanding by parents, caregivers, and teachers. Many early childhood programs require that children must be potty trained by age three to enroll in the program. This expectation is unrealistic for some children.

- Chronic stress compromises the digestive system and causes children to have stomachaches, constipation, and/or diarrhea. All of the energy resources of the body redirect to deal with the stress at hand. Digestion powers down in the face of threat.
- Some maltreated children struggle with the interoceptive sense. This means they are unaware of the internal messages related to toileting issues

communicated by their bodies. They have no awareness of their urge to go to the bathroom.

■ Chronic constipation can put pressure on the bladder, making it difficult for a child to empty his bladder. He may use the restroom and shortly thereafter insist on going again. Adults may misinterpret this behavior as "fooling around" or making things up, but it is very possible that the child is experiencing bladder issues.

■ Some children experience a lack of body integrity and struggle with the capacity to view themselves as a whole. Letting go of something produced by their body is experienced as a loss of self and is frightening. They will often hold their stool out of fear. Related to the issues of body integrity, some children also fear going down the drain or being flushed down the toilet.

■ Some children experience separation anxiety when they go to the restroom. They struggle with object constancy and the capacity to hold the image of a comforting caregiver in mind.

■ Some children may only want to go to the restroom with adult supervision. They have exaggerated fears of monsters and other scary images.

■ Children who have experienced sexual abuse have had uncomfortable sensations related to their genital areas, which may make using the toilet uncomfortable.

In any early childhood setting, bathrooms with child-sized accommodations should be in the room or directly adjacent to the room. Children should be allowed to use the restroom any time they feel the need to do so. Having designated bathroom breaks is not in the best interest of children for a couple of reasons: It is difficult for children to line up and wait for everyone to take a turn using the restroom, and the unnecessary waiting sets children up for behavior problems.

Also, making children wait to use the restroom at a designated time undermines the development of self-regulation. When a child needs to use the restroom and is told, "No, it's not time," it invalidates the messages communicated by the child's body. Eventually, the child becomes numb to those internal messages. Maltreated children have already been put into situations that violate and compromise physical sensations and internal messages. They need support in learning to pay attention to their bodies.

Toileting issues, therefore, must be handled with a great deal of sensitivity and compassion. Adults should never shame a child for having a toileting accident or ridicule a child who struggles with potty training. Telling a child that he is supposed to be a "big boy" and not wet his pants is inappropriate.

Meeting children's individual needs in the context of rituals and routines is a key element of a trauma-informed environment; however, it can be challenging to caregivers. A common objection I often hear is that if something is done for one child, it should be done for all. When a child complains about someone getting something that he doesn't get, I simply say, "Everyone gets what they need in our classroom, not necessarily what they want. You don't need what Joey has. You have other needs, and when you need something you will get it."

Rethinking Group Time

In a typical day in the early childhood classroom, beginning at age three, children come together for group time or circle time. This is a teacher-directed activity in which specific activities and experiences meet learning goals and teach concepts and skills. I like to think of large-group time as sort of a "family" time when children come together, participate in shared activities, and experience a sense of community. This is, however, often a difficult time for children from hard places. But before addressing the challenges, I first want to comment on group time with infants and toddlers.

It is inappropriate to expect children under three to participate in a mandatory large-group time. With infants and toddlers, we have what I call spontaneous group times. Young children are naturally herders; they tend to cluster together around an attachment figure, much like chicks cluster around a mother hen. A caregiver might sit down on the floor with a book, a talk box, or a puzzle, for example, and children will come and go as their interest waxes and wanes. There is no expectation for all to participate nor is there an expectation for them to remain for a designated length of time. A spontaneous group activity, despite its name, is thoughtfully planned. Teachers and caregivers intentionally choose activities to teach specific concepts and skills as determined by the developmental needs of the children. With infants and toddlers, there will be many spontaneous group times occurring throughout the day.

As children grow and mature, their capacity for self-regulation and focused attention increases. At three years of age, it is appropriate to expect them to come together for a short period of time to engage in group activities that are interesting and developmentally appropriate.

When children are disruptive during group time, we have to think like detectives and figure out what the behavior is telling us. I want to caution you, however, about immediately assuming there is something amiss with the child. Ask yourself some questions: Am I contributing to the problem? Are my group times too long or too boring? Are the activities developmentally appropriate for the age? Am I tapping into the children's interests? Are my expectations appropriate? Do my activities include movement and sensory input? Once those questions are addressed, then you need to think about the environment or the context. Is the meeting space too cramped? Do I help children define their space? Does group time take place at a time of day when children are alert? Are the children hungry or tired? Do I transition the children well into group time?

Lastly, we can make some educated guesses as to what might be going on with an individual child. Is there a sensory issue? Does the child need a fidget or to sit in a rocking chair rather than on the floor? Am I planning activities that appeal to this particular child's interest and ability? Thoughtfully plan your group times with developmental milestones and early learning guidelines, as well as the needs of children, in mind. Children from hard places often have difficulty with group time, however, for a number of reasons:

- **Spatial awareness:** Children with proprioceptive issues have difficulty knowing where their bodies are in space. It is not unusual for this child to sit on other children or invade another child's personal space. Bumping into other children is an attempt to define the boundaries of her body and know where she is in space. This behavior is often misconstrued as antisocial or aggressive. It is important to provide tools for the child to identify personal space. Listed below are strategies for helping a child with proprioceptive issues.
    - Provide a carpet square for the child to sit on.
    - Let the child sit inside a large plastic hoop.
    - Let the child hold a sand baby or a lap buddy. These are small, weighted, pillow-like forms usually filled with sand, rice, or beans. They should weigh 3 to 4 pounds.
    - Let the child sit on a therapy ball or partially inflated beach ball.
    - Let the child sit on a large pillow or towel.
    - Let the child sit inside a clothesbasket with a pillow or in a small cardboard copy-paper box.
- **Difficulty focusing:** Children with a history of trauma are often hypervigilant and can get distracted by every movement or sound in the environment. It helps some children to hold a fidget or stuffed animal. Activities should be sensory rich and include things to see, hear, touch, smell, and taste. Include opportunities to wiggle and move.
- **Blurting out:** Children with impulse control often blurt out answers to every question.

- Practice group conversation skills. Explain to children that what they say is important, but when everyone talks at once it is difficult to hear anyone. Ask the group several simple questions such as, "What is your favorite ice cream?" or "What is your favorite color?" and have them all answer at the same time. Point out how difficult it was to hear anyone speak. Then introduce activities that give children an opportunity to practice group conversations.
- Use a talking stick. A rain stick or glow ball also works well for this purpose. The stick or glow ball gets passed from person to person as they take turns talking.
- Use answer tickets. For the child who likes to dominate, give her a designated number of tickets. Each time the child answers a question, she has to give you a ticket or put one in a jar. When her tickets are gone, she can no longer answer questions. This gives very concrete learners a visual cue that reminds them to think about what they say and to control their impulse to speak.
- Put each child's name on an ice-pop stick, and draw sticks out of a can to let them take turns talking. If a child wants to "pass," draw another name.
- Use thumbs up and thumbs down. Ask agree-or-disagree questions, and have the children respond accordingly with their thumbs. You can also have children stand up or sit down.
- Make individual flannel boards using pieces cut from cardboard boxes and felt. Instead of having one child come to a large flannel board to create a pattern, illustrate directionality, or create a shape picture, each child can create his own response on his own flannel board.
- Paint small sections of plywood or inexpensive cookie sheets with chalkboard paint or magnetic paint. Children can respond on their personal chalk boards or magnet boards.
- Think, Pair, Share is a common strategy whereby children respond to questions and discuss with a neighbor.

- **Difficulty sitting in group time**: Hypervigilant children sometimes have a hard time maintaining focused attention and managing their behavior in group time. It is not uncommon for some to get up and walk away or completely disrupt the group. The goal is to help them find ways to self-regulate and participate for short periods of time and to gradually increase the time they are expected to participate. Once again, keep in mind that many children from hard places are emotionally and psychologically about half of their chronological ages, and expectations must be adjusted accordingly.

The goal is to help children find socially appropriate ways to get their needs met and replace the inappropriate behavior with appropriate behavior.

For example, I once encountered a child with a fierce need to control everything in her environment. She was five years old but could only handle group time for about five minutes. She would get up and wander the room and do as she pleased. This was obviously very distracting and disruptive to the other children. I made an agreement with her that she didn't have to stay in group time if she didn't want to, but she had to ask permission to leave the group, and she could no longer do as she pleased. She could either draw with markers or play with playdough. I chose these two activities because I knew they were enjoyable to her. This wasn't entirely successful as she made a big production when she left the group by wanting to say goodbye to everyone. The one success that I celebrated in this situation was the fact that the child no longer roamed the room. Keep in mind that we gently nudge children toward healing and behavioral change; it rarely comes overnight. After further brainstorming, I gave her two tickets and told her that instead of asking permission to leave group time she could simply hand me a ticket each time she wished to leave. When her tickets were gone, she would need to stay in group time. Little by little her capacity to self-regulate increased. I can't guarantee this would happen with every child, but the tickets were a concrete symbol of both choice and limits. Over time, the expectation to participate increased as the child's capacity grew.

When you are working with a child to self-regulate in group time, do a behavioral rehearsal. At a time when other children are not around, role-play a group-time experience, and let the child practice asking appropriately, leaving group time quietly, and going to another part of the room for the alternate activity. Then practice quietly re-entering the group.

On the opposite end of the spectrum, some children are so withdrawn that they find it very threatening to participate in group experiences. The child may sit on the fringes with her head down or even sit at a distance from the group and just watch. Some children are naturally slow to warm up by temperament, but, typically, once a shy child finally decides to enter an activity, she is all in. With a child who has a trauma history, however, fear—not temperament—likely drives the withdrawn behavior. Group activities put this child in freeze or flight mode. Emotional safety is critical for her. Invite the child to sit next to you. Give her a job to do, such as holding the book as you read or passing out the rhythm instruments. Do not overwhelm her and push too hard.

You also will encounter children with such a high need for control that they try to usurp group time. They may do so overtly and literally pull the book out of your hands, or they may beg to pass out materials. Some are very good at hijacking group discussions to talk about their own agenda. Every time you come together, state your expectations for behavior. Remind the child that you are the "boss," and remind him when it is your turn to do something. For example, I enjoy playing the autoharp with children, but when I first introduce it in a group-time setting, the more aggressive children literally jump up to play it. For several weeks, every time I get the instrument out, I explain to them that it's their turn to play it during interest-center time, but I play it during group time. Children who struggle with self-regulation have difficulty with this concept, but over time they manage.

Types of Group Times

Over the years, I have often seen "calendar" dominate group time. Not only do we need to think differently about guidance, but we also need to rethink traditional approaches to the content. In some settings, learning the days of the week and months and noting the weather is all that is accomplished in large group. This ritual has little meaning for children under the age of seven, as calendar time is a developmental concept that young children do not yet understand. There are many more important things to talk about and do in large group.

Group time should be rich in content with social-emotional understandings woven throughout. Therapeutic programs offer many purposes and formats for group-time experiences. Theraplay uses Sunshine Circles; a Trust-Based Relational Intervention (TBRI) approach uses nurture groups and life-skill groups to teach social-emotional skills; the Alert Program uses group activities to develop self-regulation. More information about these programs is listed in the appendix on page 243.

The needs, interests, and attention spans of the children should inform what you do in group time. Some broad categories of activities appropriate for group time in a trauma-informed classroom include the following:

- **Check In:** This approach is discussed in detail on pages 142–143. In the beginning of this ritual, many children will ask for lots of bandages, but the novelty quickly wears off and they begin to target specific hurts. Often, their reports become more about their emotional hurts rather than their physical hurts. The purpose in this activity is for children to give and receive empathetic care and to learn to share emotions. Caregivers and teachers should expect for children to share uncomfortable things. For example, a foster child might blurt out, "It hurts when they say you can't be a part of this family anymore." Or, another child might say, "I was scared last night because my dad threw the ladies out of the house. He threw all of their clothes in the front yard and yelled at them to get out." In situations like this, adults can acknowledge the child's feelings and assist the rest of the children to find ways they can help. In the example of the foster child, you could ask how it made her feel and then ask the children to think of ways that they can be good friends and help her feel better today. Discussing the details of a situation with a group of young children would not be appropriate, but you could—and should—talk with the foster child privately and get other professionals involved to help her.

■ **Creative movement and music:** Music and rhythmic movement are great ways to bring children together and help them to emotionally and cognitively organize. They are also ways of developing certain regulatory skills. Sing songs that involve starting and stopping or a variation of volume or tempo. Give children streamers, scarves, ribbons, or construction tape to move and dance with to music. March or sing with rhythm-band instruments. Dance on a gathering drum.

■ **Games:** Play games that involve starting and stopping, mimicking one another, moving at different speeds, or working together. For example, play Simon Says; turn on a metronome and have the leader make movements that coordinate in time with the metronome while the rest of the group mimics; pair the children and give them a towel and a fidget or ball. They each hold on to one end of the towel and use it to toss the fidget or ball into the air. The goal is to catch it with the towel.

■ **Feeding each other a bite of food:** This activity can seem strange and may feel uncomfortable at first, but it targets a need of maltreated children and is a recommended Theraplay practice. Most maltreated children have difficulty accepting nurture from someone else because they are accustomed to taking care of themselves. Get some kind of food that can easily be fed to another child with a straw, fingers, or small fork. For example, get a package of Life Savers (or any kind of candy that has a hole in the middle) and straws. Give every child a straw. Pass around a plate of candy, and let the children take turns asking one another if they would like one. If a child says yes, the nurturer feeds her a Life Saver with a straw. Another strategy is to serve a crunchy food and listen for the loudest crunch. For example, pass around a plate of pretzels and each child asks another, "Would you like a bite of a pretzel?" If the second child says yes, the nurturer holds the pretzel so her friend can take a bite.

■ **Novelty:** The brain takes notice of novel experiences, and this is a way of capturing the attention of reluctant children. I collect trinkets from the party section of discount stores and use these as interest grabbers and ways to practice self-regulation. For example, I bought tiny flying saucers that we can launch into the air. Of course the children found these very attractive and immediately wanted to launch them. But before I passed the saucers out, I explained that we were going to stick together and launch them all at once. I made a big deal about waiting for everyone to get a saucer so we could all launch. I intentionally heightened their expectation and enthusiasm while expecting them to inhibit their impulse to play until the appointed time. This is a difficult thing for all children, but especially for children with a trauma history. I showed them what to do, and on the count of three, we launched them in the air. Small experiences such as this can help children learn to manage intense emotion.

- **Reading:** Read social stories that you have created about situations in your room. Role-play strategies for solving problems. Use puppets to act out appropriate interactions. Read and discuss books about emotions and social dilemmas. Make shared reading an interactive opportunity, not just a passive listening experience. Provide ways for the children to participate and respond to the story. Some stories lend themselves to movement experiences, some to sound effects, and others to active response. For example, children can indicate how a character feels throughout the story by drawing a feeling face on his individual chalkboard or by placing a felt feeling face on the board. Active involvement holds children's interest.
- **Sharing news:** Ask children to share daily news. This gives children opportunity to share personal stories and narratives about their lives.

In group time, I have had moments with children that almost seem magical, but these pleasant memories don't happen without a great deal of planning and thoughtful preparation. When you are working with a new group of children, especially if you have several children with a history of trauma, the first weeks and months will be spent focusing on basic skills related to listening, speaking, and self-regulation.

Chapter 10

Implications for Approaches to Learning

During a conference, a child care director pulled me aside and asked for some help and insight into a four-year-old child who seemingly didn't know how to play. During interest centers and outdoor play, she stood by the adults and refused to engage, despite coaxing from the teachers. I probed into the child's background and quickly discovered that her mom and dad were in the midst of a messy divorce. Her mom did not have an adult support group, so she used her daughter as her confidante and looked to her for comfort. This little girl knew all of the sordid details of her parents' sexual escapades and their volatile relationship. Sadly, this four-year-old was expected to bear an inappropriate burden for which she was psychologically unprepared, and the weight of it was robbing her of her childhood. Preoccupation with psychological or physical survival consumes children's inner resources and inhibits their curiosity and desire to play.

Play-Based Curriculum

Open-ended, child-initiated play has long been at the heart of developmentally appropriate practice. However, in our current culture of accountability and standardized testing, play is often disregarded in favor of "real" learning—even at the youngest ages. Three- and four-year-old classrooms in child care centers and public schools may look like elementary classrooms. In at-risk schools where there is typically a large population of children who have experienced trauma, the argument is often made that because these children are "behind," they need more skill-and-drill time to increase their academic performance. Others reject play-based environments on the premise that the children would run wild if they were allowed to play. The truth is that a healing environment is a play-based environment.

> A healing environment is a play-based environment.

Dr. Stuart Brown has spent his life researching and studying play. As part of his work, he studied the lives of violent offenders incarcerated in Texas prisons and found that the absence of play in childhood is a strong predictor of criminal activity. On the other hand, he found that the tendency toward violence among at-risk children diminished when they were given opportunities for open-ended, child-initiated play.

There are three basic elements of open-ended play that set it apart from more structured forms.

- Open-ended play activities are freely chosen by the child and based on individual interests and abilities. A developmentally appropriate and healing environment provides a variety of choices that give children the chance to participate in many different forms of play. For a significant portion of the day, the children are involved in child-initiated activity during interest-center time and outdoor play.
- The sheer pleasure of the play experience motivates the child to pursue and remain engaged in the play, often repeating a certain activity over and over again. There is nothing more enjoyable to me than seeing young children totally absorbed in play. It is as if time stands still and a child's entire being is caught up in the experience. These are sacred moments.
- Children make the rules of open-ended play. At first glance, it may seem that open-ended play has no rules. However, if you watch closely you will realize that there are unspoken rules that are clearly understood by all of the children. Adults usually don't know the rules until someone breaks one; then, it becomes very clear. For example, the children are playing "pizza shop" in the dramatic play center. Everyone is happily engaged, carrying out their roles until Henry suddenly stops sweeping the floor of the restaurant, waves the broom

in the air, and declares that he is Zorro. The play stops. All eyes turn to Henry and words of protest erupt: "You can't do that!" "That's not your job." The child must either negotiate a new role, return to sweeping, or leave the play. Children who consistently break the unspoken rules are often excluded from play.

The Benefits of Play

Therapists and psychiatrists have long recognized the therapeutic value of play. They use different forms of play therapy to help children heal. A trauma-informed classroom is one where rich, open-ended opportunities for child-centered play are at the heart of the curriculum.

- **Play disarms fear**. In a play-based environment, children have an element of control that helps them feel safe. They are free to choose activities that allow them to gain a sense of mastery that builds their self-confidence.

- **Play mimics important and purposeful behavior**. For example, as children play "house," not only do they approximate the behaviors involved in being an adult, but they also practice important life skills, such as negotiation and planning.

- **Play allows children from hard places to regain their voice**. The child's voice refers to his needs, desires, wishes, interests, and abilities. The cry of a baby is his legitimate voice and his way to signal for help from his caregiver. When no one responds to a baby's cry or when his cry is met with abuse, his voice will slowly silence because he learns that no one will respond. In the most extreme cases, a baby will stop crying altogether. As the baby moves into toddlerhood, his curiosity can provoke anger and abuse from fragile parents, who see the toddler's natural desire to explore the world and practice developing skills as "making a mess" or even disobedience. When children hear *no* every time they initiate an activity, or their curiosity is met with shame, humiliation, or abuse, they will stop exploring. The message they internalize is that their preferences, interests, and individuality don't matter. Their voice is taken away.

  A play-based environment gives children the opportunity to regain their voice because it gives them a safe place to assert their will, act upon their desires and interests, and hone their skills and abilities. They can make choices regarding what and who to play with. Their interests and areas of skill are validated as they have opportunities to engage in activities with high appeal.

■ **Play reduces shame and helps children regain a sense of competence.** When children grow up in homes with domestic violence, neglect, and abuse, their legitimate needs take a back seat to the addictions, conflicts, and dysfunctions of the adults in the home. They interpret their circumstances as an indication that something is wrong with them, and the burden of shame takes root. Self-confidence is undermined, and they develop a sense of profound helplessness that they are not effective enough to get even their basic needs met.

In a rich, play-based environment, children have the opportunity to master and accomplish many things. As they choose materials that are of personal interest, they experience the satisfaction of completing a challenging puzzle, painting a picture, successfully telling a story with puppets, or creating an intricate structure with blocks. They gain confidence in their skills to make things happen. When other children join in and help them build a fort or help them with a collage, they gain the confidence that they can make and be a friend.

■ **Play gives children an avenue for self-expression.** Authentic play bubbles up from the inner life of the child and gives him creative opportunities to express his true self. Through dramatic play, art, writing, and construction, children can find creative outlets to find their true identity. It is a way for them to bring order out of chaos and make a shattered life whole.

Scientists have noted that mammals play more prolifically during times of rapid brain development. This is believed to be true for humans as well. Playful activity facilitates the organization of the brain. Early in the development of the human brain, cells organize and migrate to different regions where they become differentiated and assigned a particular task. However, there is a group of cells that has no determined function. When playful activity activates these cells, they spring into action to help the brain organize. Because play originates in the brain stem and extends throughout the limbic brain and cortex, play is critical to the formation of the brain architecture.

Components of a Trauma-Informed Play-Based Environment

A Musical Climate

Music and creative movement have long been key components of a quality early childhood environment. The research of Perry and others has confirmed the restorative powers of music for children who have suffered trauma and indicates that rhythmic movement helps organize a disorganized brain.

Rhythm and movement begin in the prenatal experience as the infant floats in a cocoon of fluid, experiencing the movement of his mom's body and listening to the steady and constant beat of her heart. Our heartbeat and breathing have a rhythm. Our bodies function according to predictable rhythmic cycles, including menstrual cycles, diurnal cortisol cycles, and sleep cycles. Rhythm and movement activate the brain stem and help a disorganized brain to organize. Singing in a group increases endorphins and oxytocin in the brain. These chemicals are associated with pleasure and happiness and serve to relieve stress and anxiety. Perry asserts that rhythmic experiences harken back

to the safety experienced in the womb. For example, a child care provider told me about a foster child in her care. During nap time, he asked to climb in her lap as she rocked in the rocking chair. He said, "I want to hear your heart because it makes me feel safe."

Musical experiences are an important piece of a trauma-informed environment. Instead of thinking of music as a special program or activity designated for a specific period of the day, think of creating a musical climate. Musical experiences should infuse the entire day. Singing, walking, dancing, and moving together increase cooperativeness and sense of belonging to a group, elements that are important for maltreated children. Throughout the day, have both spontaneous and planned experiences involving rhythm and movement.

- Sing to infants and toddlers as you rock and diaper them.
- Sing a greeting to children when they arrive in the morning.
- Sing a goodbye song when they leave in the afternoon.
- Sing to signal transitions.

- Sing just for fun.
- Sing instructions to children.
- Play quiet music during rest times.

Good classroom management requires the ability to manage the energy levels of the classroom. Throughout the day, effective caregivers and teachers bring children together much like a mother hen gathers her chicks for brief moments of orientation and calm and then sends them out again to explore the world. Musical songs, games, and activities are a great way to "gather the chicks," help them to regulate, and then send them out again.

- March with rhythm-band instruments.
- Provide a variety of music.
- Do rhythm-stick activities.
- Have children echo a rhythm created with rhythm sticks.
- Dance with scarves, ribbons, or construction tape.
- "Skate" to music on paper plates.
- Sing call-and-response songs.
- Have children jump to a rhythmic beat on a gathering drum.
- Teach children simple folk dances.

Language-Rich Environment

It is well established that children who come from hard places typically have a language delay. Children who experience significant neglect and abuse don't have a consistently available attachment figure to motivate and facilitate language.

A baby learns to speak out of a desire to communicate with those who take great delight in him. In an attachment relationship, children listen to and begin to mimic those who provide loving care. The baby begins to coo, babble, and make initiations to interact out of an innate drive to connect. However, when adults are unavailable or hurtful, the drive to connect shuts down, and language does not develop in a typical fashion.

In a healthy attachment relationship, a baby and his caregiver develop a partnership whereby they begin to share joint attention. This means that as babies become increasingly aware of their surroundings, they begin to point out things in their environment to their caregivers. Typically a baby will point at something, look at the caregiver, and perhaps even grunt as if to ask, "What is it?" Attuned parents and caregivers notice these gestures and join the baby in looking at an object, typically saying something like, "Bird. The bird flies in the sky and says, 'Tweet, tweet.'" The adult labels the object, describes its function, and provides additional facts. Through these short interactions, day in and day out, the baby begins to label and organize his world and to develop conceptual understandings of how the world works.

Children who experience abuse and neglect often lack this basic orientation to the world. Primary caregivers are either not present at all or are too overwhelmed with life's challenges to engage in these short interactions. For others, mom or dad may be passed out on the couch from substance abuse. In other instances, babies spend long hours alone in a crib with little human interaction. No one interprets and labels the world for them.

As a result, language development lags behind before it ever gets started. They enter child care or kindergarten without the most basic vocabulary. They don't know the words for basic household items, fruits, vegetables, animals, and ordinary things found in the environment. And not only do they lack basic vocabulary, but they may not know the function of the most ordinary objects. They don't know animal sounds and can't identify the most basic sounds in the environment because no one has taken the time to label and organize their world. They live in a world of chaos that makes little sense.

Therefore, a trauma-informed environment gives children a lot to talk about. A play-based environment is a language-rich environment; academically oriented environments are not. The academically oriented curriculum focuses narrowly on letters, numbers, colors, sounds, and shapes. Such an impoverished learning context does not meet the real needs of children from hard places. There is not a lot to talk about when the focus of daily activities is narrowed to a few skills.

> A play-based environment is a language-rich environment.

Yet another reason maltreated children lack language is limited life experiences. We need to provide children a rich and varied life experience to give them lots to talk about. We can take them to the zoo, to the grocery store, to the park, and to church. We can go on walks in the neighborhood, visit relatives, and watch worms crawl in the dirt. Maltreated children often lack these most basic experiences. They may sit in dimly lit rooms in front of a television or in a crib and are typically isolated from neighbors and extended family. They rarely go anywhere and encounter very few people. I had a six-year-old foster child in my home who had never seen a Christmas tree and did not know what "the things" on the tree were. Her understanding of the world and how it works was very limited.

Errorless Learning

I once observed a class of three-year-olds in a child care setting. The children went to another room to participate in music. At the end of the session, the teacher announced that it was time to choose the "star student" of the day. She invited a little girl to the front of the group to give her a sticker to attach to her clothing because she had supposedly followed all of the rules and was the best behaved of all the children. I watched the crestfallen faces of the remaining three-year-olds.

I am not suggesting that all of the children should have received a sticker. Quite the contrary. We have decades of research to indicate that punishment and reward do little to create real change in young children's behavior or academic performance. Our goal is to help children meet developmental milestones and reach their potential so they can make a contribution to the world. Mistakes and errors provide opportunities for children to problem solve and find solutions—not to receive a grade, a star, or score on a test. Behavioral issues are opportunities for correction and instruction, not reward and punishment. Standardized tests don't tell astute teachers anything they don't already know through observation. Stickers and stars won't fix children's behavior.

I first heard the term *errorless learning* from Purvis, and it sums up what good early childhood classrooms are about. Errorless learning means that making mistakes is okay. Children can try again until they master a skill. When children live in fear of failing an evaluation or not getting an award, valuable psychological energy shifts away from learning and only further pushes maltreated children deeper into a fear-based, shame-based orientation to life. Take time to celebrate children's daily accomplishments. Take pictures of children's "I did it!" moments, and post them on the wall. At the end of the day, bring children together to share new things they learned or accomplished that day.

Conceptually Rich Curriculum

Maltreated children often have very limited life experiences. Poverty and neglect can force them into an existence focused on survival. Sometimes the abusive or neglectful adults in children's lives intentionally limit their experiences outside the home to prevent anyone from finding out what is going on behind closed doors. Also, such adults are often isolated themselves and have very few connections in the community. Therefore, their children are isolated, too, and don't have the opportunity to engage in the most basic moments of life that many of us take for granted. A trauma-informed classroom introduces children to the world and how it works.

One time, I was in a facility playing with a five-year-old foster child. He had a collection of dinosaurs to which he assigned family roles. For an hour, we played with the dinos, packing up the dinosaur family and moving them from place to place. At each new "home," I asked the child what the mom and dad dinosaur were doing, and he always replied, "Sleeping on the couch." This child was removed from the home because of drug use, so I can only imagine how often he saw his parents sleeping on the couch. While they were passed out, this little boy had to fend for himself, and he obviously had very few typical life experiences.

We provide a conceptually rich curriculum through books and discussion, topics of investigation, and sensory-rich experiences. I often hear developmentally appropriate practice defined as "hands-on" and "fun;" however, a lot that is hands-on and fun that has little educational value to the child. I like to think of developmentally appropriate practice as being "minds-on" and engaging.

In the early childhood classroom, several large group times are infused throughout the day. In a skills-driven environment, one common activity is calendar time. Children come together to identify the day of the week and usually put some kind of marker on the particular day. Children sing songs and chant the days of the week or months. The weather is addressed in some way, usually with cartoonish characters. Children may also be drilled on colors, numbers, letters, or shapes using flash cards or charts.

A group time of this nature is impoverished in conceptually rich understandings and very limited in scope. The typical child does not understand calendar time until somewhere between ages six and seven. They may memorize the days of the week but have no understanding of what *week* means with regard to the passing of time.

Group time should introduce children to conceptual understandings and not just skills. Carefully choose books, activities, and discussion on a variety of topics. The following ideas will give you a framework for choosing learning activities that are rich in concepts.

- **Form and Function:** This would include books and materials related to simple machines; vehicles; movement of people, animals, and things; human and animal bodies; and habitats.
- **Systems:** This would include books and materials related to families; communities; the human body; life cycles of plants, insects, birds, and animals; ecosystems such as desert, mountain, farm, jungle, ocean, city, and country; systems of production and delivery such as the mail system or the process of moving milk from the farm to the store; habitats; and cultures.
- **Growth and Change:** This would include books and activities related to seasons, life cycles, weather, and human growth and development.
- **Alike and Different:** This would include books and activities related to making comparisons of size, shape, color, texture, form, function, association, and culture.
- **Cause and Effect:** This would include books and activities related to emotions, simple machines, cooking experiences, and movement.

An inquiry-based curriculum encourages children to think, make connections between ideas, and investigate the world in a hands-on fashion.

Chapter 11

Organizing the Trauma-Informed Classroom for Play

Open-ended play does not mean chaos prevails. A play-based learning environment should offer enough structure for the children to feel safe and contained—especially the traumatized child. That includes a consistent and predictable schedule and thoughtfully chosen, organized materials. Divide the room into smaller cozy corners with themed materials grouped together to evoke a particular kind of play.

The Dramatic Play Center

Most early childhood classrooms have a dramatic play center or a place in the room called "housekeeping." In this spot, one typically finds child-sized kitchen appliances, a table and chairs, and dolls and doll accessories. This is designed to represent "home," but for children from hard places, home is the context of abuse, neglect, and trauma. The housekeeping center often can be the backdrop for children to play out the events and scenarios of their lives and can serve as a therapeutic setting to help them process the anxiety, fear, and sadness that they carry deep inside.

Adults often fear encouraging traumatized children to talk about their emotions and worry when children begin to enact the trauma that they have experienced—perhaps the child will become hysterical or overwhelmed by her emotions and scare the other children. This usually is not the case, however. Dramatic play provides a safe and containing context in which children can freely explore and express emotions and real-life events. Because the child has control over the storyline, the scripts, and the images that are created, the play only becomes as intense as the child can handle. As children enact the events over and over again, they can process the events in smaller, more manageable portions until the power diminishes and they can absorb the impact.

If we don't provide the context and issue invitations for children to play out the themes of their lives, we will have to deal with the fallout of unresolved anxiety and emotions in a more disruptive way. Children's emotions constantly brew below the surface and will spill over into classroom life. The meltdown on the playground may not really be about someone breaking in line but about the feelings of fear and vulnerability sparked by the domestic violence the child witnessed the night before. Someone pushing her aside and taking her rightful place in line is yet another indication to the child that she doesn't matter and is invisible.

Depending upon the situation and the strength of the relationship with family members, teachers can discuss children's concerns with parents or guardians and work together to help the child feel safe. But often this is a delicate situation. It is also imperative that teachers *document, document, document* the child's behavior and conversations to help other professionals who may be involved get a clear picture of what is taking place and the effects on the child. Teachers need to continually monitor the play and step in when needed to help the child process the emotion. Here are some questions and comments that teachers can ask to help the child make sense of the experience:

- Who was there?
- What happened?

- What was it like for you?
- Is there anyone or anything that helped make it better?
- Is there anyone or anything that made it worse?
- Is there anything that you would like to say to Mom? Dad? another person?
- What would have helped you feel safe when this happened?
- Is there anything you need now?
- Let's make a plan for what you can do if this happens again.

For example, if a child reports that Mom and her boyfriend yell and scream a lot, the teacher can help the child think of a place in her house where she feels safe. She might suggest that the child keep a blanket or other items of comfort in this area. When the yelling begins, she can go to this spot and wait until the arguing ends. Obviously, if the child reports abuse, the teacher needs to contact the authorities.

Symbolic Representation

Dramatic play has many benefits, but facilitating the development of symbolic representation is one of the most important. The capacity to represent one object with another lays the foundation for more complex ideas, such as understanding the alphabet, a complex, visual symbol system representing the discrete sounds of language. Before a child can master the alphabet, she must handle basic symbol systems such as those experienced in dramatic play.

Young children have a natural interest in exploring the themes of power and powerlessness, good and evil, justice and injustice, and love and hate. Although most children, especially four-year-olds, typically embrace these themes to one degree or another, these themes dominate the play of traumatized children. In a safe and containing environment, children can personify evil in terms of monsters, villains, bad guys, or witches. They can master their fears by taking on the persona of good guy, police officer, army person, or a more powerful other. Often, they role-play the superheroes

they see on TV. For many traumatized children, television functions as an electronic baby sitter and defines the scope of their world. They can watch whatever and whenever they please as long as they don't bother the adults.

There has been debate over the role that TV superheroes should play in an early childhood classrooms. Some insist that TV superheroes have no role at all, while others suggest they can serve a purpose in the lives of young children. My primary objections to superheroes conceived in the minds of adults are these:

- Commercialized superheroes are created to market products to our very youngest children. They are not created with the purpose of helping children deal with existential issues.

- Commercialized superhero figures come with very scripted and restricted storylines that squelch imagination. The themes of superhero cartoons are high on action, power, and violence and low on creativity and problem solving. Saturating children in adult-created media restricts the imaginative play that bubbles up from the inside of children.

So how do we solve this dilemma? Do we allow superhero or pretend gun play in the classroom with traumatized children? If dramatic play can help children process the often troubling and difficult events of their lives, how do we do it appropriately?

When children have the opportunity and freedom to create personifications of good and evil that are psychologically safe for them, it becomes an emotionally healing experience.

Instead of encouraging adult-created superheroes, invite the children to create their own. Talk about what superheroes do—they help people and keep them safe. Give children the opportunity to invent their own superhero identities and decide what each superhero does to help people. Give them towels or pieces of fabric and some clothespins to make capes. Let each child design a logo for her superhero identity.

The dramatic play center does not have to remain just a housekeeping center. In fact, if materials never change, children will lose interest and avoid playing there. As teachers listen to the conversations of children and observe their interactions, they can gain insight into the things that weigh on children's minds and inform daily life in the classroom. If, for example, the police showed up at a child's door late at night, or if a child heard gunshots and saw red and blue lights outside, the teacher could place props such as police uniforms, CB radios, police badges, walkie-talkies, clip boards, and pencils in the dramatic play center. Add books related to police officers as well. If you have enough room, the housekeeping equipment can stay in place, and you can set up a police station in another part of the room. If space is an issue, the home-living center can be moved out or repurposed for inclusion in another setting. Here are some other ideas for props that invite children to play:

- Firefighter coats (yellow raincoats or ponchos)
- Fire hoses (old garden hose)
- Fire-hose mounts (mount hose reel on the wall in the classroom or outside on the playground equipment near the fire hose)
- Firefighter hats
- Oxygen tanks (Make oxygen tanks out of 2-liter pop bottles fastened together with tape, and attach plastic tubing.)
- Doctor kit
- Stethoscope
- Elastic bandages
- Adhesive bandages
- Gloves
- Shoe coverings and hair nets donated by a hospital
- Check-in desk in a hospital setup
- Teddy bears
- Blankets
- Sterile masks
- Nurse outfits
- Cots
- Baby dolls
- Sheets
- Pillows

Language Development

According to Weitzman and Greenberg, dramatic play engages children in complex forms of language that are linked to success in school. In the course of play, children use language to make plans and predictions, explain their actions and points of view, solve problems, and negotiate roles. For this reason, dramatic play is especially important for traumatized children. As previously discussed, traumatized children typically have a language delay from lack of nurturing relationships and limited life experiences.

When setting the stage for dramatic play and choosing materials and props, consider the background knowledge of the children. When children have not had real-life exposure or a great deal of second-hand exposure to ideas, settings, and experiences of life through books, video clips, and virtual field trips, they will struggle with how to use the props and story lines. For example, children may have some vague knowledge of fire trucks. They may know that they are red, have a loud siren, drive through red lights, and help put out fires. At the same time, children may not know about the different kinds of fire trucks, the tools they carry, and their functions. They may know that firefighters wear special

hats but they not know about the tools they carry into a fire and the oxygen tanks they wear. Children may be unaware of how firefighters receive calls, where they stay when they aren't putting out fires, or what they do when they get to a fire.

Before creating dramatic play settings, ensure that children have adequate background knowledge to know how to play in complex and creative ways with the materials. Firsthand experience is always the best, but when that is not possible, books, pictures, video clips, and the Internet can help children become familiar with the details of the setting. Make sure children know the names of all of the props and tools available for them to play with. Role-play the different actions, language, and behaviors people in those settings use with the children. For example, demonstrate how someone calls 911 and talks to the dispatcher, giving a name, address, and information about the emergency. Demonstrate how the dispatcher contacts the fire station, and act out the sequence of events that unfolds. This kind of modeling and background knowledge inspires more complex play that engages children for longer lengths of time.

Background knowledge particularly matters when creating typical scenes from daily life. Because of limited life experience, traumatized children may never have been to a bakery, a post office, or a lemonade stand. Teachers need to be very sensitive to this dynamic. If a child never or rarely engages in dramatic play, consider that a lack of background knowledge in how to use the materials may drive the child's behavior.

Self-Awareness

Children from hard places are often delayed in the development of self-awareness, particularly when they have experienced abuse and neglect in the first year of life. As previously discussed, traumatized children often lack nurturing relationships in which they feel "felt" by others and experience authentic emotional attunement. Therefore, many grapple with the concepts of *self* and *other*. When children engage in pretend play, they can try on the roles of other people. They can vicariously experience what it feels like to be a doctor who saves someone who has been shot or to be the police officer who captures the robber. They can experience what it is like to be a nurturing mom or dad or the baby who is loved and rocked.

The Math and Manipulative Center

I observed a five-year-old who had suffered horrific abuse as an infant. By the time he was two months old, he had suffered fifteen broken bones. He was placed into a very loving foster home, but for two years court-ordered visits with his abusive biological parents traumatized him over and over. After each visit, he would scream for days on end. A jury trial finally terminated parental rights, and he was adopted by his new loving family.

As I watched this child play with his Legos, I saw an unusual intensity to his play—as if he were playing for dear life. With each Lego that he so purposefully and painstakingly added to his sculpture, I got the sense that he was attempting to restore order to the chaos of his young life. As I watched him that day, it was clear that play was an important component to this child's healing.

Legos are an example of *manipulatives*, multisensory materials used to teach important basic concepts such as fine-motor skills, problem solving, spatial awareness, and number sense.

Closed Manipulatives

- Puzzles
- Peg boards

Open Manipulatives

- Legos
- Tinkertoys
- Brio blocks
- Lincoln Logs
- Window Blocks
- Pattern blocks

Open and Closed Manipulatives

There are two basic kinds of manipulatives, closed and open. A closed manipulative has a single "right" way to use the materials. For example, a puzzle is a closed manipulative because there is only one way to correctly put it together to form a whole. Other closed materials include nesting cups, stacking rings of graduated sizes, and many Montessori materials. Children from hard places generally like these materials because they don't require a great deal of creativity or interaction with other children. They are self-correcting, and the child can achieve a sense of satisfaction upon completion.

An open-ended manipulative allows children to configure and reconfigure materials in many different and creative ways. There is no right or wrong way to use the materials. Magnetic blocks, Tinkertoys, and Legos are open ended. It is not unusual to see fragile children compulsively put together and take apart different manipulative materials. In doing so, these children can experience the empowerment of bringing order out of chaos. A scattered pile of Legos becomes a well-organized and recognizable structure.

A healing classroom provides a wide variety of manipulative materials for children to explore and create. Because children from hard places often struggle with spatial awareness, it is important to help them define their space. Using mats, large trays, area rugs, scatter rugs, or large plastic hoops provides the definition needed to help a child know that his structure needs to stay within a given area.

Dramatic Play

Not only do manipulatives give children the experience of bringing order out of chaos, they also work as tools for dramatic play. I once visited a classroom of four-year-olds in an urban school for at-risk children. Two little girls sat at a table playing with Legos. One of the children fashioned a gunlike object out of the blocks, pointed it at her friend, and said, "Pow, pow! I'm going to shoot the policeman." This definitely caught my attention, so I sat down at the table to observe. Because this school had a no-tolerance policy toward violence, technically I should have immediately shut this kind of play down and admonished the child that "We don't do that here." But because I was familiar with the community that this school served, I knew that this child's play likely was an attempt to process a real-life event.

I said nothing to the children when I first sat down. I wanted to see where this child would go next. A few seconds later, she said it again: "Pow, pow! I'm going to shoot the policeman."

"Why do you want to shoot the policeman?" I asked.

"Because he is a bad man," she replied.

"Why do you think policemen are bad?" I asked.

"Because they took my uncle to jail," she responded.

"Why did they take him to jail?"

"Because he shot someone."

This led to a lengthy conversation regarding the role of police officers and the laws that govern adult behavior. We discussed the fact that when adults break the rules they have to go to jail, which is kind of like time out for big people. But the most important aspect of this conversation was that, despite the fact that her uncle broke the rules, it still didn't change the fact that he loved her and she loved him. No matter what he did, he would always be her uncle and they would always have a loving relationship.

These spontaneous, teachable moments are critical in the lives of traumatized children. Each time caregivers and teachers seize the moment for conversations such as these, we gently nudge a child further down the path toward emotional healing.

Issues of Ownership

The issue of ownership matters to most young children but even more so to children from hard places because they have lost so much. When the state takes children into custody, they are typically removed abruptly with nothing but the clothes on their backs and whatever they happen to have in their hands at the moment. Sometimes they are given a bag and allowed to grab whatever they can before they are whisked out the door to the patrol car or into a state vehicle. Beloved toys, teddy bears, and all that is important to the child stay behind.

A child who has spent concentrated effort creating a complex design or structure with the manipulatives may have a difficult time pulling that structure apart and putting it back in the storage tub. Relinquishing something that is "mine" can be very difficult because these children have had to relinquish so much in their short lives. Show respect for their work by keeping it for display to show other children or the child's parents or guardians. Often keeping it for the day is enough. You can put it back into storage later.

Another way to celebrate their work is to take a digital photo to display in the room, give to parents or guardians, or keep in the child's portfolio. What better way to say, "I'm proud of what you've done!" Extend the learning experience by having the child dictate a story about the object or invite the child to write it himself.

Manipulatives are usually small enough to fit in a child's pockets. Children from hard places may enjoy the manipulatives so much that they want to take them home in their pockets or backpacks. *It is critical to not accuse the children of stealing.* Traumatized children are still very much in the process of developing and understanding mine and yours. You can deal with this in a few ways:

- Playfully have a "pocket check" at the end of the day, and ask the children to check their pockets and backpacks for any toys that may be trying to hitchhike home with them.
- Allow families to check out popular sets of materials to use at home.
- Give the child a small number of parts and pieces to keep and use at home.
- Suggest popular toys to parents and guardians for birthday or Christmas presents. People usually welcome this kind of input.

The Art Center

Tony was a delightful, well-adjusted child born to young parents who seemingly adored him. Mom was a very involved parent and often helped out in the preschool program that I directed. From all outward appearances, this family was the epitome of happiness. Unfortunately, Dad came home one evening and announced that he no longer wanted to be married. He packed his bags and left, leaving his wife reeling. Overnight, happy three-year-old Tony became sullen, angry, and aggressive.

Tony's mom regularly updated me on the situation and Tony's behavior at home. I occasionally opened the door for Tony to talk about his feelings and the unfortunate changes at home, yet he never uttered a word about what was going on.

One morning on the playground, I noticed Tony having a particularly bad day. He was pushing and shoving, obviously in a foul mood. I pulled him aside and guided him to sit with me on the bench. I said, "Tony, you seem to be having a very hard day. Is something bothering you?" He stared at the ground in silence, but I could see his lip start to quiver. I reached for the crayons and paper nearby and said, "Tony, can you draw me a picture of how you are feeling today?" He picked up black and purple crayons and began to vigorously scribble across the paper. As he scribbled, tears began to roll down his cheeks. Finally he whispered, "I miss my daddy." I held him on my lap, and he began to tell me that he only got to see his daddy "sometimes" and he wished he would come back home. After we dried his tears, I asked, "Would you like to draw a picture of how you are feeling now?" He nodded, chose some bright colors, and began to draw.

Self-Expression

Art is a universal language children use to communicate their deepest feelings. Young children often have difficulty finding the words to share their experiences and emotions. Art helps traumatized children find their voice and communicate their emotions and reflections on the world.

In helping children find their voice, you should provide open-ended art experiences and not "crafts." An open-ended art experience involves art materials that are not aimed at producing a particular product. There is no right or wrong way to configure the materials, which allows the children the freedom to create whatever is on their minds. A craft, on the other hand, has a specific product in mind as the end result. There is a right and wrong way to configure the materials to create an easily recognizable object to hang on the wall or send home. Crafts do not give children a voice; they take away the opportunity for self-expression and creativity.

Drawing and painting are two of the easiest and most common art experiences to give children a voice. Easel painting, water colors, markers, colored pencils, pastels, chalk, and crayons are just a few of the tools that children can use and explore.

Though the typical early childhood professional is not a trained art therapist, some common characteristics and signs in children's drawings can indicate emotional pain and trauma. When these signs and symbols are present, save the child's work for a trained professional to evaluate. Children's drawings can add great insight into issues and dynamics to address in therapy. Some of the things to notice include the following:

- Consistent use of dark colors. Traumatized children often use black, brown, and purple to the exclusion of all other colors, and their paintings and drawings have a noticeably dark tone to them. The occasional colorless drawing is not something to be concerned about, but when children consistently create dark paintings and drawings it should be noticed and documented.
- The child is always absent from the picture, but other family members and friends are consistently present.
- The faces of the people always look sad.

It is crucial that early childhood professionals keep things in perspective and look at the whole child. If you happen to have a child who draws or paints dark pictures but demonstrates no other behavior problems or issues of concern, certainly note it but don't get alarmed and immediately conclude something is amiss.

After children paint or draw a picture, offer to take dictation, or if they are able, encourage them to use invented spelling to document their thoughts about the pictures. Keep the artwork in a portfolio or take a picture to print and keep. A child's portfolio can provide significant insight to therapeutic professionals working with a child.

Dough and clay, collage materials, and three-dimensional creations help children reclaim their voice and provide an outlet for self-expression. I was once talking with a young child who was experiencing a very difficult and traumatic divorce. As we talked, he worked with clay. As we wrapped up our discussion, he held up his creation and said, "This is a lonely palm tree sitting on an island all by himself." This comment shed more insight into this child's emotional state at the moment than all the words he expressed in the conversation before.

The Library Center

In early childhood, we often use books to teach the concepts of print and the structure of a story or to point out rhyming words and predictable phrases. Good children's literature, however, plays an important role in a healing environment for children. *Bibliotherapy* is a way of using books to deal with emotional issues and the everyday challenges of young children. Books are carefully chosen to address topics of daily concern. For example, *Thunder Cake* by Patricia Polacco deals with a little girl's fear of thunderstorms. Her wise old grandmother helps her cope with her fear by sending her out and about on the farm to gather the ingredients to make a thunder cake. She goes to the henhouse to gather eggs, to the garden to get tomatoes, and to the barn to get milk. In the process, the little girl finds her courage to deal with her fear of storms.

Selecting Books

Stories are powerful tools that appeal to young children. Well-chosen stories can inspire courage and new ways of thinking and behaving in children of all ages. Through stories, children encounter others who have the same fears and challenges in life, and they find new solutions to their own dilemmas. They encounter worlds that they have never seen, requiring them to use their imaginations. Children from hard places often struggle with a sense of hope, which is born in a mind with the capacity to imagine a better life and a different way of living. Books and the imaginative journeys they inspire plant the seed of hope in a struggling child's heart.

Through reading stories, children can process and make sense of their lives in small, palatable doses. They have the tools to think about and manage often disturbing forces in their lives. A wicked stepmother or the Big Bad Wolf become symbols of the destructive forces that often operate in their lives. The story of *The Ugly Duckling* by Hans Christian Andersen can encourage the foster child who feels unlovable or different. *The Rag Coat* by Lauren Mills encourages empathy and the capacity to look at life from another person's perspective. *The Kissing Hand* helps children know that others struggle with separation from people they love.

In choosing books for your library center, include a wide selection on specific topics:

- Managing strong emotions, such as anger, disappointment, sadness, and fear
- Separation anxiety
- Making friends
- Grief and loss
- Positive emotions, such as thankfulness, peace, and calmness
- Foster care
- Adoption
- Jealousy
- Sibling struggles
- Death of a beloved person
- Transitioning to a new foster or adoptive home
- Divorce

Unfortunately, many of our beloved fairy tales have been used to promote the commercialization of childhood. *Beauty and the Beast*, *Cinderella*, and a long list of others have been repackaged on the big screen to entertain and to sell products. This does not mean that we should not use these stories; however, it preferable to read the classic versions of these tales, which often differ from the versions on the screen. In fairy tales and classic stories, children encounter the war between good and evil, the power of love and friendship. They realize that the hope of redemption and transformation is real, and they encounter the forces of life and death. Stories such as *The Three Little Pigs* illustrate the importance of planning ahead and looking out for family and friends. Fairy tales and classic stories help children grapple with the realities of their difficult lives.

Creating a Welcoming Space

The library center should feel warm and cozy and invite both children and adults to curl up and read a book. If the library center does not keep adult needs in mind, caregivers and teachers will be less likely to take the time to read to children on an individual or small-group basis. Overstuffed chairs, love seats, adult-sized rocking chairs, large pillows, and bean-bag chairs create inviting spaces. Afghans, stuffed animals, blankets, pillows, and quilts beckon children and adults to curl up together and read. These moments of emotional connection while sharing a story are the glue that holds relationships together.

Including Specific Content

The collection should also include teacher-made books. A child may be dealing with a particular issue not specifically addressed by a commercially produced book. For example, one adoptive mom of a traumatized child reported the struggle that bedtime presented. The child had meltdowns and temper tantrums nearly every night. I created a book about bedtime rituals specific to the child's situation and behavior. The book addressed the inappropriate responses that the child had to this daily routine and gave some socially appropriate alternative responses and behaviors. To illustrate the story, I used pictures that I downloaded from a website designed for teachers to use in creating visual prompts and stories for children who need and require visual cues. Other sources of illustrations include calendars, magazines, drawings, cards, and photographs of the children themselves.

Not only can adults create homemade books, but children may also want to create their own. If the children cannot write on their own, caregivers and teachers can take dictation of the text. Subject matter for homemade books may include topics such as the following:

- Termination of parental rights and the feelings involved
- Death of a parent or loved one
- Transitioning to a new foster home
- Arrival of a new baby or foster child in the home
- Jitters about going to a new school
- Divorce
- Court-ordered visitation with biological parents

- Cessation of visitation with biological parents
- A traumatic event such as a fire, natural disaster, or witnessed act of violence
- Domestic violence
- Strong emotions and emotional meltdowns

The library center can also provide tools and materials that invite children to tell their own stories about their experiences. Adults sometimes feel reluctant to encourage children to talk about traumatic events for fear that it will upset other children or cause the child to become emotional. However, discouraging or stifling children's need to tell their stories sends the message that it's not okay to talk and only causes their emotions to lie below the surface. Eventually these feelings will fester to the point that they suddenly bubble up and spill over into the classroom through aggression, emotional meltdowns, and other disruptive forms of behavior. We must create classrooms that encourage and support children in finding the words to share and process their life events.

By providing a variety of materials for storytelling, we send the message, "I want to listen to you." Here are some suggestions for story telling materials:

- A doll house with family figures of all ethnicities and physical challenges represented in your group
- Flannel-board figures
- Puppets and a puppet theater
- Drawing materials

The Science Center

The importance of the science center for traumatized children may not seem obvious, but it is a critical part of a healing environment. Because many maltreated children have such limited life experiences, they are fascinated by and drawn to the novelty and richness of the materials and the experiences. For this reason, the science center must be more than an afterthought with a box of seashells and a magnifying glass sitting on shelf. Purposefully and thoughtfully plan science displays, investigations, and materials to support a healing environment.

Reverence for Life

The harsh world of violence and neglect communicates to children a fundamental disregard for life. Interactions with the natural world and observation of life cycles help them learn respect for living things and, most importantly, learn to respect their own lives and those of others around them.

Young children have a natural interest in and affinity for plants, animals, insects, birds, rocks, soil, and other elements of the natural world. Hunting for roly-polys on the playground, creating a worm farm in a galvanized tub, or documenting the changes in a particular tree over the course of different seasons teaches children about life cycles and the needs of living things. It also develops a reverence for life.

Children learn to nurture by being nurtured. This critical dynamic often is absent in the life of a maltreated child. Healing environments nurture the children and, in turn, give them opportunities to practice nurturing other living things. Gardening is one of the ways that children can learn about the natural world and learn how to care. When children have the responsibility to plant, water, and weed a garden, they gain firsthand experience in nurturing living things. When they must meet the needs of animals in their classroom, they actively participate in nurturing care. As they learn about and care for the natural world, they start to understand the fragility of life and what is required to sustain it.

Gentleness

Caring for plants and animals helps children develop the concept of *gentle touch*. The world of violence and abuse is often harsh and abrupt; gentleness is not a common trait of abusive parents and caregivers. Pulling weeds from among tender shoots of plants allows the child to practice gentleness. Picking up a worm or stroking the fur of a pet rabbit gives children firsthand experience with gentle touch.

The physical and psychological benefits of caring for pets is well established. Interactions with a pet offer a number of benefits:
- Lower blood pressure
- Release endorphins that are essential for calming stress
- Improve communication
- Reduce anxiety
- Decrease feelings of isolation and depression
- Improve focus
- Reduce loneliness
- Increase self-confidence

A Sense of Hope

The process of planting seeds and watching for them to sprout helps children learn what it means to wait for the future with hope and anticipation. Gardening helps develop a future orientation and the capacity to hope.

Encourage the children to keep a journal to document the process of growth and change over time. Every day or two, have children observe and then document what they see in the garden. Even three-year-olds can draw pictures of the growth process that occurs over time. Ask the children to predict and draw a picture of what they think they will see when the plants are fully grown. Take photos of the growth and change over time and have children arrange the images in sequential order.

Cause and Effect

The egocentric nature of children's thinking often leads young children to make erroneous cause-and-effect relationships between seemingly unrelated events. For example, a child may secretly wish that her abusive dad would go away. Her dad gets drunk that night and has a car accident. The child may think that her "bad" thoughts caused the wreck.

Children who cannot link an action or behavior to the likely outcome will struggle with understanding right and wrong and with their own behavior. Traumatized children have difficulty understanding the rippling effects of their behavior on the reactions and behavior of other people. They live in a world that doesn't make sense, and they repeat the same dysfunctional behaviors over and over again because they can't make these mental leaps.

A compromised ability for cause-and-effect thinking is a hallmark of fetal alcohol exposure. Prenatal exposure impacts the development of the corpus callosum, which is the conduit of communication between the two hemispheres of the brain. Children with significant alcohol exposure usually have a smaller corpus callosum, so the two sides of their brains don't communicate as efficiently, resulting in a compromised ability to grasp cause-and-effect thinking. Neglect in the first year of life is also a cause of impaired cause-and-effect thinking, as it comes online in the daily attachment dance between a caregiver and a child. When a baby cries and he is responded to in a timely fashion, the foundation of cause-and-effect thinking is established. But when caregivers respond inconsistently, let the baby cry for inordinate lengths of time, or fail to respond at all, cause-and-effect thinking is compromised.

Cause-and-effect thinking will become more complex throughout the early childhood years as new and different experiences are provided. For this reason, the early childhood environment needs to be rich in experiences that expose children to cause-and-effect thinking, which give them a chance of recovering as much as possible. Sometimes results are not immediate, and the cumulative effects of early experiences are not realized until later in childhood.

A healing environment rich in opportunities for children to manipulate and experiment with materials helps them make cause-and-effect associations between events. Scientific activities and investigations develop this thinking. When children roll a car down an incline, they learn that they can change the speed of the car by raising or lowering the ramp. When children pull down on a rope attached to a pulley, they learn that the bucket of sand at the end moves upward. When children blow through a straw, they learn that they can make a cotton ball roll across the table at different speeds by varying the strength of the air stream.

Through interactions such as these, children learn that cause-and-effect outcomes will happen when certain conditions are present. The capacity to make cause-and-effect associations is the foundation of a moral conscience. Understanding the Golden Rule requires an understanding of cause and effect. When I mistreat others, I am likely to receive aggression and dislike from others. When I treat other people as I would want to be treated, I likely will receive kindness and respect.

Caregivers and teachers must recognize the importance of interaction in scientific investigations. Materials cannot simply sit out for children to play with without any adult interaction. Much of the learning will be lost if adults are not present to hang the language on children's experiences and ask "I wonder" questions. For example, "Johnny, what do you notice when you add more blocks to the top end of the ramp?" "Susie, I wonder what would happen if you put a tennis ball on the end of the pendulum instead of a golf ball?" These interactions help clarify the cause-and-effect associations being made in children's minds.

A World of Order and Predictability

Because of their home life, maltreated children believe the world at large is unpredictable and chaotic. Science investigations help children recognize that the patterns, principles, and laws that govern how things work always remain in place. They learn that there is predictability and order in the natural world, which helps create a sense of emotional security. When I throw something up in the air, gravity will inevitably bring it back down. When I pour popcorn into a sieve with tiny holes, the popcorn cannot sift through; however, if I pour flour in the sieve, the consistency will allow me to sift it. If I fail to water the plants, they will always die. A pendulum will always swing in an elliptical fashion.

Self-Regulation

In most early childhood environments, the sensory and water tables stay in the science center. These materials allow children to explore and experiment with the various attributes and characteristics of a wide variety of solids and liquids. They can mix, pour, measure, and sift. They experience different textures of materials and observe what happens when materials mix. Interactions with materials in the sensory table calm the central nervous system and benefit agitated and stressed children. When children arrive at child care in an agitated state, starting the day with a few moments at the sensory table can help to regulate and calm them. An angry child can visit the sensory table to calm herself before sitting down at the conflict-resolution table to problem solve.

Problem Solving

One of the primary goals of an early learning environment is to grow and develop children who can solve problems. Knowing how to recognize and generate solutions to problems encountered in everyday life is a basic skill critical to success in life. Unfortunately, in a world of accountability and standardized testing, more focus is placed on conformity and right answers than on creativity and problem solving.

Recognize that children from hard places are often very good at solving the daily dilemmas they face related to survival. In fact, they often have a precocious ability for self-care born out of a drive to survive. Four-year-olds figure out how to open a can of soup and heat it up on the stove to feed themselves or their siblings. Five-year-olds learn how to change  a diaper or make a bottle for a baby brother or sister. Don't underestimate the ability of maltreated children to problem solve. However, when it comes to cognitive tasks versus daily tasks of survival, their limited life experiences sometimes makes it difficult for them to transfer this ability into other settings.

The science center offers lots of manageable challenges for which children can find answers. When they successfully solve problems, their self-esteem grows, and they develop a sense of competence. Children realize that they indeed do have what it takes to make their way in a world that often tells them otherwise.

Manageable challenges such as creating a waterway with funnels and plastic tubing, making a pinball machine with cardboard and paper towel rolls, or figuring out how to make a homemade boat float down the gutter improve children's problem-solving abilities.

The Block Center

An important part of any healing environment, the block center gives children another voice with which to symbolically represent their world. They create their homes, schools, and communities and reenact the events of their lives with small figurines and props. They build and tear down, build and tear down, over and over again. After the violence of September 11, 2001, teachers reported lots of destructive block play. Over and over, children built and crashed block towers as they processed the events they had seen on television or heard adults discussing. Blocks are a tool for expressing the strong and sometimes scary emotions held inside in a way that allows children to come to grips with their inner life.

As do manipulatives, blocks give children a way to bring order out of disarray and structure out of chaos. The block area is often the first place hesitant children will play because of the open-ended nature of the materials and the lack of a "right" way to use them. The block corner provides a good place for adults and children to play together when trying to establish a connection.

Blocks also offer opportunities for understanding cause-and-effect relationships. When teetering towers tumble, children learn that a tall tower needs a wide base to stay steady. They learn that the form of something determines its function. A triangular block serves a different function than a rectangular one does. Children encounter the predictable, unchanging force of gravity when structures fall. Healing environments seek to give children the variety of experiences they need to encounter the world from many different angles.

Gun Play in the Block Center

Many early childhood teachers report the common phenomenon of children using blocks and other manipulatives to create imaginary weapons. Understandably, there is a great deal of controversy regarding gun play in child care centers and classrooms. Many school districts take a no-tolerance stance even with their pre-K and kindergarten students. But is this really in the best interest of children and, most especially, of maltreated children?

I do not advocate that we allow children to play with realistic toy guns in child care or school settings, but my understanding of children has grown and deepened over the forty years of my career. In my early days of working with children, I worked in an inner-city setting that ran after-school programs for teenagers. I soon learned that the guitar cases I saw kids carrying did not hold guitars; they held sawed-off shotguns. Guns and violence were an everyday reality for these children, and in my four-year-old classroom, gun play was a common occurrence. As a young teacher, I was not sure how to handle it. At first I tried to squelch it altogether and forbade them to use blocks and Legos as weapons, but they soon resorted to using their fingers. I couldn't cut off fingers, so I had to rethink my plan. Since that time, I have come to recognize that gun play is a legitimate form of play for young children, but we can address it in the classroom in either a healthy way or an unhealthy way.

An unhealthy approach is to simply let children do what they want without any adult guidance or conversation—"kids will be kids," with no attempt to understand the messages that children are trying to communicate and the life events that motivate the play. A healthy approach to gun play in the classroom takes into account the following:

- If play, and in particular, dramatic play is a way that children make sense of and process real-life events, then it stands to reason that young children growing up in a violent world will play in violent ways.
- Maltreatment causes children to feel a profound sense of helplessness. Gun play allows them to express their feelings toward real and imaginary sources of fear and hostility and to gain mastery over them. As they lock the bad guy up at gunpoint, they gain a sense of safety. When they pretend to shoot the bad guy, they gain a sense of power and mastery over the forces that potentially overwhelm and threaten them.

- Gun play requires close supervision by teachers, and children need a great deal of interaction with teachers to help them process the meaning behind the play. Children should never be left to play it out without adult intervention. Note: This idea is from Nancy Carlson-Paige, author of *Taking Back Childhood*.
    - Talk to children about what makes a bad guy bad and what makes a good guy good. Compare and contrast the differences.
    - Ask children why they think bad guys do bad things. Ask children what they think bad guys do when they aren't out doing bad things.
    - Talk to children about ways to stop bad guys besides shooting them. Brainstorm both real and imaginary ways, such as calling the police, making a trap, or using imaginary guns that turn people into statues or make them melt.
    - Talk to children about the things that threaten them and the things that they are afraid of.
    - When a child shoots a bad guy, tell him he needs to call an ambulance. Even when people do wrong things, we still take care of them when they are hurt. Set up a hospital to care for wounded people, even the bad guys.
    - Ask children if they think bad guys are scared when they are being chased.

Trauma-informed teachers stay vigilant and alert to teachable moments and the messages children communicate through play and behavior. The keys are communication and interaction—asking good questions, redirecting play, introducing new ideas, and using play as a springboard for understanding the world and how it works.

Afterword

There is nothing more rewarding than watching children with a history of trauma and all of the accompanying challenging behaviors make baby steps toward progress and healing. The paycheck of teachers and caregivers will probably never reflect the importance of the job, but the satisfaction and privilege of changing the world one child at a time make it all worthwhile. Caregivers and teachers must not remain islands unto themselves. The amount of expertise and knowledge needed to create healing environments is beyond the scope of any one individual. We have to be team players and lifelong learners, recognizing the limits of our own understanding. We each hold a piece of the puzzle, and partnering with professionals in other disciplines is good for us and good for children. When we link arms with parents, foster parents, occupational therapists, therapists, case workers, and psychiatrists and work together for the good of the child, miracles can happen. Enjoy the journey.

Recommended Children's Books

Aliki. 1984. *Feelings*. New York: Greenwillow.

Bailey, Carolyn. 2001. *The Little Rabbit Who Wanted Red Wings*. New York: Grosset and Dunlap.

Bang, Molly. 2004. *When Sophie Gets Angry—Really, Really Angry*. New York: Scholastic.

Berry, Joy. 2010. *Let's Talk About Feeling Angry*. New York: Joy Berry Enterprises.

Brown, Margaret. 1972. *The Runaway Bunny*. New York: HarperCollins.

Cain, Janan. 2000. *The Way I Feel*. Seattle, WA: Parenting Press.

Curtis, Jamie Lee. 1998. *Today I Feel Silly: And Other Moods that Make My Day*. New York: HarperCollins.

Cusimano, Maryann. 2010. *You Are My I Love You*. New York: Philomel.

Duksta, Lauren. 2009. *I Love You More*. Naperville, IL: Sourcebooks Jabberwocky.

Emberley, Ed. 1997. *Glad Monster, Sad Monster*. New York: Little, Brown Books for Young Readers.

Emberley, Ed. 1992. *Go Away, Big Green Monster*! New York: Little, Brown Books for Young Readers.

Fox, Mem. 1993. *Time for Bed*. New York: Harcourt.

Henkes, Kevin. 2006. *Lilly's Purple Plastic Purse*. New York: Greenwillow.

Janisch, Heinz. 2012. *"I Have a Little Problem," Said the Bear*. New York: North-South Books, Inc.

Joosse, Barbara. 2014. *Mama, Do You Love Me?* San Francisco, CA: Chronicle.

Kachenmeister, Cherryl. 1989. *On Monday When It Rained*. New York: Houghton Mifflin.

Katz, Karen. 2002. *The Colors of Us*. New York: Square Fish.

Lewis, Rose. 2000. *I Love You Like Crazy Cakes*. New York: Little, Brown Books for Young Readers.

Lionni, Leo. 1973. *Swimmy*. New York: Random House.

Lovell, Patty. 2001. *Stand Tall, Molly Lou Melon*. East Rutherford, NJ: Penguin.

Mayer, Mercer. 1985. *I Was So Mad*. New York: Random House.

McBratney, Sam. 1994. *Guess How Much I Love You*. Somerville, MA: Candlewick.

McCourt, Lisa. 2003. *I Love You, Stinky Face*. New York: Scholastic.

Mills, Lauren. 1991. *The Rag Coat*. New York: Little, Brown Books for Young Readers.

Mitchell, Lori. 2001. *Different Just Like Me*. Watertown, MA: Charlesbridge.

Munsch, Robert. 2000. *Love You Forever*. New York: Random House.

Ormerod, Jan. 2003. *If You're Happy and You Know It*. New York: Star Bright.

Parr, Todd. 2004. *Do's and Don'ts*. New York: Little, Brown Books for Young Readers.

Parr, Todd. 2003. *The Family Book*. New York: Little, Brown Books for Young Readers.

Parr, Todd. 2009. *The Feel Good Book*. New York: Little, Brown Books for Young Readers.

Parr, Todd. 2005. *The Feelings Book*. New York: Little, Brown Books for Young Readers.

Parr, Todd. 2011. *The I'm Not Scared Book*. New York: Little, Brown Books for Young Readers.

Parr, Todd. 2001. *It's Okay to Be Different*. New York: Little, Brown Books for Young Readers.

Parr, Todd. 2014. *It's Okay to Make Mistakes*. New York: Little, Brown Books for Young Readers.

Parr, Todd. 2005. *The Peace Book*. New York: Little, Brown Books for Young Readers.

Parr, Todd. 2012. *The Thankful Book*. New York: Little, Brown Books for Young Readers.

Penn, Audrey. 1993. *The Kissing Hand*. Terre Haute, IN: Tanglewood.

Penn, Audrey. 2004. *A Pocket Full of Kisses*. Terre Haute, IN: Tanglewood.

Pfister, Marcus. 1992. *The Rainbow Fish*. New York: North-South.

Piper, Watty. 1978. *The Little Engine that Could*. New York: Penguin.

Polacco, Patricia. 1990. *Thunder Cake*. New York: Penguin.

Rotner, Shelley. 2003. *Lots of Feelings*. Minneapolis, MN: Millbrook.

Rotner, Shelley. 2009. *Shades of People*. New York: Holiday House.

Rylant, Cynthia. 1997. *Silver Packages*. New York: Scholastic.

Seuss, Dr. 1998. *My Many Colored Days*. New York: Knopf.

Tarpley, Natasha. 2001. *I Love My Hair*! New York: Little, Brown.

Tillman, Nancy. 2013. *I'd Know You Anywhere, My Love*. New York: Feiwel and Friends.

Tillman, Nancy. 2006. *On the Night You Were Born*. New York: Feiwel and Friends.

Tillman, Nancy. 2010. *Wherever You Are My Love Will Find You*. New York: Feiwel and Friends.

Vail, Rachel. 2005. *Sometimes I'm Bombaloo*. New York: Scholastic Books.

Viorst, Judith. 1972. *Alexander and the Terrible, Horrible No Good Very Bad Day*. New York: Simon and Schuster.

Willems, Mo. 2005. *The Pigeon Has Feelings, Too!* New York: Disney-Hyperion.

Wilson, Karma. 2008. *Bear Feels Scared*. New York: Simon and Schuster.

Bibliography and Recommended Readings

Bailey, Becky. 1997. *I Love You Rituals*. New York: Harper Collins.

Bath, Howard. 2008. "The Three Pillars of Trauma-Informed Care." *Reclaiming Children and Youth*. 17(3): 16–21.

Belcher, Harolyn. 2012. "Prenatal Exposure to Substances and Trauma: Fostering Parent and Child Well-Being." Presentation of the National Center for Child Traumatic Stress.

Bilmes, Jenna. 2004. *Beyond Behavior Management: The Six Life Skills Children Need to Thrive in Today's World*. St. Paul, MN: Redleaf.

Booth, Phyllis, and Ann Jernberg. 2001. *Theraplay: Helping Parents and Children Build Better Relationships through Attachment-Based Play*. 2nd ed. San Francisco: Jossey-Bass.

Brown, Stuart, and Christopher Vaughan. 2009. *Play: How It Shapes the Brain, Opens the Imagination, and Invigorates the Soul*. New York: Penguin.

Bukowski, William, and Lorrie Sippola. 1996. "Friendship and Morality: (How) Are They Related?" In *The Company They Keep*. Cambridge, MA: Cambridge University Press.

Carlson, Frances. 2009. "Rough and Tumble Play 101." *Exchange* July/August: 70-73.

Carlson, Vicki, Dante Cicchetti, Douglas Barnett, and Karen Braunwalk. 1989. "Disorganized Attachment Relationships in Maltreated Infants." *Developmental Psychology* 25(4): 525–531.

Carlson-Paige, Nancy. 2009. *Taking Back Childhood: A Proven Roadmap for Raising Confident, Creative, Compassionate Kids*. New York: Penguin.

Center on the Developing Child at Harvard University. 2012. "The Science of Neglect: The Persistent Absence of Responsive Care Disrupts the Developing Brain" Working Paper 12. Cambridge, MA: Center on the Developing Child. http://www.developingchild.harvard.edu

Child Welfare Information Gateway. 2009. *Understanding the Effects of Maltreatment on Brain Development*. Issue brief. Washington, DC: U.S. Department of Health and Human Services, Administration for Children and Families, Administration on Children, Youth, and Families, Children's Bureau. https://www.childwelfare.gov/pubPDFs/brain_development.pdf

Epstein, Ann. 2000. *Me, You, Us*: *Social-Emotional Learning in Preschool*. Ypsilanti, MI: HighScope.

Field, Tiffany. 1994. "Infant Massage." *The Journal of Perinatal Education* 3: 7–14.

Fisher, Sebern. 2014. *Neurofeedback in the Treatment of Developmental Trauma*: *Calming the Fear-Driven Brain*. New York: W.W. Norton.

Forbes, Heather, and Bryan Post. 2009. *Beyond Consequences, Logic, and Control*: *A Love Based Approach to Helping Children with Severe Behaviors*. Boulder, CO.: Beyond Consequences.

Ganz, Jennifer, and Margaret Flores. 2010. "Implementing Visual Cues." *Young Children* 65(2): 78–83.

Gaskill, Richard, and Bruce Perry. 2013. "The Neurobiological Power of Play: Using the Neurosequential Model of Therapeutics to Guide Play in the Healing Process." In *Creative Arts and Play Therapy for Attachment Problems*. New York: Guilford.

Gershon, Michael. 1999. *The Second Brain*: *A Groundbreaking New Understanding of Nervous Disorders of the Stomach and Intestine*. New York: HarperCollins.

Gill, Tim. 2005. "If You Go Down to the Woods Today." *Playing with Nature*. Concord, NH: Natural Playgrounds Company. http://naturalplaygrounds.com/documents/NaturalPlaygroundsDotCom_Go-Woods.pdf

Gilkerson, Linda, and Rebecca Klein, eds. 2008. *Early Development and the Brain*: *Teaching Resources for Educators*. Washington, DC: Zero to Three.

Greenwald, Ricky. 2005. *Child Trauma Handbook*: *A Guide for Helping Trauma-Exposed Children and Adolescents*. New York: The Haworth Maltreatment and Trauma Press.

Groves, Betsy. 2002. *Children Who See Too Much*: *Lessons from the Child Witness to Violence Project*. Boston: Beacon.

Gunnar, Megan. 2000. "Early Adversity and the Development of Stress Reactivity and Regulation." In *The Minnesota Symposia on Child Psychology Vol. 31*: *The Effects of Early Adversity on Neurobehavioral Development*. Mahwah, NJ: Lawrence Erlbaum.

Gunnar, Megan, and Charles Nelson. 1994. "Event-Related Potentials in Year-Old Infants: Relations with Emotionality and Cortisol." *Child Development* 65(1): 80–94.

Hirsh-Pasek, Kathy, Roberta Golinkoff, Laura Berk, and Dorothy Singer. 2009. *A Mandate for Playful Learning in Preschool*: *Presenting the Evidence*. New York: Oxford.

Hyche, Karen, and Vickie Maertz. 2014. *Classroom Strategies for Children with ADHD, Autism, and Sensory Processing Disorders*. Eau Claire, WI: PESI.

Hyson, Marilou. 2003. *The Emotional Development of Young Children*: *Building an Emotion-Centered Curriculum*. New York: Teacher's College Press.

Kaplan, Stephen. 1995. "The Restorative Benefits of Nature: Toward an Integrative Framework." *Journal of Environmental Psychology*. 15(3): 169–182.

Karen, Robert. 1994. *Becoming Attached*: *Unfolding the Mystery of the Infant-Mother Bond and Its Impact on Later Life*. New York: Warner.

Karr-Morse, Robin, and Meredith Wiley. 1997. *Ghosts from the Nursery: Tracing the Roots of Violence*. New York: Grove Atlantic.

Kohn, Alfie. 1993. *Punished by Rewards: The Trouble with Gold Stars, Incentive Plans, A's, Praise, and Other Bribes*. New York: Houghton Mifflin.

Koplow, Lesley. 2002. *Creating Schools that Heal: Real-Life Solutions*. New York: Teachers College Press.

Koplow, Lesley. 2007. *Unsmiling Faces: How Preschools Can Heal*. New York: Teachers College Press.

Kranowitz, Carol. 1998. *The Out-of-Sync Child*. New York: Penguin.

Kranowitz, Carol. 2003. *The Out-of-Sync Child Has Fun*. New York: Perigee Trade.

Kuban, Caelan, and William Steele. "Restoring Safety and Hope: From Victim to Survivor." *Reclaiming Youth* 20(1): 41–44.

Lieberman, Alicia, and Patricia Van Horn. 2011. *Psychotherapy with Infants and Young Children: Repairing the Effects of Stress and Trauma on Early Attachment*. New York: Guilford.

Lillas, Connie, and Janiece Turnbull. 2009. *Infant/Child Mental Health, Early Intervention, and Relationship-Based Therapies: A Neurorelational Framework for Interdisciplinary Practice*. New York: W. W. Norton.

Louv, Richard. 2008. *Last Child in the Woods: Saving Our Children from Nature-Deficit Disorder*. Chapel Hill, NC: Algonquin.

Malchiodi, Cathy, and David Crenshaw, eds. 2013. *Creative Arts and Play Therapy for Attachment Problems*. New York: Guilford.

Maroney, Dianne. 2003. "Recognizing the Potential Effect of Stress and Trauma on Premature Infants in the NICU: How Are Outcomes Affected?" *Journal of Perinatology* 23(8): 679–683.

Maxwell, Lorraine. 1996. "Multiple Effects of Home and Day Care Crowding." *Environment and Behavior* 28(4): 494–511.

McEwen, Bruce, and Elizabeth Lasley. 2002. *The End of Stress as We Know It*. New York: Dana.

Nachmias, Melissa, et al. 1996. "Behavioral Inhibition and Stress Reactivity: The Moderating Role of Attachment Security." *Child Development* 67(2): 508–522.

The National Child Traumatic Stress Network. 2008. *Child Trauma Toolkit for Educators*. Los Angeles, CA, and Durham, NC: National Center for Child Traumatic Stress. http://nctsn.org/sites/default/files/assets/pdfs/Child_Trauma_Toolkit_Final.pdf

The National Child Traumatic Stress Network, Physical Abuse Collaborative Group. 2009. *Child Physical Abuse Fact Sheet*. Los Angeles, CA, and Durham, NC: National Center for Child Traumatic Stress.

Nathanielsz, Peter. 1999. *Life in the Womb: The Origin of Health and Disease*. Ithaca, NY: Promethean.

Nelson, Charles, Nathan Fox, and Charles Zeanah. 2014. *Romania's Abandoned Children: Deprivation, Brain Development, and the Struggle for Recovery*. Cambridge, MA: Harvard University Press.

Neufeld, Gordon, and Gabor Maté. 2006. *Hold On to Your Kids: Why Parents Need to Matter More than Peers*. New York: Random House.

Nicholson, Simon. 1971. "How Not to Cheat Children: The Theory of Loose Parts." *Landscape Architecture* 62(1): 30–34.

Parker, Jeffrey, and Steven Asher. 1987. "Peer Relations and Later Personal Adjustment: Are Low-Accepted Children at Risk? *Psychological Bulletin* 102(3): 357–389.

Pellegrini, Anthony. 1987. "Rough-and-Tumble Play: Developmental and Educational Significance." *Educational Psychology* 22(11): 23–43.

Pellis, Sergio, and Vivian Pellis. 2007. "Rough-and-Tumble Play and the Development of the Social Brain." *Current Directions in Psychological Science* 16(2): 95–98.

Perry, Bruce. 2001. "Curiosity: The Fuel of Development." *Early Childhood Today*. (15)6: 22–23. http://teacher.scholastic.com/professional/bruceperry/curiosity.htm

Perry, Bruce. 2001. "The Neurodevelopmental Impact of Violence in Childhood." In *Textbook of Child and Adolescent Forensic Psychiatry*. Washington, DC: American Psychiatric Press.

Perry, Bruce. 2003. *Effects of Traumatic Events on Children*. Houston, TX: The ChildTrauma Academy. http://childtrauma.org

Perry, Bruce. 2006. "Applying Principles of Neurodevelopment to Clinical Work with Maltreated and Traumatized Children: The Neurosequential Model of Therapeutics." *Working with Traumatized Youth in Child Welfare*. New York: Guilford.

Perry, Bruce. 2013. *Neurosequential Model in Education*. Child Trauma Academy Webinar Series.

Perry, Bruce. 2014. *Neurosequential Model of Therapeutics*. Child Trauma Academy Webinar Series.

Perry, Bruce, and Maia Szalavitz. 2006. *The Boy Who Was Raised as a Dog*. New York: Basic Books.

Perry, Bruce, and Maia Szalavitz. 2010. *Born for Love: Why Empathy Is Essential—and Endangered*. New York: HarperCollins.

Porges, Stephen. 2011. *The Polyvagal Theory: Neurophysiological Foundations of Emotions, Attachment, Communication, and Self-Regulation*. New York: W. W. Norton.

Purvis, Karyn, and David Cross. 2007. *The Connected Child: Bring Hope and Healing to Your Adoptive Family*. New York: McGraw-Hill.

Purvis, Karyn, and David Cross. 2009. *TBRI Professional Training Program*. Fort Worth, TX: Texas Christian University, Institute of Child Development.

Purvis, Karyn, and David Cross. 2013. *Leading Nurture Groups*. Fort Worth, TX: Texas Christian University, Institute of Child Development.

Purvis, Karyn, and David Cross. 2013. *TBRI Professional Training Program*. Fort Worth, TX: Texas Christian University, Institute of Child Development.

Purvis, Karyn, and David Cross. 2014. *The Hope Connection: A Place of Hope for Children from the "Hard Places."* Fort Worth, TX: Texas Christian University, Institute of Child Development.

Quesenberry, Amanda, Mary Louise Hemmeter, and Michaelene Ostrosky. 2011. "Addressing Challenging Behaviors in Head Start: A Closer Look at Program Policies and Procedures." *Topics in Early Childhood Special Education* 30(4): 209–220.

Rasmussen, Carmen. 2005. "Executive Functioning and Working Memory in Fetal Alcohol Spectrum Disorder." *Alcoholism: Clinical and Experimental Research* 29(8): 1359–1367.

Riley, Dave, Robert San Juan, Joan Klinkner, and Ann Ramminger. 2008. *Social and Emotional Development: Connecting Science and Practice in Early Childhood Settings*. St. Paul, MN: Redleaf.

Schieffer, Kay. 2013. *Sunshine Circles Teacher Resource Manual*. Evanston, IL: The Theraplay Institute.

Scott, Janny. 2000. "When Child's Play Is Too Simple: Experts Criticize Safety-Conscious Recreation as Boring." *New York Times*, July 15.

Seefeldt, Carol. 1974. "Creative Activities and Materials." Class discussion. College Park, MD: University of Maryland.

Shanker, Stuart. n.d. *Self-Regulation*. Canadian Self-Regulation Initiative. http://www.self-regulation.ca/download/pdf_documents/magforbooklet.pdf

Shore, Allan. 1999. *Affect Regulation and the Origin of Self: The Neurobiology of Emotional Development*. Mahwah, NJ: Lawrence Erlbaum.

Siegel, Daniel. 2001. *The Developing Mind: How Relationships and the Brain Interact to Shape Who We Are*. New York: Guilford.

Siegel, Daniel, and Tina Bryson. 2011. *The Whole-Brain Child: 12 Revolutionary Strategies to Nurture Your Child's Developing Mind*. New York: Random House.

Siegel, Daniel, and Tina Bryson. 2014. *No-Drama Discipline: The Whole-Brain Way to Calm the Chaos and Nurture Your Child's Developing Mind*. New York: Random House.

Siegel, Daniel, and Mary Hartzell. 2003. *Parenting from the Inside Out: How a Deeper Self-Understanding Can Help You Raise Children Who Thrive*. New York: Penguin.

Sroufe, Alan, Byron Egeland, and Elizabeth Carlson. 1999. "One Social World: The Integrated Development of Parent-Child and Peer Relationships." In *Relationships as Developmental Contexts*. Mahwah, NJ: Lawrence Erlbaum.

Streissguth, Ann. 1997. *Fetal Alcohol Syndrome: A Guide for Families and Communities*. Baltimore: Brooks.

Tantam, Digby. 2009. *Can the World Afford Autistic Spectrum Disorder? Nonverbal Communication, Asperger Syndrome, and the Interbrain*. London: Jessica Kingsley.

Taylor, Andrea, Frances Kuo, and William Sullivan. 2001. "Coping with ADD: The Surprising Connection to Green Play Settings." *Environment and Behavior* 33(1): 54–77.

Thompson, Curt. 2007. *Anatomy of the Soul: Surprising Connections between Neuroscience and Spiritual Practices That Can Transform Your Life and Relationships*. Carol Stream, IL: Tyndale House.

Thompson, Gill. 2003. *Supporting Communication Disorders: A Handbook for Teachers and Teaching*. New York: David Fulton.

U. S. Department of Health and Human Services. 2012. *Child Maltreatment 2012*. Washington, DC: Department of Health and Human Services, Administration for Children and Families. http://www.acf.hhs.gov/sites/default/files/cb/cm2012.pdf

van der Kolk, Bessel. 2014. *The Body Keeps the Score: Brain, Mind, and Body in the Healing of Trauma*. New York: Penguin Group.

van der Kolk, Bessel. n.d. *Developmental Trauma Disorder: Towards a Rational Diagnosis for Children with Complex Trauma Histories*. http://www.traumacenter.org/products/pdf_files/preprint_dev_trauma_disorder.pdf

van Ijzendoorn, Marinus, Carlo Schuengel, and Marian Bakermans-Kranenburg. 1999. "Disorganized Attachment in Early Childhood: Meta-Analysis of Precursors, Concomitants, and Sequelae." *Development and Psychopathology* 11(2): 225–249.

Voskamp, Ann. 2011. *A Thousand Gifts: A Dare to Live Fully Right Where You Are*. Grand Rapids, MI: Zondervan.

Walker, Aimée, and David MacPhee. 2011. "How Home Gets to School: Parental Control Strategies Predict Children's School Readiness." *Early Childhood Research Quarterly* 26(3): 355–364.

Weitzman, Elaine, and Janice Greenberg. 2002. *Learning Language and Loving It: A Guide to Promoting Children's Social, Language, and Literacy Development*. Rev. ed. Toronto: Hanen Centre.

Wells, Michael. 2013. *Relationships Matter: Qualitative Interviews with Head Start Preschool Teachers on Turnover Rates*. Presentation at the Thirty-ninth Annual Head Start Association Conference, Nashville, TN, February 2013.

Wells, Nancy, and Gary Evans. 2003. "Nearby Nature: A Buffer of Life Stress among Rural Children." *Environment and Behavior* 35(3): 311–330.

Werner, Emmy. 2005. "Resilience and Recovery: Findings from the Kauai Longitudinal Study." *Research, Policy, and Practice in Children's Mental Health* 19(1): 11–14.

Williams, Mary Sue, and Sherry Shellenberger. 1994. *How Does Your Engine Run?* Albuquerque, NM: Therapy Works.

Willis, Judy. 2009. "What You Should Know about Your Brain." *Educational Leadership* 67(4): 1–3.

Zahn-Waxler, Carolyn, Marian Radke-Yarrow, Elizabeth Wagner, and Michael Chapman. 1992. "Development of Concern for Others." *Developmental Psychology* 28(1): 126–136.

Zero to Three. 2012. *Safe Babies Court Teams: Building Strong Families and Healthy Communities*. DVD. Washington, DC: Zero to Three.

Internet Resources

Alert Program

http://www.alertprogram.com

An approach to teaching self-regulation awareness.

Center for Social and Emotional Foundations for Early Learning

http://csefel.vanderbilt.edu

CSEFEL is a national resource center funded by the Office of Head Start and Child Care Bureau for disseminating research and evidence-based practices to early childhood programs.

Harvard Center on the Developing Child

http://www.developingchild.harvard.edu

This website has many articles and videos on early brain development and trauma.

Sensory Processing Disorder Resource Center

http://www.sensory-processing-disorder.com

This site offers basic information on sensory processing disorder.

Theraplay for Educators

http://www.theraplay.org

Theraplay is a play-based approach to supporting attachment relationships.

Trust-Based Relational Intervention (TBRI)

http://www.child.tcu.edu

This is a forty-five-hour professional development course offered through Texas Christian University.

Zero to Three

http://www.zerotothree.org

This website offers webinars, articles, parenting materials, and videos related to child development and trauma.

Instructions for Making a Sand Baby

Materials:

play sand

2 gallon-sized ziplock freezer bags

duct tape

cotton fabric, 15" x 36"

scissors

needle and thread

muslin

Styrofoam ball, 3-inch diameter

ribbon

baby blanket

Directions

1. Fill a gallon-sized ziplock freezer bag with sand.
2. Close the bag and seal it, then wrap the bag in duct tape.
3. Place the duct-taped bag inside a second ziplock freezer bag and close.
4. Make a small pillowcase out of a piece of fabric.
5. Put the bag of sand inside the pillowcase.
6. Wrap a square of muslin around a 3-inch Styrofoam ball to make a head.
7. Tuck the gathered fabric at the bottom of the ball into the open end of the pillowcase.
8. Gather the open end of the pillowcase and the fabric at the bottom of the head, and tie together tightly with a ribbon.
9. Wrap the sand baby in a piece of fabric or baby blanket.

Index

National Child Traumatic Stress Network, 16, 105
    Physical Abuse Collaborative Group, 14
Natural disasters, 13, 225
Neglect, 25, 61, 63, 73–74, 118, 120, 142, 151, 178, 187,
    191–192, 204, 207–208, 217, 226–227
    defined, 15
    identifying, 8
    statistics in the U.S., 8
    transcends socioeconomic barriers, 18–19
    vestibular system and, 82–83
Nelson, Charles, 17–18, 55, 118
Neufeld, Gordon, 47, 74–75, 153, 183
Nicholson, Simon, 174
Night terrors, 111
Nightmares, 13
Noise levels, 166–167, 185
Noncompliance, 129–132
Nonverbal cues, 68, 71–73, 103–104, 139–140
Norepinephrine, 31
Novelty, 199–200, 225
Number sense, 217
Nurture groups, 76, 198

O

Object constancy, 155–157, 159, 193
Object permanence, 155–157, 159, 169
Obsessive compulsive disorder, 8
Open-ended play, 120, 159, 211
Oppositional behavior, 21, 26, 43, 57
Oppositional defiant disorder, 8, 41, 122
Organization of time, 177–200
    entry into care, 183–184
    group time, 194–200
    managing transitions, 181–183
    morning arrival, 185–188
    nap time, 189–190
    principles, 177–181
    snack time, 190–192
    toileting, 192–194
Orientation voids, 75, 183
Ostrosky, Michaelene, 128
Outdoor spaces, 166, 171–176, 179–181
    creativity and, 173–174
    elements for, 174–176
    healing, 171–172
    natural environments, 172–173
Overcrowding, 165–166
Ownership issues, 145, 219–220
Oxytocin, 205

P

Paint, 69, 96, 175, 196, 221
Painting, 221–222
Parachutes, 68, 95, 135–136
Parallel steppage, 83
Parentese, 71–72
Parker, Jeffrey, 138
Pellegrini, Anthony, 140
Pellis, Sergio, 140
Pellis, Vivian, 140
Perceptual perspective taking, 140
Perry, Bruce, 8–9, 11–12, 16, 33, 41, 45, 58, 60, 75, 111,
    148, 151, 183, 205
Perseverance, 102
Personal space, 15, 69–70, 195, 218
Phenylethylamine, 31
Photo sequencing, 121–123
Physical abuse, 8, 14–15, 18–19, 25, 63, 79, 120, 139,
    151, 154, 156–157, 178, 184, 187, 191–192, 203–204,
    207–208, 217
Physical environments, 163–176
    aromatherapy, 94, 112, 168
    art center, 220–222
    block center, 230–232
    conceptually rich, 208–210
    dramatic play center, 212–217
    errorless learning, 208
    fostering independence, 170
    language-rich, 206–207
    library center, 222–225
    math and manipulative center, 217–220
    musical, 205–206
    noise levels, 166–167
    organizing for play, 211–232
    organizing materials, 169
    organizing space, 164–166
    outdoors, 171–176
    play-based, 205–210
    science center, 225–230
Physiological regulation, 102
Pinching, 23, 38–39
Plastic hoops, 68, 70, 190, 195, 218
Play, 56
    benefits of, 203–204
    child-directed, 179
    child-initiated, 202
    dramatic, 121, 159, 161, 173–175, 176, 203–204,
    212–219, 231–232
    erratic, 21

Terror state, 36–38
    disorganized attachment, 59
Texas Christian University, 12, 27
TheraBands, 93, 95
Therapists, 8–9
Theraplay, 123, 198–199, 243
Therapy balls, 92, 97–98, 195
Thompson, Curt, 51–52, 57–59, 73
Thompson, Gill, 178
Tickling, 70
Time
    organization of, 177–200
    sequence of, 161–162, 177
Time outs, 131–132
Tinkertoys, 218
Toileting, 76, 86, 91, 192–194
Tone of voice, 63, 71–72
Touch, 63, 110, 142, 182, 184, 190
    avoidance, 20, 63–65, 67, 77, 87, 89
    importance of, 66–69
    school policies, 67
    sensory processing disorder, 80–81
Towels, 96, 136, 195, 199, 214
Transitional objects, 159
Transitions, 33, 38, 101, 113, 122, 134, 142, 178, 191, 205, 223
    difficulty with, 23
    entry into care, 183–184
    managing, 181–183
    minimizing, 179–180
    morning arrival, 185–188
Trauma
    acute, 13
    characteristics, 20–24
    chronic, 29
    complex, 13–14
    defining, 13–24
    exposure in early years, 8
    ignorance about, 9–10
    medical, 14–15
    relational, 13–14
Trust, 14, 47–49, 73, 152
Trust-Based Relational Intervention, 198, 243
Tulsa Sunshine Center Sensory Processing Disorder Resource Center, 90
Turn taking, 143–145, 198
Turnbull, Janiece, 101

U
U.S. Department of Health and Human Services, 8, 24, 178
V
van der Kolk, Bessel, 13, 19, 40
Van Horn, Patricia, 14, 60, 80
van Ijzendoorn, Marinus, 55
Vertigo, 82, 90
Vestibular sense, 89–90, 81–85, 102, 112, 165
    activities, 97–98
Violence, 10, 59
Visual cues, 128–129, 178, 182, 184, 192
Visual-spatial processing, 84
Voice modulation, 134–135
Voskamp, Ann, 177
Vygotsky, Lev, 76, 128

W
Walker, Aimée, 153
Water play, 133, 175, 229
Weighted neck buddies, 93
Weighted vests, 94
Weitzman, Elaine, 173, 215
Wells, Michael, 26
Wells, Nancy, 172
Whining, 58, 102
Williams, Mary Sue, 142
Willis, Judy, 78
Withdrawal, 21, 59, 61–62, 70, 103, 110, 135, 197
Working memory, 118–119
Wrist weights, 94
Writing, 204

Z
Zahn-Waxler, Carolyn, 141
Zeanah, Charles, 12, 18, 118
Zero to Three, 104–105, 243
Zip lines, 95
Zone of proximal development, 76